Foreword

Early in 2001, photographer Christopher Hirsheimer and I—a couple of California natives—drove south on Interstate 5 from Grants Pass, across the Oregon border down into the Golden State. This was the start of a 10-day journey, following a largely improvised itinerary that took us jagging back and forth from the coastline to the Central Valley, through tiny towns and major cities, past flat farmlands and rocky seaside cliffs, all the way to the edge of Mexico—eating and drinking and occasionally cooking along the way. (Our report of the trip appeared in the May/June issue of our magazine, *Saveur*, that year.)

It was one of the most memorable trips of my life, and I dream sometimes about making it again. In the meantime, Brigit Binns has done it for me—for all of us—but in her case, beginning in the south and heading north and not stopping when she got to Grants Pass but pushing on all the way up almost to the Canadian border.

Brigit divides her own itinerary into a dozen easily manageable, food-filled routes, punctuated with stops at farm-stands, markets, bakeries, and dairies, but most of all at great places to eat. With a few exceptions, these aren't big-name restaurants: They're local treasures, the real thing, establishments with names like Oink and Moo Burgers and BBQ, and Franny's Cup & Saucer, and New Sammy's Cowboy Bistro, where folks with good stories behind them and sizzling griddles and bubbling pots in front of them prepare real food—not fancy show-off chefs' stuff, but dips and hashes and scrambles, sandwiches and salads, tacos and burritos, fried fish and fried oysters, crab Louis, and tri-tip steak.

The best part? Brigit gives us clearly written, irresistible recipes for many of the specialties she devoured with great joy along the way, from homemade focaccia (and homemade English muffins!) to mango-strawberry flambé with coconut ice cream, from sweet potato fries with honey-maple drizzle to truffled cheese tortelli with butternut squash and *pepitas*, from Dungeness crabcakes to bacon-wrapped pork tenderloin with Worcestershire butter.

If you have no plans to take a West Coast road trip, read this book and cook some of these recipes instead—but I'll bet you'll be thinking plane flights and rental cars before you're halfway through.

COLMAN ANDREWS
Co-founder of *Saveur* magazine and editorial director of *TheDailyMeal.com*

Introduction

Some people drive just to arrive. Getting there is most of the fun for me; I drive because the lure of the open road is irresistible. And because the diversity of people, sights, and food I encounter along the way are, well, just as captivating as finding what I'd consider the best of the best: eating perfect Dungeness crabcakes with a glass of crisp rosé on a sunny day, while perched at a cliffside cafe overlooking the crashing waves of the Pacific.

In 2006, I began a tradition that lasted for six years: Every fall, I would drive from New York to California. A few months later, I would drive back. (This was winter-avoidance by someone who'd vowed never to put her dog on an airplane.) Mostly, I was solo—with Stella, of course, but she doesn't drive. I always took my sweet time, and in 12 cross-country drives, I never once ate in a chain restaurant. Routes, lunches, and overnight stops were meticulously planned around dining opportunities. So when the folks at *Sunset* suggested I apply this algorithm to the entire West Coast, I literally burst into (happy) tears.

By then I was living full time back in my native California, and had begun to miss those semiannual drives. Inspired by a roomful of precious back issues of *Sunset* but also ravenous for new sights, people, and tastes, I pestered the magazine's travel and food editors for recent discoveries, and mysteries that were rumored but yet to be revealed.

Next, I commenced the delicate dance of deciding where to stop, what to eat, and which sights and experiences merited my attention—always leaving myself open to on-the-fly encounters of the captivating kind, of course. I wanted a range of eateries: from dress-up fine dining to walk-in-straight-from-the-car/paper-napkin joints (plus everything in between). Big urban areas were no-go zones on this trip. It was a spectacular smorgasbord: Is there anywhere else on Earth as quirky, romantic, and delectable—in short, iconic—as the route along the edge of America's West Coast?

And then the fun began. Meeting mother-daughter bakers—one with purple hair—in their jewel-like shop front, in a one-horse town on the wild Mendocino coast. Standing at the prow of a ferry as it approached Whidbey Island, sun glinting on water. Rediscovering gold in Southern California—in the form of a meat-centric menu and pig-themed patio in the small town of Fallbrook. Frolicking with Stella on the deepest beach I'd ever seen, just north of Newport, Oregon. Visiting the new-millennium incarnation of a burger-and-shake shack I'd once frequented as a college student, in Portland, Oregon (see photo, bottom right). Sinking my teeth into ethereal roast chicken and crisped rustic bread—on a salad, so quintessentially SoCal—in a teensy town north of Santa Barbara. Scribbling down excellent restaurant tips from a well-traveled gent at the tiny bar of a tiny tiki hut on the Oregon Coast.

My belly was always full, and I was never starved for companionship: Everyone I met was warm and generous with spirit, sustenance, and best of all, their precious recipes. Stella was always sanguine, waiting patiently in countless dog-friendly hotel rooms; she knew there would be food, toys, and episodes of wild dancing before the next morning's departure.

Back home, I set to work re-creating the dishes I'd found, often phoning and emailing (okay, bugging) chefs and restaurateurs from Mexico to Canada. Eventually, the recipes were reproduced in a home-kitchen-friendly form, and then passed on to the exacting folks in the *Sunset* Test Kitchen for further refining. Occasionally, we tweaked things away from restaurant style, always retaining the spirit of the dish. The painstaking results are offered here, and they're keepers—recipes you'll return to time and again.

I invite you to ride along with me (and Stella) on our tasty culinary adventure. You don't even have to leave your kitchen.

Route 1

ALMOST WITHIN HAILING distance of the Mexican border, I make my first stop in *Vista*, a small city at the northernmost edge of the massive zone coyly referred to as the San Diego Metropolitan Area. It may not be cute, historic, or scenic, but with its large Latino population, Vista is a great place to find truly authentic Mexican food.

My desire to stay off the beaten track ("OTBT") leads me inland, away from the teeming coastal sprawl of Southern California, and I head east on State 78 toward the "mountain" town of *Julian*. In the Gold Rush of the 1870s, a disgruntled miner hauled a load of young apple trees up to Julian, and the apple-based economy has been thriving ever since—mostly by serving pie to tourists. Julian is above 4,000 feet and there are pine trees, but the softly rolling terrain feels more like hills than mountains. It's ranching country and you'll pass cattle, horses, scrubby prickly pear cactus, and towering eucalyptus trees.

Julian is cute. Structures are clapboard, and businesses sport names like Pistols and Petticoats, Miner's Diner, and Hog Heaven Leather Goods in Gold Rush/cowboy-esque fonts. You can stay at the Apple Tree Inn, or mine your own gemstones. But I'm not here to stop or shop—I'm here for the pie.

Heading west again toward *Fallbrook*, the countryside becomes Farmstand Central. Where and when there is access to water, this is one of the best growing climates in the world. Fallbrook is—according to locals—a well-kept secret: an *American Graffiti*–like town right next door to Temecula's polished wine country but sans the glitz.

LAKE ELSINORE

74

The Lookout
Roadhouse
p. 29

Oink and
Moo Burgers
and BBQ
p. 24

TEMECULA

15

Pala Mesa Nursery
p. 26

FALLBROOK

76

Vamos
a Texcoco
p. 14

San Diego Zoo
Safari Park
p. 16

76

Julian Tea &
Cottage Arts
p. 23

VISTA

Oasis Camel
Dairy
p. 23

ESCONDIDO

78

JULIAN

RAMONA

Fran's Original
Farm Stand
p. 16

Apple Alley
Bakery
p. 20

8

SAN DIEGO

950 E. Vista Way
Vista, CA

(760) 758-3313

VAMOS A TEXCOCO

Vista

The city of Texcoco—located about 20 minutes northeast of Mexico City—has long been famous for its exquisite, long-cooked *barbacoa de borrego* (lamb barbecue). The name of this restaurant—opened by Roberto and Hortensia Cuin and their daughters—echoes the cry that arises when myriad souls who've worked hard all week long finally emerge from church, look eagerly at one another, and cry *"Vamos a Texcoco!"* Don't be put off by the lack of curb appeal of Vamos's mini-mall-like location. There is perhaps no more authentic Mexican restaurant in this area—which is saying a great deal, considering it's pretty easy to *vamos* straight to the border from here. You'll find an unusual selection of legit Mexican classics, including ingredients, dishes, and drinks hardly seen in more quotidian spots: *huitlacoche*, freshly made *horchata* and lemonade with chia seeds, and melt-in-your-mouth *birria* (goat stew). On a hungry day (or, for your second visit, after your initial *barbacoa* appreciation visit), sample the legendary Martinez Special: lamb *barbacoa* plus garbanzos, rice, avocado, and *nopales*.

Fresh Corn Tortillas

MAKES 16 6-IN. TORTILLAS ❧ 1 HOUR, 10 MINUTES

Homemade tortillas are far better than store-bought, and easy to make once you get into a rhythm. In fact, you may find yourself making them every time you serve tacos! Masa harina can be found at any well-stocked supermarket. You'll need a tortilla press to make these.

4 cups finely ground deep yellow masa harina, such as Maseca

1 tsp. fine sea salt

Canola or other vegetable oil

1. In a large mixing bowl, combine the masa harina, salt, and 2¾ cups hot water; work with your hands until a dough forms. The dough should be slightly sticky, firm, and springy. Cover and let stand for 15 minutes, to hydrate. Test the consistency: Flatten a small ball of dough between your palms. If the edges crack, you'll need to add hot water to the dough, 1 tsp. at a time, until a test piece does not crack. If too wet and sticky, add masa harina, 1 tsp. at a time, until it feels like soft cookie dough.

2. Divide the dough into 16 pieces and roll into balls. Cover with plastic wrap to keep from drying out. Line the bottom of a tortilla press with a single sheet of waxed paper or plastic wrap and place the dough ball in the center. Place another sheet of waxed paper or plastic wrap over the top and close the press to flatten the ball of dough to about ⅛ in. thick and about 6 in. in diameter. Remove the dough disk and the sheets of waxed paper; layer between fresh sheets of waxed paper. Repeat to make 15 more tortillas.

3. Place a large cast-iron or nonstick skillet or a griddle over medium-high heat and brush with a little oil. Cook the tortillas until charred in places, and the edges start to curl, about 2 minutes. Turn over with a metal spatula and cook on the other side, about 1 to 2 minutes. Transfer to a kitchen towel and fold towel over to keep warm. Repeat to cook the remaining tortillas. Use immediately.

PER TORTILLA 162 Cal., 44% (71 Cal.) from fat; 3 g protein; 8 g fat (4.6 g sat.); 21 g carbo (2 g fiber); 95 mg sodium; 0 mg chol. GF/LS/VG

San Diego Zoo
Safari Park

ESCONDIDO

Kids of all ages love to hang out with the
goats (that includes brushing their hair),
see a cheetah run like the wind, and ride
the feed truck to get up close and personal
with giraffes and rhinos. This is a free-range
haven set on terrain that looks and
feels remarkably like wildest Africa itself.
15500 San Pasqual Valley Rd.;
sdzsafaripark.org

Fran's Original
Farm Stand

ESCONDIDO

One of the last vestiges of San Diego
County's once-huge agricultural industry,
Fran's offers superb, hyper-local fruit
and vegetables grown and sold by the same
family that's owned this land since 1924.
Ripe and luscious avocados, berries, persim-
mons, tomatoes, stone fruit, white corn, and
lots more. Hours vary with the season.
1980 Summit Dr.; thefarmstandwest.com

Mushroom Quesadillas

MAKES 4 QUESADILLAS ❖ 30 MINUTES

At Vamos a Texcoco, the lamb *barbacoa* (page 18) comes with a trio of rather unconventional—but hugely popular—quesadillas, all using housemade corn tortillas (page 15): mushroom, *huitlacoche* (corn fungus), and zucchini flowers. Since the last two contain ingredients that can be difficult to find, I'm sticking with just the mushroom quesadillas (plenty tasty!). If you can find *huitlacoche* and zucchini blossoms, by all means make all three. (You'll need very little of either—about 1/4 cup after chopping—as the key to a great, crispy-light quesadilla is to keep the filling ingredients to a minimum.)

Mushrooms

2 tsp. extra-virgin olive oil

8 oz. cremini or brown mushrooms, brushed clean, ends trimmed, and coarsely chopped

3 garlic cloves, minced or pushed through a press

1/4 tsp. red chile flakes

1/4 tsp. fine sea salt

Pinch of pepper

1 tbsp. finely chopped cilantro leaves and tender stems

1/2 cup (about 2 oz.) *each* shredded Monterey jack cheese and shredded cheddar cheese

Eight 6-in. corn tortillas, homemade (page 15) or purchased

2 tbsp. extra-virgin olive oil

Lime wedges

1. **PREPARE THE MUSHROOMS:** In a frying pan, warm the oil over medium-low heat. Add the mushrooms and sauté, stirring occasionally, until softened and juicy, about 4 minutes. Add the garlic, chile flakes, salt, and pepper. Cook until the pan is almost completely dry, 2 to 3 minutes more. Remove from the heat and stir in the cilantro.

2. Combine the jack and cheddar cheeses. Sprinkle about 2 tbsp. of the cheese mixture on 1 tortilla, followed by 2 tbsp. of the mushroom mixture, and then another 2 tbsp. of the cheese mixture. Top with a second tortilla to enclose the fillings. Repeat with the remaining tortillas, cheese, and mushrooms.

3. Preheat the oven to its lowest setting and place a paper towel–lined baking sheet on a rack in the oven. Place a large nonstick or cast-iron skillet over medium-high heat and add 1 tbsp. oil. When it's hot, add 2 of the quesadillas and cook until lightly browned on the bottom and a little cheese oozes out of the edges, pressing down on the top occasionally, 2 to 3 minutes. Turn over and cook until lightly browned on the other side, 1 to 2 minutes more. Transfer to the baking sheet in the oven. Repeat with the remaining 2 quesadillas, adding the remaining tbsp. of oil to the pan when it becomes dry. Cut the quesadillas in half or in wedges, and serve with lime wedges on the side.

PER QUESADILLA 535 Cal., 57% (304 Cal.) from fat; 15 g protein; 34 g fat (8.1 g sat.); 47 g carbo (4.9 g fiber); 453 mg sodium; 28 mg chol. GF/V

Barbacoa de Borrego (Lamb Barbecue)

SERVES 8 TO 10 ❈ 30 MINUTES, PLUS AT LEAST 7¹/₂ HOURS TO CHILL AND GRILL MEAT

Roberto Cuin serves his *barbacoa* with a brick red pasilla salsa, a fire-engine red salsa made with dried Japones chiles, and the green tomatillo salsa you see here. This is a simplified version of his legendary, labor-intensive dish. I do highly recommend using a charcoal grill, if you have one, for this rewarding project. For the full-on Vamos effect, serve the ethereal lamb with homemade tortillas and mushroom quesadillas (pages 15–17).

Tomatillo Salsa

¹/₂ lb. tomatillos, husked, washed, and cut into quarters

1 to 2 large jalapeño chiles, stemmed, seeded if desired, and roughly chopped

¹/₄ medium white onion, cut in half

2 cups chopped cilantro

2 tsp. fine sea salt

Lamb Adobo

6 dried ancho or guajillo chiles, stemmed and seeded

3 garlic cloves, sliced

1 medium onion, thinly sliced

¹/₂ tsp. dried oregano

1¹/₂ tsp. ground cumin

1 tbsp. firmly packed brown sugar

¹/₄ cup *each* white vinegar and lemon juice

1 tbsp. tomato paste

1¹/₂ tsp. fine sea salt

¹/₂ tsp. pepper

4-lb. boneless shoulder of lamb, fat trimmed, cut into 3-in. chunks

About 1¹/₂ lbs. fresh avocado or banana leaves (if using banana leaves, cut them into 11- by 14-in. rectangles)*

Steaming Broth

1 medium onion, finely chopped

2 carrots, finely chopped

¹/₂ head green cabbage, roughly chopped

1 (14.5-oz.) can diced tomatoes, undrained, or 1 large tomato, seeded and cut into dice

6 bay leaves

1 tsp. fine sea salt

Corn tortillas, homemade (page 15) or purchased

1 (14.5-oz.) can garbanzo beans, rinsed and well drained

2 cups cooked white rice

2 cups chopped cilantro

3 canned chipotle chiles in *adobo* sauce, finely chopped

1 tsp. fine sea salt

¹/₂ head green cabbage, shredded

1. **MAKE THE SALSA:** Purée the tomatillos, jalapeño, and ¹/₄ cup cold water in a blender just until chunky. Add the onion, cilantro, and salt and purée 1 minute more, until no large chunks remain.

2. **PREP THE LAMB ADOBO:** In a bowl, soak the chiles in warm water for about 15 minutes. Drain, then put in a blender with the garlic, onion, oregano, cumin, sugar, ¹/₂ cup water, vinegar, lemon juice, tomato paste, salt, and pepper. Purée to a smooth paste, adding a tsp. or more of water if necessary to thin. Rub it all over the lamb chunks, working it into the nooks and crannies. Chill on a baking sheet, uncovered, for 4 to 6 hours.

3. Prepare a charcoal or gas grill for indirect low heat (275° to 325°): *If using a charcoal grill,* light the charcoal. When the coals are covered with ash, in about 20 minutes, bank them on opposite sides of the firegrate, leaving space between for a wide, sturdy, grill-safe pot. Remove the lamb from the refrigerator. In the pot, combine 1 qt. water and the ingredients for the broth. Loosely wrap 1 lamb chunk in each avocado leaf, folding over slightly; use more than 1 leaf if necessary. Place the leaf packages on a metal rack large enough to put on top of your pot (if using banana leaves, put a layer of leaves on the rack, top with lamb chunks, nestling them together, and top with another layer of leaves). Place the pot of broth on the firegrate between the mounds of charcoal. Put the rack holding the leaf packages atop the pot of broth; close the grill lid. Grill for 2¹/₂ to 3¹/₂ hours, replenishing coals once or twice, until the lamb is falling-apart tender and an instant-read thermometer registers 170°. *If using a gas grill,* turn all burners to high, close the lid, and heat for 10 minutes. Then, turn off one burner and reduce the heat for the other(s) to low. Remove the lamb from the refrigerator. In a large pot or dutch oven, combine 1 qt. water and the ingredients for the broth. Bring to a boil, then reduce the heat to a low simmer. Cover and simmer 20 minutes or until the vegetables are tender. Transfer to a heavy-duty foil pan. Loosely wrap 1 lamb chunk in each avocado leaf, folding over slightly; use more than 1 leaf per

chunk if necessary. Put the foil pan with the broth directly on the ceramic coals (or flame tamers) on the unlit side of the grill. Place the leaf packages on the cooking grate on unlit side. (If using banana leaves, put a layer of leaves on the grate, top with lamb chunks, nestling them together, and top with another layer of leaves.) Close the grill lid. Grill for 2¹/₂ to 3¹/₂ hours, until the lamb is falling-apart tender and an instant-read thermometer registers 170°.

4. Wrap the tortillas in foil and warm on the grill for 10 minutes (or wrap in a damp towel and warm in a microwave 10 to 20 seconds). Stir the beans, rice, half

the cilantro, the chipotles, and salt into the broth; ladle into bowls and serve. Unwrap the lamb; pull apart slightly with forks and serve atop the leaves. Assemble the tortillas, cabbage, salsa, and remaining cilantro for making tacos. Enjoy!

* Find fresh avocado and banana leaves at Asian and Latino markets. Or substitute dried avocado leaves (soak them in hot water for 20 minutes before using).

PER SERVING 847 Cal., 43% (366 Cal.) from fat; 42 g protein; 41 g fat (11 g sat.); 81 g carbo (11 g fiber); 1,298 mg sodium; 114 mg chol.

APPLE ALLEY BAKERY

Julian

2122 Main St.
Julian, CA

(760) 765-2532

Six months after Debbie Gaudette started working at Apple Alley in 1993, she took the place over. "It was either that or be out of work," she says. Although she'd never worked in public food service, cooking and baking had been a passion forever. In 1993, Apple Alley was just a small courtyard: The street-front space now occupied by the dining room used to be a yarn shop, and pie sales occurred at a small counter down the alley behind it. Debbie and her husband, Keith, added the dining room in 2005, and a popular-with-locals-and-visitors-alike "soup-sandwich-pie" lunch special fills up all available indoor space—plus the pretty flower-decked side patio—daily. Debbie's caramel apple pecan pie was a ground-breaking first for the town, and she's not blind to evolving tastes: Hers is the only bakery in Julian (and there are quite a few) to offer a gluten-free crust, which she makes with rice flour. "And I still go home every night and cook or bake," she says.

Pumpkin Cookies with Cream Cheese Frosting

MAKES ABOUT 56 COOKIES
25 MINUTES, PLUS 45 MINUTES TO BAKE AND COOL

The drive up into what counts as mountains in Southern California, to reach the idyllic town of Julian, is a true scenic pleasure. But not a short one. What, then, accounts for the slavish devotion of the hordes who make this drive just for Debbie's famous pumpkin cookies? If possible, get to Julian with a long afternoon at your disposal, and find out for yourself. If that's not in the cards, make our version.

1. **MAKE THE FROSTING:** In a mixing bowl, beat the cream cheese with a handheld blender until smooth and creamy. Add the butter, 1 piece at a time, beating it in well. Scrape down the sides of the bowl, then sift the powdered sugar over the top and beat in well. Stir in the vanilla.

2. **MAKE THE COOKIES:** Preheat the oven to 375° and butter a large baking sheet. In the bowl of a mixer, beat the butter and sugar on medium speed until pale and fluffy. Beat in the eggs until incorporated. Thoroughly blend in the pumpkin, then sift the flour, baking powder, baking soda, salt, and cinnamon over the top. Blend in, then fold in the raisins and walnuts.

3. Using a small ice cream scoop or a soupspoon, drop the dough in 2-tbsp. portions onto the baking sheet, leaving about 1 in. between each. Bake until set and golden, 14 to 16 minutes. Cool about 2 minutes, then transfer to a wire rack. When completely cool, spread each cookie with some of the frosting.

PER COOKIE 121 Cal., 46% (56 Cal.) from fat; 1.7 g protein; 6.3 g fat (3.1 g sat.); 15 g carbo (0.6 g fiber); 103 mg sodium; 21 mg chol. LC/LS/V

Cream Cheese Frosting

8 oz. cream cheese, softened

½ cup unsalted butter, cut into 4 pieces and softened

1 cup powdered sugar

1 tsp. best-quality vanilla extract

Cookies

½ cup unsalted butter, softened, plus extra for preparing the pan

1½ cups granulated sugar

2 large eggs, lightly beaten

1 (15-oz.) can pumpkin purée (not pumpkin pie mix)

2½ cups cake flour

2½ tsp. baking powder

1 tsp. baking soda

1 tsp. salt

1½ tsp. ground cinnamon

1 cup raisins

1 cup walnuts, roughly chopped

Apple-Boysenberry Crumble Pie

MAKES ONE 10-IN. PIE; SERVES 10

25 MINUTES, PLUS 1 HOUR, 20 MINUTES TO BAKE AND 1 HOUR TO COOL

Here, then, is what it's all about in Julian, home of ethereal apples, and of exquisite apple pie. If at all possible, take the time to drive the winding road all the way up from the coast past safari parks and palm tree nurseries, past biker havens and sere vistas, to see Debbie and taste her legendary pie. There is something almost magical in this marriage of earthy-sweet apples and tart, purple boysenberries. And don't get me started on the crumble topping!

Pie Dough

1½ cups all-purpose flour

½ cup cold unsalted butter, cut into pieces

¼ tsp. salt

5 to 6 tbsp. ice water

Crumble Topping

¼ cup unsalted butter, melted

½ tsp. vanilla extract

¾ cup all-purpose flour

⅔ cup granulated sugar

¼ tsp. fine sea salt

1½ lbs. (3 large) Granny Smith or other cooking apples, peeled, cored, sliced, and halved crosswise

1 lb. (3 cups) fresh or thawed frozen boysenberries or blackberries

1 cup granulated sugar

2½ tbsp. cornstarch

½ tsp. ground cinnamon

Cinnamon or vanilla ice cream, for serving

1. **MAKE THE PIE DOUGH:** Combine the flour, butter, and salt in a bowl. Cut the butter into the flour with a pastry blender or two knives until the mixture resembles small peas. Sprinkle the ice water, 1 tbsp. at a time, over the mixture in the bowl. Stir with a fork until the dry ingredients are moistened. Shape into a flat disk, then wrap in plastic wrap and chill for at least 1 hour and up to overnight.

2. Preheat the oven to 375° and position a rack in the lower third of the oven. Roll the dough into a 14-in. circle on a lightly floured surface. Fit into a 9-in. deep-dish pie pan, fold the edges under, and crimp. Chill while preparing the filling.

3. **MAKE THE CRUMBLE:** In a small bowl, stir together the melted butter and vanilla. In another bowl, combine the flour, ⅔ cup sugar, and salt and stir together with a fork. Add the butter mixture and stir until evenly blended and crumbly.

4. In a large bowl, combine the apples, boysenberries, 1 cup sugar, cornstarch, and cinnamon. Toss together until thoroughly and evenly blended. Mound the fruit mixture into the pie shell, pressing slightly to make sure it all fits securely. Scatter the crumble topping evenly over the top of the pie, pressing it into the gaps and crevices slightly to help it adhere. Place on a baking sheet and bake for 1 hour and 20 minutes, until the fruit is tender and bubbly and the crust and topping are deep golden brown. Watch the pie and, if the topping or crust edges seem to brown too quickly, cover it loosely with foil. Cool on a rack for 1 hour. Serve warm, cut into wedges, each accompanied by a scoop of ice cream.

PER SERVING (NOT INCLUDING ICE CREAM) 416 Cal., 30% (126 Cal.) from fat; 3.7 g protein; 14 g fat (9 g sat.); 70 g carbo (2.7 g fiber); 99 mg sodium; 37 mg chol. LS/V

Oasis Camel Dairy

RAMONA

Yes, you can ride a camel here, but the animal-loving family that owns and runs this place also teaches all levels of camel training, grooming, and care; the emphasis is on helping your camel (not that most people have a camel) have so much fun that he/she wants to learn! There are exotic birds doing fun tricks, and camel's-milk hand lotion to die for. State 78, about 1/4 mi. west of intersection with Old Julian Hwy; cameldairy.com

Julian Tea & Cottage Arts

JULIAN

Every possible kind of tea, plus vessels for brewing and serving tea, and myriad things floral and cute that might possibly be associated with tea, all riotously populate this two-story Victorian. Afternoon tea is served with scones and clotted cream, just as in Jolly Old England. Bonus: excellent pumpkin soup and scrummy finger sandwiches. 2124 Third St.; juliantea.com

Stop 3

OINK AND MOO BURGERS AND BBQ

Fallbrook

121 N. Pico Ave.
Fallbrook, CA

(760) 451-6005

oinkandmoo.com

Fallbrook feels like it was slightly bypassed by the mall-ification that surrounds it, and the locals are happy to keep it that way. But they also want tasty and festive nosh; Oink and Moo mightily (and meat-ily) satisfies that need. But there's a palpably pork-centric—and definitely wacky— sense of humor in evidence too: Witness the borderline kitschy animal decor of the outdoor patio, and the cow paintings in the cozy, colorful little bar. These culinary and design sensibilities flow straight from the active minds of husband-and-wife owners Jonathan and Jennifer Arbel, who hail from the East Coast but met in San Francisco. Finding this "secret" place, they tell me, felt like discovering a new frontier. They set out to make a stand, carve out a niche, and circle the wagons. (Yeee-haw!) Jennifer runs the front of the house with the kind of vital hospitality that's a pleasure to encounter, and Jonathan wields impossibly sharp knives and cutting-edge humor in the kitchen, where he chooses names for his dishes that will have you doing a double take. The first time.

Sweet Potato Fries with Honey-Maple Drizzle

SERVES 4 ❖ 30 MINUTES

Chef Jonathan's trick of dusting these fries lightly with cornstarch yields a tender, just lightly crispy fry, quite unlike—and superior to—the hard-shelled fast-food fries you may (somehow) be intimately familiar with. Whenever you are deep-frying at home, I recommend banishing children and animals from the kitchen until serving time.

About 2 qts. canola or vegetable oil, for deep-frying

3 lbs. sweet potatoes (2 to 3 large potatoes), washed, peeled, and sliced into ½-in. by 3- to 4-in. sticks

2 tbsp. cornstarch

1 tbsp. maple syrup

1 tbsp. honey

Fine sea salt and pepper

2 tsp. finely chopped fresh flat-leaf parsley

1. Fill a deep-fryer or deep, heavy pot no more than one-third full of oil and heat until it registers 375° on a deep-fry thermometer. Preheat oven to 200°. Line a large baking sheet with a double layer of paper towels and set in oven to warm. In a large bowl, toss half the sweet potatoes with half the cornstarch; ideally, there should be a light dusting on all sides of the fries. In a small bowl, combine the maple syrup and honey.

2. In a mesh skimmer or a fryer basket, gently lower the dusted sweet potatoes into the hot oil, then stir with a slotted spoon to prevent them from clumping together. Fry until cooked through, stirring occasionally, about 8 minutes. Transfer to the warm baking sheet, immediately sprinkle with salt and pepper, and keep warm in the oven. Return the oil to 375°. Toss the second half of the sweet potatoes with the remaining cornstarch, then fry as before (if the oil is not hot enough, the potatoes will absorb too much oil and be greasy). Again, transfer to the baking sheet and sprinkle with salt and pepper.

3. Transfer the fries to a serving bowl or platter and drizzle with the maple-honey mixture. Scatter the chopped parsley over the top.

PER SERVING 332 Cal., 24% (79 Cal.) from fat; 3.9 g protein; 8.9 g fat (0.1 g sat.); 61 g carbo (7.4 g fiber); 136 mg sodium; 0 mg chol. LS/VG

Pala Mesa Nursery

FALLBROOK

The Fallbrook area is home to many specimen tree, succulent, and palm nurseries, but not a lot of them also provide knowledgeable "counseling" to reassure home gardeners about to make an important purchase (it's almost like getting a puppy!). The folks here will happily walk you through your new friend's needs. 3235 Old Hwy. 395; palamesanursery.com

Goat-a-licious Burgers with Apricot Chutney

SERVES 4 ❖ 30 MINUTES, PLUS 30 MINUTES TO CHILL

Initially, I thought this was going to be a burger made with ground goat meat, but actually it's an American-style classic, topped with piquant goat cheese and a radical earthy-sweet chutney. For a tender and juicy burger, keep the meat crumbly, not compressed; remember to use a light hand when transferring the meat from the food processor and forming the burger patties. The air pockets left in an uncompressed burger patty are the perfect place for delicious juices to hide.

Burgers

1⅓ lbs. well-marbled beef chuck, cut into 1-in. cubes

½ tsp. fine sea salt

½ tsp. pepper

Chutney

1 tsp. extra-virgin olive oil

2 small garlic cloves, minced

1 tbsp. sun-dried tomato paste (or minced oil-packed sun-dried tomatoes)

½ tsp. white wine vinegar or red wine vinegar

4 fresh basil leaves, finely chopped

Pinch of red pepper flakes

½ cup apricot jam

Sauce

½ cup mayonnaise

1 tbsp. Thousand Island dressing or ketchup

⅛ tsp. fine sea salt

Pinch of pepper

Pinch of Cajun seasoning or hot chile powder

Goat Cheese Spread

½ cup fresh goat cheese, softened

4 fresh basil leaves, roughly chopped

4 best-quality buns or rolls, split

2 tsp. extra-virgin olive oil, plus extra for brushing burgers

1 cup mixed greens

2 tsp. balsamic vinegar

4 slices thick-cut smoked bacon, halved crosswise and cooked until crispy

1. Place the cubes of beef in a single layer on one or two baking sheets that will fit into your freezer. Freeze, uncovered, for 20 minutes, or until firm. (While freezing, make the chutney, sauce, and spread.)

2. **MAKE THE CHUTNEY:** In a small skillet, warm the oil over low heat. Add the garlic and sauté, stirring frequently, until softened, about 20 seconds. Stir in the sun-dried tomato paste, vinegar, basil, and pepper flakes; remove from the heat and stir in the apricot jam.

3. **MAKE THE SAUCE AND THE SPREAD:** In a small bowl, whisk together all the ingredients for the sauce. In another small bowl, stir together the goat cheese and basil.

4. **MAKE THE PATTIES:** In a large food processor, add about a third of the meat. Pulse about 12 times, until the meat is coarsely chopped; don't let it turn to mush. (You may have to remove the processor's top and redistribute the meat to achieve an even chop.) Scrape out into a bowl without compacting the meat, and continue with the second and third batches in the same way. Using a fork, mix in the salt and pepper. With a light hand, form 4 loosely packed patties, then gently flatten to 1 in. thick and about 3 in. in diameter. Chill for 15 minutes.

5. **COOK THE BURGERS:** Preheat the broiler and assemble all the ingredients. Toast the bun halves cut sides up until golden. Place a large, well-seasoned cast-iron skillet over medium-high heat. When it is very hot, reduce the heat to medium, brush one side of the burgers with oil and season generously with salt. Add the burgers oiled side down, and cook without disturbing for 3 minutes. Oil and salt the top sides, then turn the burgers with a metal spatula. Cook until a meat thermometer at the thickest point reads 145°, 1½ to 2 minutes more, for medium (or to taste). Transfer to a platter and place in the turned-off oven.

6. **TO SERVE:** Let the burgers stand for 5 minutes while you toss the mixed greens with the oil and balsamic vinegar; season with salt and pepper. Assemble the goat-a-licious burgers as follows: Spread some sauce on the bun base, then top with the burger, a quarter of the goat cheese, 2 halves of bacon, and some chutney. Top with the dressed greens. Serve open-face.

PER SERVING 974 Cal., 59% (576 Cal.) from fat; 44 g protein; 64 g fat (23 g sat.); 57 g carbo (1.6 g fiber); 1,145 mg sodium; 146 mg chol.

BBQ Pork Lettuce Cups

SERVES 6 TO 8 ❧ 20 MINUTES, PLUS 3½ HOURS TO BRAISE

I think of this immensely appealing dish as a sort of low-carb taco. But that's just me. Pork shoulder, combined with Asian-spiced yumminess and subjected to a low-and-slow easy braise, becomes unctuous and addictive. No wonder Oink and Moo is the hottest ticket in small but fabulous Fallbrook. Are you in the car yet? If you like, make your own barbecue sauce (see page 86).

Pork

4 garlic cloves, peeled and smashed with a heavy knife

¼ cup of your favorite barbecue sauce

¼ cup Asian plum sauce

¼ cup rice vinegar

3 tbsp. soy sauce, preferably low-sodium

3 tbsp. low-sodium beef or chicken broth

¾ tsp. fine sea salt

2 lbs. pork shoulder, trimmed, cut into 3 large chunks

4 star anise pods

4 thick slices fresh ginger, unpeeled

2 small heads iceberg lettuce, wilted leaves pulled off, cored, and pulled apart into 2 rough halves

1 cup Thai sweet red chili sauce

¼ cup minced English cucumber

6 green onions, ends trimmed, finely chopped

¼ cup chopped salted peanuts

¼ cup roughly chopped cilantro

2 limes, quartered

1. **BRAISE THE PORK:** Preheat the oven to 300°. In a small, heavy dutch oven or covered baking dish just large enough to hold the pork in a single layer, combine the garlic, barbecue sauce, plum sauce, vinegar, soy sauce, broth, and salt. Add the pork chunks and turn to coat evenly with the sauce. Cover the pot, and cook in the oven for 1 hour. Turn the pork pieces over and baste with the pan juices. Cook for 1 hour more, then turn and baste again. Add the star anise and ginger and cook until the meat is falling-apart tender, 1 to 1½ hours more (ideally, basting with the pan juices every 45 minutes or so). When the meat is cool enough to handle, pull off and discard any large, visible pockets of fat; discard the ginger slices and star anise. Use two forks to shred the meat right in the pot, mixing it with the rich pan juices.

2. To crisp the lettuce cups, fill a large bowl with ice water and immerse the halved heads of lettuce in the water, open sides up (be sure water gets in between all the leaves). In a small bowl, combine the sweet chili sauce, cucumber, and half the green onions (this is the dipping sauce). In a medium serving bowl, fold together the pulled pork (with all the juices), remaining green onions, peanuts, and cilantro. Separate the lettuce into small cups, shaking off the excess water and reserving the larger outer leaves for another use. On a large platter, arrange piles of lettuce cups, the pulled pork, and the dipping sauce. Squeeze a little lime juice over the pork, then place the remaining lime quarters in a bowl on the platter. Provide spoons or chopsticks, so guests can assemble their own lettuce cups, dip into the sauce, and enjoy.

PER SERVING 372 Cal., 43% (160 Cal.) from fat; 24 g protein; 18 g fat (6 g sat.); 26 g carbo (2.3 g fiber); 817 mg sodium; 83 mg chol. LC

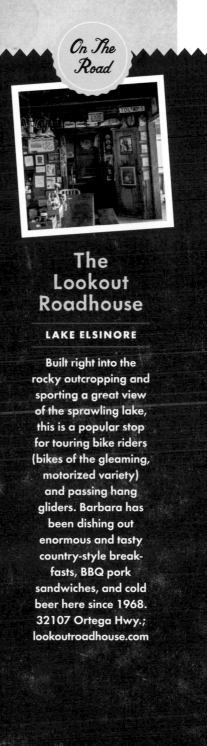

The Lookout Roadhouse

LAKE ELSINORE

Built right into the rocky outcropping and sporting a great view of the sprawling lake, this is a popular stop for touring bike riders (bikes of the gleaming, motorized variety) and passing hang gliders. Barbara has been dishing out enormous and tasty country-style break-fasts, BBQ pork sandwiches, and cold beer here since 1968. 32107 Ortega Hwy.; lookoutroadhouse.com

Route 2

Guadalupe-
Nipomo Dunes
Preserve
p. 53

TO AVOID THE HUGE BLOB of Los Angeles, I begin Route 2 after leaving Interstate 5 and heading west toward Fillmore. Instant reward: myriad farmstands and the box-grown birthplace of those huge palm trees that dot the Southern California landscape. Fillmore is the darling of Hollywood location managers: picturesque, historical, agricultural—it's an intact slice of Old California.

For a fantastic OTBT experience, drive north on State 150 toward *Ojai* from Santa Paula. Small family ranches, orchards, and iconic views line the winding 19 miles to Ojai, a now-gentrified artists and theosophists haven of leafy drives, mission architecture, and many a Hollywood location manager's weekend home.

Bypassing the moneyed slopes of Santa Barbara, this strikingly scenic route follows Casitas Pass Road west of Ojai, paralleling the coast and skirting inland of Montecito, to join State 154 over the San Marcos Pass and straight down into polished, farmstand-chic *Los Olivos*.

We're now finished with the overpopulated terrain of the south, and the road jogs mostly inland, leaving the coast until just north of Route 2's end. Back on the 101 is once-gritty *Los Alamos*; a few years ago, you could see tumbleweeds on the main street—now there are galleries, tasting rooms, and more great restaurants per capita than in Greenwich Village. You Have Entered Wine Country.

Little *Nipomo*, "gateway to the Central Coast," was an important stop on El Camino Real, the route from mission to mission, in the mid-1800s. More recently, it was the setting for Dorothea Lange's iconic photo *Migrant Mother*, a harsh reminder of the dust bowl conditions of the Depression.

Ember
p. 53

Jocko's
Steak House
p. 50

ARROYO GRANDE

NIPOMO

Full of Life
Flatbread
p. 49

Bell Street
Farm
p. 44

GUADALUPE   166

1

Los Olivos
p. 40

The Ranch
House
p. 32

Ojai Hiking
Trails
p. 34

LOS ALAMOS   101

LOMPOC   246

LOS OLIVOS

Sides Hardware
and Shoes
p. 38

SANTA YNEZ

1

154

Knead
Baking
Company
p. 34

OJAI   150

SANTA BARBARA   192   101

33

La Purisima
Mission
p. 40

S.Y. Kitchen
p. 37

THE RANCH HOUSE

Ojai

The Ranch House has remained virtually the same for decades. Why, then, does it not feel dated? In fact, it may be the most perfect place for a date in this entire book. More marriage proposals have taken place at table 101 than anyone can count (the award-winning wine cellar may help with this). Random tall stands of bamboo make many of the tables into idyllic islands of their own, and little ponds teem with koi as big as dachshunds—and almost as feisty. Small, arched bridges over the ponds are perfect for posing upon. ("Honey? Did you bring the camera?")

Alan Hooker—member of the Theosophical Society in Ojai—tried to open this former boardinghouse as a vegetarian restaurant in 1953, but it didn't fly. He famously asked Krishnamurti (the philosopher who'd led the society), "What shall I do?" Krishnamurti responded, "Do you want to stay in business? Then it's okay to serve fish and meat." So in 1958, he did, and the restaurant has been open ever since. It's a quintessentially California story. And restaurant.

Coffee and Rum Crème Brûlée

SERVES 4 ❈ 45 MINUTES, PLUS 3 TO 24 HOURS TO COOL

This adults-only concoction could be the reason why dessert is so popular at The Ranch House. At least the coffee content will keep everyone perky enough for some midnight rambles.

2 cups (1 pint) premium coffee ice cream

4 large egg yolks

3 tbsp. sugar, plus 8 tsp. for topping

1 tsp. vanilla extract

2 tsp. dark Jamaican rum, such as Myers's

1. Preheat the oven to 325°F. In a saucepan, melt the ice cream over low heat, stirring, just until it reaches 160° on an instant-read thermometer; it will be steaming, but do not allow it to boil. Remove from the heat. In a bowl, combine the egg yolks and 3 tbsp. sugar. Beat with a whisk until the sugar has dissolved and the mixture is thickened and pale.

2. Whisking constantly, slowly pour the melted ice cream into the egg mixture. Pour the mixture through a fine strainer into a large glass measuring pitcher. Stir in the vanilla and rum.

3. Place four 4-oz. ramekins or custard cups in a baking pan large enough to hold the ramekins in one layer. Divide the custard between the ramekins; it should come to about 1/4 in. below the rim. Pour boiling water into the pan to reach halfway up the sides of the ramekins. Transfer the pan to the oven and bake until the edges of the custard are set and the centers are slightly jiggly, about 30 minutes.

4. Let cool to room temperature in the water bath. Remove the ramekins and cover each with plastic wrap. Chill for at least 2 hours and up to overnight.

5. When ready to serve, sprinkle 2 tsp. sugar in an even layer over each custard. For best results, use a small handheld torch to melt and caramelize the sugar. Or, preheat a broiler and place the ramekins underneath until the sugar melts, rotating the ramekins so the sugar melts and caramelizes evenly.

PER SERVING 372 Cal., 47% (176 Cal.) from fat; 6.7 g protein; 20 g fat (12 g sat.); 40 g carbo (0 g fiber); 68 mg sodium; 285 mg chol. GF/LS/V

Ojai Hiking Trails

OJAI

Just south of the Los Padres National Forest, Ojai is an idyllic inland refuge from the busy coast, and hiking trails range from easy to challenging, along creekbeds and through citrus and avocado groves to mountain peaks—always with excellent views. You may even see some Chumash pictographs. Choose from Shelf Road Trail, Pratt Trail Loop, and Last Chance Trail. Shelf Rd.: alltrails.com; Pratt: trails.com; Last Chance: ventura countytrails.com

Knead Baking Company

OJAI

This tiny, family-run bakery oozes passion from every croissant (especially the chocolate-nutella!). Bobbi, Leah, Rachel, and Jake have taken the concept of artisanal baking to heart, and incorporate the edible bounty of this jewel-like, historic, old-California community in every bite. The breakfast sandwich has so many devoted admirers that securing one on a weekend may take a little time. Persevere. 469 E. Ojai Ave.; (310) 770-3282; kneadbakingcompany.com

Wild Mushroom Strudels

MAKES 28 MINI STRUDELS; SERVES 6 TO 8 AS AN APPETIZER

1 1/2 HOURS, PLUS 4 HOURS TO THAW FILO

At The Ranch House, these bite-size mushroom strudels are served with a decadent wine-cream sauce and sprinkled with diced green onions and red peppers, but you can also serve them as finger food as part of a buffet, or pass them on a platter.

Mushroom Filling

1/2 oz. dried wild mushrooms (morel, porcini, or shiitake)

1/3 cup madeira wine

12 oz. button mushrooms

12 oz. portobello mushrooms

4 tbsp. butter

1 large shallot, peeled and finely chopped

1 cup finely chopped yellow onion

1/2 tsp. dried thyme

3/4 tsp. fine sea salt, plus more to taste

1/4 tsp. pepper, plus more to taste

1/8 tsp. grated nutmeg

7 (14- by 18-in.) sheets filo dough, thawed*

1/4 cup warm melted butter

1. MAKE THE MUSHROOM FILLING: Rinse the dried mushrooms and combine in a small bowl with the madeira. Let stand for 1 hour. Brush the fresh mushrooms, and clean and trim off the woody ends of the stems. In a food processor, pulse the fresh mushrooms until very finely chopped. Place a large pan over low heat and add the butter. When it has melted, add the shallot and onion, cover the pan, and cook gently, stirring occasionally, until tender and slightly golden, about 25 minutes.

2. Add the fresh mushrooms, thyme, salt, pepper, and nutmeg to the skillet. Increase the heat to medium-high and cook uncovered, stirring, until the mushrooms have rendered their juices, about 5 minutes. Meanwhile, transfer the reconstituted dried mushrooms and any soaking liquid to the food processor and pulse until finely puréed and smooth. Add the purée to the pan, reduce the heat and cook, stirring occasionally, until the mixture is reduced and thickened, about 40 minutes. Near the end, pay close attention, as the mixture can scorch; it should be quite dry. Remove from heat, correct the seasonings with salt and pepper, and cool to room temperature. Cover and chill, about 1 hour or up to overnight.

3. Preheat the oven to 400° and lightly oil two rimmed baking sheets. Unwrap the thawed filo and separate out 7 sheets*. Place on a work surface with one long end facing you and cut the whole stack crosswise into quarters—each strip will be approximately 3 1/3 in. wide. Cover the strips with a barely damp kitchen towel. Working with 1 filo strip at a time, and keeping the others covered with the damp towel, place the strip on a dry work surface. Brush lightly but thoroughly with the melted butter. Place about 1 tbsp. of the filling 1 in. from the bottom edge. Fold the lower right corner of the pastry up and over the filling, forming a triangle, and continue folding back and forth (as though you were folding a flag) until you reach the end of the strip. Transfer to the baking sheet and brush the top of the triangle with a little more of the butter. Make the remaining triangles in the same way, dividing them between the baking sheets.

4. Bake until the triangles are crisp and golden brown, 15 to 20 minutes. Let cool 5 minutes, then serve.

*Filo pastry takes about 4 hours to thaw at room temperature. Reroll the unused sheets of filo and wrap them securely with plastic to exclude any air. Return to the box, chill, and use within 1 week. Or refreeze and use within 2 months.

MAKE AHEAD: The strudels can be frozen for up to 1 week in airtight containers, separated by layers of parchment or waxed paper. When ready to serve, cook them straight from frozen, adding 5 minutes or so to the cooking time.

PER SERVING 252 Cal., 63% (159 Cal.) from fat; 4.3 g protein; 18 g fat (9.2 g sat.); 19 g carbo (1.9 g fiber); 742 mg sodium; 35 mg chol. V

Grilled Quail Salad
with Honey-Mustard Vinaigrette

SERVES 4 ❖ 30 MINUTES, PLUS AT LEAST 3 HOURS TO MARINATE AND STAND

The Ranch House is delightfully and unapologetically Old California. But back in the days when my mother attended school in the still-small town of Ojai, the quail would have been caught outside the back door and served simply with mashed potatoes. It never would've experienced this wine-rich marinade, then be grilled and served atop a fresh salad. In the case of this dish, progress is good. Note: If the quail have been boned out, you obviously will not need to spatchcock them (cut out the backbones, to lie flat, as described in the recipe).

4 quail, 3 to 4 oz. each

Marinade

¾ cup Pinot Noir or other dry red wine

⅓ cup honey

2 tbsp. Dijon mustard

2 tsp. chopped fresh thyme

½ tsp. fine sea salt

¼ tsp. pepper

⅓ cup canola or vegetable oil

Vinaigrette

½ cup canola or vegetable oil

2 tbsp. toasted sesame oil

1 tsp. grated or minced fresh ginger

¼ cup rice vinegar

1 tbsp. honey

½ tsp. Dijon mustard

¼ tsp. fine sea salt

Salad

¼ cup pine nuts

4 cups mixed baby greens

1 cup cherry tomatoes, halved

1 carrot, thinly sliced crosswise

1. Rinse the quail and pat dry thoroughly with paper towels inside and out. With kitchen shears or a heavy, sharp knife, cut out the backbones and press down on the breastbones with the palm of your hand to flatten them. Cut each quail in half lengthwise (through the breast bone). If desired, remove the thigh bones and part of the breast cage (this will make them easier to eat), scraping as much meat off the bone as you can.

2. **MAKE THE MARINADE:** In a large resealable plastic bag, combine all the ingredients for the marinade. Add the quail and turn to coat all sides. Chill at least 2 hours and up to 6 hours. Return to room temperature for 1 hour before grilling.

3. **MAKE THE VINAIGRETTE:** In a small bowl, whisk together all the ingredients until smooth.

4. Prepare a charcoal or gas grill for high heat (450° to 550°) and oil the cooking grate. Grill the quail, until dark grill marks show and meat is firm but still a little pink at the bone, about 5 minutes, turning once or twice. Do not overcook, or they will be tough. Let stand for 5 to 10 minutes.

5. Meanwhile, in a small pan over medium heat, cook the pine nuts until lightly toasted, about 3 minutes. In a bowl, toss together the greens, tomatoes, and carrot. Add the pine nuts. Re-whisk the vinaigrette and drizzle a little over the salad. Toss to coat all the ingredients evenly, and divide among four plates. Top each salad with a grilled quail and serve. Pass the remaining vinaigrette.

PER SERVING 641 Cal., 78% (499 Cal.) from fat; 22 g protein; 56 g fat (6.9 g sat.); 17 g carbo (1.9 g fiber); 266 mg sodium; 67 mg chol. GF/LS

These succulent little birds are still a proud part of California's cuisine, just as they were when my mother roamed these hills in her dusty cowboy boots and pigtails.

On The Road

S.Y. Kitchen

SANTA YNEZ

At this sleek, modern-farmhouse joint in wine country—within spitting distance of LA-LA Land—you're definitely going to eat well. The big draw here is rustic, flavor-forward Italian cuisine, with a focus on what's local, both on the plate and in the glass. The owners also helm Brentwood's tony Toscana, and both their chef-partner Luca and maestro mixologist Alberto are straight out of Verona (cue the "two gents of" jokes). There's a wood-fired oven, so get ready to tear into impeccable pizza and oak-scented meat. Buona Notte! 1110 Faraday St.; (805) 691-9794; sykitchen.com

Stop 2

SIDES HARDWARE AND SHOES

Los Olivos

2375 Alamo
Pintado Ave.
Los Olivos, CA

(805) 688-4820

sidesrestaurant.com

The owners of this eatery are brothers Matt and Jeff Nichols. They opened the sunshine-filled space after closing their über-popular space at the historic Mattei's Tavern, just around the corner. The name is in honor of the store that occupied this building more than 100 years ago. Locals were thrilled the brothers would be reopening anywhere nearby, though at first controversy simmered about the name. Now, everyone just calls it Sides, and lines the rustic, brick-studded sidewalk waiting for a chance to sample a Hammered Pig sandwich or salad ("hammered," because of the hardware connection, natch), the outrageous albacore, or the pork belly tacos. In the high-ceilinged dining room bordered by an airy, classy bar (yes, of course I ate at the bar), there's a large black-and-white photo of the original clapboard store. Los Olivos long ago shed its identity as a dusty ranching hub. In fact, it's outstripped nearby Santa Ynez as the hippest little burg in the SB/SY (Santa Barbara/Santa Ynez) wine country. Loved the movie *Sideways*? Then you're already a fan of this area, but beware: *Sideways* country has gotten really sophisticated.

Fried Brussels Sprouts with Sherry Vinegar and Capers

SERVES 4 TO 6 ❈ 10 MINUTES

Sure, you could roast these amazing little miniature cabbages rather than deep-frying them, but when the result is as sublime as in this crispy-salty-sour dish, it's best to just give in. At Sides, these function as addictive bar food par excellence.

Canola or vegetable oil, for deep-frying

1½ lbs. small brussels sprouts

2 tbsp. sherry vinegar

½ tsp. sugar

¾ tsp. fine sea salt, or to taste

1 tbsp. drained capers

1. Prepare a deep-fryer or a deep, heavy pot no more than one-third full of oil for frying at 350°. Trim away any loose or discolored leaves from the base of each sprout, leaving the root intact. Cut the sprouts in half through the root.

2. In batches, fry the brussels sprouts for 1½ to 2 minutes, until golden brown with crispy bits on the outside but not burned. Lift from the oil with a skimmer, drain for a moment, and immediately toss with the sherry vinegar. Season with sugar and salt, then add the capers and toss again; serve at once.

PER SERVING 98 Cal., 48% (47 Cal.) from fat; 2.7 g protein; 5.4 g fat (0.4 g sat.); 8.9 g carbo (4.1 g fiber); 266 mg sodium; 0 mg chol. GF/LC/LS/VG

La Purisima Mission

LOMPOC

Founded in 1787 and once commanding 470 square miles, this pink adobe compound has been extensively restored—it's a superb example of the string of Franciscan missions that once lined El Camino Real exactly one day's horseback ride apart. Take a self-guided tour and get up close and personal with Old California. 2295 Purisima Rd.; lapurisimamission.org

The Charming Town of Los Olivos

LOS OLIVOS

Named for the 5,000 olive trees planted at a nearby ranch in 1885, this town now boasts a plethora of small, independent art galleries, studios, and boutiques arranged in bucolic, magazine-ready fashion along wide, sidewalk-free streets. One of my favorites is Los Olivos General Store, in one of the first gas stations in the state. losolivosca.com

Hammered Pig Salad

SERVES 4 ❖ 35 MINUTES

Full disclosure: I put Sides on my must-visit list because of the name of this dish. I had visions of a rather tipsy porker, fetchingly waving lettuce leaves over his or her head. The reality is every bit as enticing (well, a tipsy porker is enticing to me). The crust is shatteringly crisp and thick with promise, while the lemony-garlicky vinaigrette drizzles down gently into all its nooks and crannies. Sitting at the bar, thinking of the old-time hardware store that stood on this spot more than 100 years ago, I reveled in my favorite kind of spiritual, retro-California heaven.

Lemon Garlic Vinaigrette

4 garlic cloves, peeled

2 tbsp. lemon juice

1/2 cup canola or vegetable oil

1/2 tsp. fine sea salt

1 tsp. finely grated lemon zest

Pork

1 1/4 lbs. pork tenderloin*, cut into 4 equal portions

1 tsp. fine sea salt

1/4 tsp. pepper

1 1/2 cups all-purpose flour

2 large eggs

1 1/2 cups *panko* bread crumbs

3 tbsp. unsalted butter

3 tbsp. olive oil

Salad

2 cups (2 oz.) baby arugula

1/3 cup roughly chopped pecans, lightly toasted

4 radishes, thinly sliced

1/3 cup dried cherries

About 1 cup bite-size pieces of seasonal fruit*

1/3 cup coarsely grated grana padano or parmesan cheese

Lemon wedges, for serving

1. **MAKE THE VINAIGRETTE:** In a small saucepan, cover the garlic cloves with cold water and bring to a boil. Immediately drain in a colander, then cover the garlic again with cold water, bring to a boil, and drain. Repeat a third time. In a blender or mini food processor, combine the garlic, lemon juice, canola oil, and salt. Blend until creamy. Stir in the lemon zest.

2. On a work surface, lay a 10-in. sheet of plastic wrap. Place a piece of tenderloin in the center and lay another sheet of plastic wrap on top. Use the flat side of a meat mallet to pound lightly, gently easing the meat out into a rectangle about 1/4 in. thick. The pork should be roughly 6 to 8 in. by 3 to 4 in. Repeat with the remaining pieces.

3. Season the pork all over with the salt and pepper. Spread the flour on a plate. In a wide, shallow bowl, beat the eggs together. Place the panko on another plate; assemble all three near the stove. In a large sauté pan, heat the butter and oil over medium-high heat until sizzling. Working with 1 piece at a time, dip the pork first in the flour, shaking off any excess, and then in the beaten egg, coating it completely. Finally, dredge in the panko, making sure all sides are coated evenly, and gently shake off the excess. Place the pork in the pan and continue with the remaining 3 pieces, placing them in a single layer (work in batches if necessary). Cook without disturbing until deep golden brown on the bottom, about 3 minutes. Working in the order added to the pan, turn the pork over with a metal spatula and cook until the other side is golden, about 3 minutes more. Drain briefly on paper towels and transfer each piece to a warm plate.

4. **MAKE THE SALAD:** In a large bowl, combine the arugula, pecans, radishes, cherries, fresh fruit, and cheese. Add about 1/4 cup vinaigrette and toss quickly to coat thoroughly. Place a mound of salad on each plate. The salad should slightly overlap the pork. Serve with lemon wedges to squeeze over, and pass any additional vinaigrette at the table.

*Ideally, use locally and sustainably raised pork. For the seasonal fruit, choose from mangos, apples, pears, peaches, or berries—whatever is in season and available locally.

PER SERVING 791 Cal., 61% (479 Cal.) from fat; 39 g protein; 54 g fat (10 g sat.); 39 g carbo (5.7 g fiber); 813 mg sodium; 166 mg chol.

Grilled Toma Cheese with Caramelized Onions

MAKES 4 SANDWICHES ❖ 45 MINUTES

Now here's a truly iconic SoCal experience: Relax on the front patio of Sides and watch the beautiful people drive by (some of them alone in vehicles that could house a soccer team, others in beat-up pickup trucks accessorized with dogs), while you nibble on good honest California freshness from the kitchen. This addictive sandwich is served with a house salad and fries on the side, but would also be lovely with a very light slaw—especially if fennel were involved.

Caramelized Onions

2 tbsp. olive oil

1 large yellow onion (about 1 lb.), halved and thinly sliced crosswise

½ tsp. fine sea salt

¼ tsp. pepper

½ cup unsalted butter, thoroughly softened

8 large slices rustic sourdough bread, about ½ in. thick

14 oz. Point Reyes Toma cheese or gouda, sliced ¼ in. thick

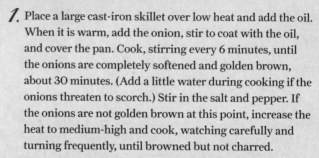

1. Place a large cast-iron skillet over low heat and add the oil. When it is warm, add the onion, stir to coat with the oil, and cover the pan. Cook, stirring every 6 minutes, until the onions are completely softened and golden brown, about 30 minutes. (Add a little water during cooking if the onions threaten to scorch.) Stir in the salt and pepper. If the onions are not golden brown at this point, increase the heat to medium-high and cook, watching carefully and turning frequently, until browned but not charred.

2. Evenly butter one side of each slice of bread. Place a large nonstick frying pan or a griddle over medium-low heat. Working in batches if necessary, place 4 slices of bread, butter side down, on the cooking surface and immediately top with half of the sliced cheese, distributing it evenly. Dollop and gently spread ¼ cup onion over the cheese on each sandwich, then top with the remaining cheese slices, dividing them evenly. Top with the remaining slices of bread, butter side up. Cook until the bottom is golden brown, 2 minutes; use a spatula to press down firmly on each sandwich to flatten slightly. Turn over and cook until golden brown and the cheese starts to ooze from the edges, 3 minutes more. Transfer to plates and cut each sandwich in half on the diagonal.

MAKE AHEAD: The onions may be caramelized up to 1 day in advance; warm through before adding to the sandwiches.

PER SANDWICH 1,217 Cal., 44% (541 Cal.) from fat; 49 g protein; 61 g fat (34 g sat.); 121 g carbo (6.6 g fiber); 2,258 mg sodium; 174 mg chol. V

The eternal quest to convey melted cheese into my mouth has rarely encountered such a true masterpiece of the sandwich-maker's art.

406 Bell St.
Los Alamos, CA

(805) 344-4609

bellstreetfarm.com

BELL STREET FARM

Los Alamos

Jamie Gluck has come full circle. His dad owned the pre-Puck classic California-French restaurant Etienne's in SoCal and Arizona, but Jamie bugged out to attend art school, and then became a successful creative director in the fashion-advertising industry. Fast forward about 12 years into his career, when Jamie and his husband, John Wentworth (a TV studio exec), bought a weekend home in the then-backwater town of Los Alamos. "We just loved it," Jamie says. "Two days felt like four." Picnic choices were slim, so the two packed delectable lunches for winery visits, and then were overrun by jealous folks dining from Trader Joe's bags. The two saw an unmet need and, inspired by Zuni Café in San Francisco, Joan's on Third in L.A., and countless fantastic French bistros, conceived and rather quickly executed what Jamie calls a "French restaurant masquerading as an American cafe." The backwater phase of Los Alamos is clearly over, if the appreciative crowds at Bell Street are any indication. "I am truly my father's son," Jamie says, with a sense of wonder. "I'm absolutely dedicated to the fullest concept of hospitality."

Farm Salad

SERVES 4 ✤ 25 MINUTES, PLUS 45 MINUTES TO BAKE

I've been having a love affair with the quirky little town of Los Alamos since I accidentally discovered it during a gas stop back in 2009. Sleepy and frontierlike, it got a small boost in both popularity and development from the film *Sideways*, but it will never be as polished and presentable as its rich sister Los Olivos. (To me, that's a *good* thing.) The arrival of the excellent and stylish Bell Street Farm cements its rep as a bona fide worth-stoppin'-off-the-101 destination. But it still doesn't detract from the sleepy charm.

1. Preheat the oven to 350°. Scrub the beets, wrap in foil, and bake about 45 minutes, or until tender when pierced with a knife. Let cool slightly, peel, and slice thinly into a bowl. Set aside to cool completely.

2. **MAKE THE CANDIED WALNUTS:** Line a baking sheet with parchment paper. In a medium saucepan, combine the sugar, 1/4 cup water, bitters, and pepper over medium heat. Stir constantly until the sugar has dissolved, then simmer, swirling occasionally, until the bubbles turn amber and break very slowly, 7 to 8 minutes. Remove from the heat and add the walnuts and salt; stir to coat the nuts evenly. Spread on the parchment and let cool.

3. **MAKE THE SALAD:** In a large bowl, combine the lettuce, arugula, and sliced apple. Add just enough vinaigrette to coat the greens lightly, and toss. Divide the salad among four plates. Toss the sliced beets with a little more vinaigrette. Top the salad with the beets, dividing them evenly, and then scatter the candied walnuts and crumbled blue cheese over the top of each salad. Pass the remaining vinaigrette at the table.

4 small beets, assorted colors, ends trimmed

Candied Walnuts

1/2 cup sugar

2 dashes Angostura bitters

1/4 tsp. pepper

1 cup (4 oz.) walnuts, coarsely chopped

Pinch of salt

Salad

1 head butter lettuce, pale inner heart only, torn into bite-size pieces

2 cups (2 oz.) wild or baby arugula leaves

1 medium Granny Smith apple, scrubbed, quartered and cored, and very thinly sliced

3/4 cup Bell Street Vinaigrette (page 48)

4 oz. Point Reyes Blue Cheese or other creamy blue cheese, crumbled

PER SERVING 685 Cal., 69% (479 Cal.) from fat; 14 g protein; 54 g fat (9 g sat.); 42 g carbo (4.7 g fiber); 672 mg sodium; 21 mg chol. GF/V

Roast Pork Sandwiches with Apple-Jicama Slaw and Pickled Onions

MAKES 8 SANDWICHES ❖ 30 MINUTES, PLUS AT LEAST 1³/₄ HOURS TO CHILL AND COOK

Much of the immense appeal of Bell Street Farm is the attention Jamie Gluck gives to his ingredients. Jamie and his husband didn't come to Los Alamos to relax; they came to make something beautiful, tasty, and community-oriented. I urge you to borrow a page from their book and find a source of sustainably raised pork, preferably from a heritage breed. Your taste buds, your friends—and the planet—will thank you.

Apple-Jicama Slaw

2 tbsp. white vinegar

2 tbsp. *each* sour cream and mayonnaise

¼ tsp. fine sea salt

¼ tsp. sugar

½ cup loosely packed fresh flat-leaf parsley leaves, finely chopped

6 oz. jicama, thoroughly peeled and cut into fine matchsticks (about 2½ cups, firmly packed)

1 large apple, such as Fuji, peeled, cored, and cut into fine matchsticks

Pork

3 lbs. boneless pork shoulder (Boston butt), trimmed

6 garlic cloves, peeled and minced

2 medium shallots, minced

Leaves from 3 small sprigs rosemary, minced

1 tsp. fresh thyme leaves

1 tsp. ground fennel seed

2 tsp. fine sea salt

1 tsp. pepper

2 tbsp. extra-virgin olive oil

8 ciabatta rolls, split

Quick Pickled Onions (page 243)

1. **MAKE THE SLAW:** In a large nonreactive bowl, whisk together the vinegar, sour cream, mayonnaise, salt, sugar, and parsley. Add the jicama and apple and toss to mix. Cover and chill for at least 1 hour and up to 3 hours, to allow the flavors to marry.

2. **MEANWHILE, PREPARE THE PORK:** Remove the pork from the refrigerator and let stand for 1 hour at room temperature, so it will cook evenly. In a bowl, combine the garlic, shallots, herbs, fennel, salt, pepper, and 1 tbsp. oil. (Alternatively, combine whole garlic and shallots with the remaining ingredients, minus 1 tbsp. oil, in a mini food processor, and pulse to a chunky paste.) Rub this mixture all over the pork, working it into all the nooks and crannies.

3. Preheat the oven to 450°. Place a large ,heavy ovenproof pan over medium-high heat on the stovetop until it is very hot (about 2 minutes); add the remaining 1 tbsp. oil to the pan. Place the pork fat side down in the pan; reduce the heat to medium and sear until deep golden brown, about 6 minutes total, turning over once or twice. Turn the pork fat side up and poke a heatproof meat thermometer into the thickest part of the meat. Transfer to the oven with the thermometer facing the glass oven door and roast for 15 minutes. Reduce the oven temperature to 325° and roast 40 minutes more. Now, turn off the oven but do not open the door. Leave the pork in the turned-off oven for 35 to 45 minutes, monitoring the temperature through the oven window; it should reach 150°. (If it does not, turn the oven back on to 325° for 5 minutes more.) If you do not have a glass oven door, check the temperature after 35 minutes, and then again every 5 minutes until meat reaches the desired temperature. Remove from the oven and let rest for 15 minutes. (For the full Bell Street effect, make the sandwiches right away with warm pork; reheat it slightly if necessary, but do not allow it to dry out.)

4. **TO SERVE:** Hollow the tops and bottoms of the rolls slightly with a fork, reserving the crumbs for another use. Carve the pork across the grain about ¼ in. thick. Lay slices on the base of each roll, dividing evenly between the rolls, then top the pork with some of the slaw and pickled onions. Sandwich the halves without losing any of the filling, and compress each firmly.

PER SANDWICH 621 Cal., 28% (174 Cal.) from fat; 55 g protein; 19 g fat (5.1 g sat.); 56 g carbo (3.9 g fiber); 3,175 mg sodium; 84 mg chol.

Roast Chicken Salad with Rosemary Croutons and White Bean Hummus

SERVES 4 ❈ 20 MINUTES, PLUS 2 HOURS TO ROAST

Once upon a time, the little town of Los Alamos might not have supported an eatery of the caliber of Bell Street Farm. (Los Angeles or San Francisco? Sure.) But Jamie and John's timing was as impeccable as the produce that they are, happily, able to source, sometimes from within a stone's throw of this adorable storefront cafe. The Middle Eastern spice blend *zaatar**   contributes fruity, faintly tart flavor (think cranberries) that's a fabulous counterpoint to the classically comforting richness of chicken. You could also use a best-quality rotisserie chicken for this deservedly popular dish.

Chicken

2 tbsp. olive oil

3 tbsp. *zaatar**

1 tsp. fine sea salt

1/2 tsp. pepper

1 (41/2-lb.) whole chicken

Cooking-oil spray

White Bean Hummus

1 garlic clove

1/2 tsp. fresh rosemary

1 (15.5-oz.) can cannellini beans, drained and well rinsed

2 tbsp. extra-virgin olive oil

2 tsp. lemon juice

1/4 tsp. *each* fine sea salt and pepper

Bell Street Vinaigrette

3 tbsp. red wine vinegar

1/3 cup canola oil

3 tbsp. extra-virgin olive oil

1/2 tsp. Dijon mustard

1/2 tsp. fine sea salt

1/4 tsp. pepper

Salad

8 oz. crustless French baguette, torn into bite-size pieces (about 4 cups)

2 tbsp. extra-virgin olive oil

1/2 tsp. fine sea salt

1/4 tsp. pepper

11/2 heads butter lettuce, pale inner hearts only, torn into bite-size pieces (about 4 cups)

1. **MAKE THE CHICKEN:** Preheat the oven to 375°. In a bowl, combine the oil, zaatar, salt, and pepper; stir to create a paste. Rub the chicken all over with the paste, rubbing it into and under the skin on the breast. Place the chicken on a roasting pan coated with cooking spray. Roast until golden brown and crispy, about 1 hour and 30 minutes or until a meat thermometer registers 165°. Let stand 15 minutes. Reduce oven temperature to 350° for croutons. Cut the chicken into 8 pieces**.

2. **MAKE THE HUMMUS:** In a food processor, combine the garlic and rosemary; pulse about 5 times or until chopped. Add the beans, oil, lemon juice, salt, and pepper. Process until very smooth, adding 2 to 3 tbsp. water if necessary, to make a nice dipping consistency. Divide the purée among four small ramekins and set aside.

3. **MAKE THE VINAIGRETTE:** In a jar, whisk or shake all the ingredients until emulsified. The vinaigrette will separate; shake again just before serving.

4. **MAKE THE CROUTONS:** In a bowl, toss the torn bread with the oil; season with salt and pepper. Transfer to a baking sheet and bake until golden brown, 16 minutes, tossing occasionally.

5. **TO ASSEMBLE:** Working quickly, in a large bowl, combine about half the vinaigrette and croutons. Toss to coat, then toss in the lettuce. Divide among four plates and top each serving with 2 pieces of chicken. Place the ramekins of hummus on the side, for dipping the chicken pieces. Pass the remaining vinaigrette on the side.

*Zaatar usually includes marjoram, oregano, thyme, sesame, and sumac.

**To easily cut a roasted chicken into serving pieces, use a good pair of kitchen shears: Cut each breast crosswise into 2 pieces, keeping the wing attached to 1 piece; cut the thighs from the drumsticks, keeping as much meat from the back with the thighs as possible. Discard the backbone or save in the freezer for stock.

PER SERVING 1,265 Cal., 58% (740 Cal.) from fat; 77 g protein; 84 g fat (16 g sat.); 50 g carbo (7 g fiber); 1,430 mg sodium; 201 mg chol.

Full of Life Flatbread

LOS ALAMOS

Owner Clark Staub revolutionized the (then-nonexistent) dining scene in this tiny town when, in 2004, he opened his temple of local, farm-to-table and wine-friendly cuisine (with a great bar and huge wood-burning oven). He's now been joined by some other fabulous eateries, but I still consider him the reigning king of coolness. 225 Bell St.; fulloflifefoods.com

JOCKO'S STEAK HOUSE

Nipomo

125 N. Thompson Ave.
Nipomo, CA

(805) 929-3565

The Knotts family has been feeding and watering Californians since the late 1800s; even Prohibition couldn't stop Ralph (aka Jocko) Knotts, who bootlegged with Bull Tognazzini (Bull's Tavern still stands and serves in San Luis Obispo). Jocko—son of Emory Knotts (also a barkeep)—opened his namesake in the 1920s. Weekend steak barbecues and horseshoes proved so popular that a restaurant was erected on the opposite corner, where it stands today.

Jocko and his wife, Mollie, raised seven children in the little red house next door. After he died in 1952, his sons Fred and George took over (it's now owned by Fred's widow, Sandy, and run by his son Mike and grandson Daniel). Not much has changed in Jocko's dining room in recent decades, and folks sometimes complain about the wait, but it's all part of the Jocko's charm. "You can't eat atmosphere," Fred Knotts once proclaimed. He preferred to pour money into serving real food: steak, butter, bacon, and, incidentally, a few salads. Plus really excellent cocktails. My advice: Get there early and enjoy the wait (and the conversation) in the bar.

Relish Tray

SERVES 4 AS AN APPETIZER ❖ 10 MINUTES

The Old California tradition of serving a relish tray before a nice meal—most often at a steak-house like Jocko's—may have originated in the belief that foods coming out of a can, jar, or bottle were intrinsically better/more luxurious than anything straight from the earth. As a kid, I had two relish-tray favorites: jumbo black ripe olives—which I would painstakingly fit onto all my fingertips before nibbling them off—and pickled watermelon rind. This quick-to-put-together dish feels like a delightful throwback, a tradition I'm happy to revive in my own kitchen.

2 large carrots, peeled and cut into 1/4-in. strips, chilled

1 (5 oz.) jar pitted jumbo California black ripe olives, chilled

12 green onions, white and light green parts only, root ends trimmed, chilled

1 (7 1/2-oz.) jar green and red pepperoncini or cherry peppers, drained and chilled

1 small jar sliced bread-and-butter pickles or spears (about 1 1/2 cups), drained, chilled

Crackers (such as saltines or oyster crackers), ideally individually wrapped, for serving

Chill four individual oval plates, preferably metal. Divide the ingredients evenly among the plates. Serve with a basket of crackers on the side.

PER SERVING (NOT INCLUDING CRACKERS) 143 Cal., 29% (41 Cal.) from fat; 2.1 g protein; 4.5 g fat (0.1 g sat.); 24 g carbo (3.8 g fiber); 567 mg sodium; 0 mg chol. LC/V

Spencer Steak from the Oak Pit

SERVES 4 ❈ 25 MINUTES, PLUS 1 HOUR TO LET MEAT STAND

Part of the sublime magic of Jocko's Spencer steak comes from sourcing the meat wisely. You may not be able to get the same steaks that they serve at Jocko's, but seek out the very best: well-marbled, nice and thick, with deep red meat (rather than bright pink, which indicates the meat has not been aged). There's another trick you can employ to approach the Jocko's effect: Try a few shakes of Jocko's Mix Seasoning, available in person at Jocko's, or at jockosmix.com.

4 well-marbled boneless Spencer or rib-eye steaks, about 1½ in. thick (about 3 lbs. total)

2 tsp. fine sea salt and/or seasoning salt, such as Jocko's Mix Seasoning

Pepper to taste

1. Pat the steaks completely dry with paper towels, then loosely cover; let stand at room temperature for 1 hour.

2. *If using a charcoal grill*, set up a fire for high heat (450° to 550°) using medium-size pieces of seasoned red oak. Light the wood and let it burn down to glowing red coals just barely covered with a layer of ash. "Season" the cooking grate: Cut off a small piece of beef fat and, holding it firmly with long-handled tongs, rub the fat along the grate. *If using a gas grill*, soak about 2 cups wood chips, such as applewood, for 30 minutes. Drain the chips and wrap them in a foil packet. Season the cooking grate with beef fat as for the charcoal grill. Heat the gas grill to high (450° to 550°) and place the foil packet on the heat element just before grilling.

3. Generously season one side of the steaks with 1 tsp. salt and/or seasoning mix. Grill the steaks salted side down over the hottest part of the fire for 2 minutes, moving around after the first minute if the fire flares. Season the uncooked sides with the remaining 1 tsp. salt and turn over; sear for 2 minutes more. Move to the edge, or the cooler part of the grill, and continue cooking for 10 to 12 minutes longer, or until a meat thermometer inserted at the center reaches 130°, for medium-rare, turning with your tongs several times to brown the crust on both sides and the edges. Season generously with pepper and rest on a warm platter, loosely tented with foil, for 5 minutes.

PER SERVING 630 Cal., 54% (338 Cal.) from fat; 70 g protein; 38 g fat (15 g sat.); 0 g carbo (0 g fiber); 903 mg sodium; 283 mg chol.

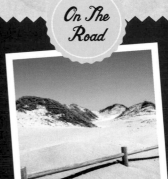

Guadalupe-Nipomo Dunes Preserve

GUADALUPE

Covering 18 miles of coastline, this is one of the largest intact coastal dune ecosystems in the world, an alien land of softly rolling, sensual sand. Large parts of the delicate ecosystem—home to many endangered and threatened species—have been set aside for conservation. Visit the Dunes Center to get your bearings. 1065 Guadalupe St.; dunescenter.org

Ember

ARROYO GRANDE

Chef Brian Collins was part of the team at Full of Life Flatbread, and he brings that wood-fired, farm-centric sensibility north to A.G., in a smallish, barn-chic restaurant that's proved such a hit with locals that the wait can be daunting. Arrive early or late, or stake out a table in the bar. 1200 E. Grand Ave.; (805) 474-7700

Route 3

DISCLOSURE: I'M BIASED when it comes to this route, because the whole area is my beloved backyard. At *Shell Beach*, U.S. 101 returns to the sparkling blue Pacific, hugging slopes and cliffs on one side while the other is all bluffs, crags, crashing surf, and tidepools. The demographic leans slightly toward retired folks who have the folding green to "afford such an idyllic spot", but there are also plenty of young families in search of the unspoiled, and lots of beach-heads (surfing and nonsurfing varieties).

Take my unorthodox route here, please. Head west from San Luis Obispo (aka SLO) on Highway 1 toward the old-fashioned town of Morro Bay, with its looming rock, duo of power towers, quiet marina, and protected bay (ideal for kayaking). Continue up Highway 1 through another, hipper sand-swept beach town, Cayucos, and re-member to brake for antiques stores. Turn east on 46 toward *Templeton* and Paso Robles, and feast your eyes on luscious rolling green-or-gold, cattle-dotted hills, topped with faraway views, wheeling hawks, and the occasional jet trail.

Ideally, stop for a day or six in Paso Robles wine country, land of dirt farmers and excellent restaurants. Turning south, follow 101 to the old boom-and-bust ranching town of *Santa Margarita*, a town now moseying real slowly toward a low-grade form of gentrification. Just north of town, on the west side of 101, you will likely have the honor of seeing a large herd of astonishingly regal Texas longhorn cattle. Measured tip to tip, many horns have a spread the size of a tall man.

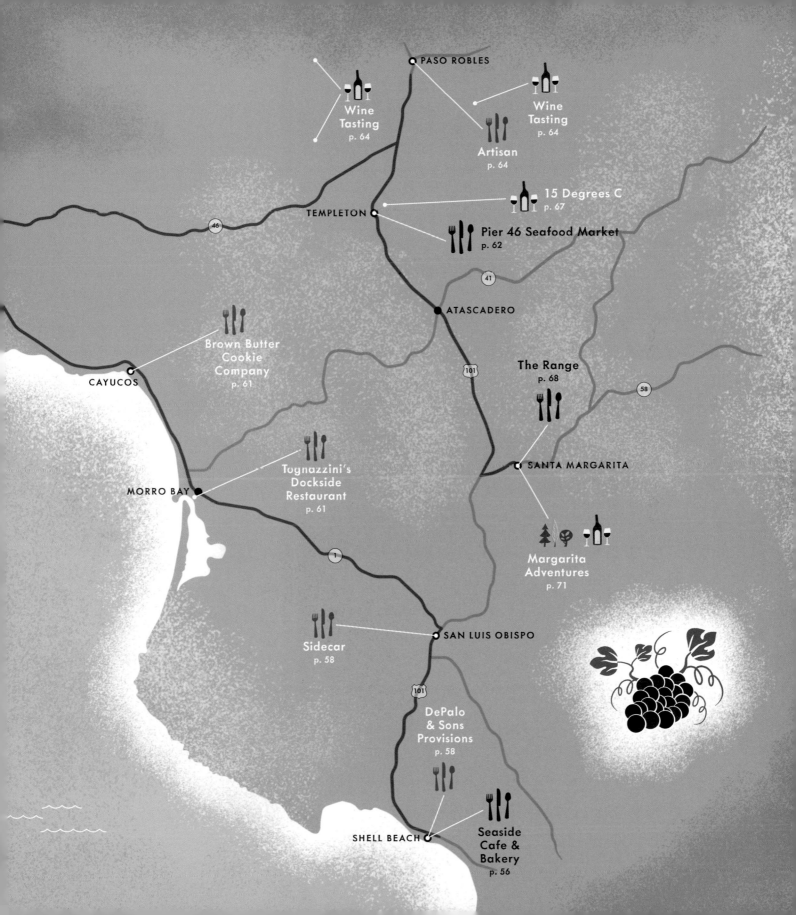

PASO ROBLES

Wine
Tasting
p. 64

Wine
Tasting
p. 64

Artisan
p. 64

15 Degrees C
p. 67

TEMPLETON

Pier 46 Seafood Market
p. 62

46

41

ATASCADERO

Brown Butter
Cookie
Company
p. 61

101

The Range
p. 68

CAYUCOS

58

SANTA MARGARITA

Tognazzini's
Dockside
Restaurant
p. 61

MORRO BAY

Margarita
Adventures
p. 71

1

Sidecar
p. 58

SAN LUIS OBISPO

101

DePalo
& Sons
Provisions
p. 58

Seaside
Cafe &
Bakery
p. 56

SHELL BEACH

Stop

1

1327 Shell Beach Rd.
Shell Beach, CA

(805) 773-4360

shellbeachcafe.com

SEASIDE CAFE & BAKERY

Shell Beach

Grab a Mimosa Growler (yes, and you can thank me later), and belly up to an outdoor table at this beachy destination for lovers of deceptively simple, fantastic fare. I am totally channeling the Beach Boys as I chat with co-owner Tim Begovich while his wife, Liz Lynch, creates the deliciousness that pours forth from their tiny kitchen. This is a millennial version of the classic mom-'n'-pop joint, and aptly enough it started life as a delivery service from the back of a VW Beetle. Liz baked professionally at Art Cafe in San Luis Obispo, but when she and Tim met in 2003, they knew they wanted to work for themselves. Having been raised in a restaurant family, Tim had the knowledge in his blood. They wanted to make a big commitment to high-quality, in-house baking. Through ups and downs they've stuck it out, and the proof of their passion is in the pudding—and the Cherry Bomb Cupcakes. OMG. And the corned beef hash!

French Onion Soup

SERVES 4 TO 6 ❧ 1 HOUR, PLUS 20 MINUTES TO SIMMER

French onion soup—an old favorite of mine—gains vastly in my estimation by the addition of lots of wine and the beefy richness of consommé. Rich? This soup is loaded! And the croutons? Radical! (Liz Lynch jettisons old-school gruyère in favor of havarti, for its superior melting properties.) With its sunny and sublime outdoor dining patio, the Seaside became an instant hit with Shell Beachers, and owners Liz and Tim have plans to expand the Seaside to accommodate more indoor and after-sundown diners. Not that there's much inclement weather in Shell Beach...

Soup

3 tbsp. unsalted butter

3 large red onions, thinly sliced

2 large shallots, thinly sliced

5 garlic cloves, thinly sliced

½ tsp. fine sea salt

½ tsp. pepper, or to taste

2 (10.5-oz.) cans *each* reduced-sodium beef broth and beef consommé (or use 4 cans beef broth total)

½ cup dry red wine, such as Pinot Noir

2 sprigs rosemary

1 bay leaf

¼ cup heavy cream

Croutons

1 tsp. minced fresh basil

¼ cup mayonnaise

12 (½-in.-thick) slices sourdough baguette

6 oz. havarti, thinly sliced

1. **MAKE THE SOUP:** Warm the butter in a large, heavy dutch oven over medium heat. Stir in the onions and shallots and cover the pan. Cook until softened but not browned, stirring occasionally, about 15 minutes. Stir in the garlic, salt, and plenty of pepper. Uncover and continue cooking, stirring frequently, until the mixture is golden brown, about 20 minutes more. Stir in the broth, consommé, wine, rosemary, and bay leaf. Bring to a simmer, partially cover, and cook for 20 minutes; the onions will be very soft. Remove the remains of the rosemary and bay leaf and stir in the cream.

2. **MAKE THE CROUTONS:** Preheat the broiler to high. Stir the basil into the mayonnaise. Toast the bread slices until golden, 1 to 2 minutes, then turn slices over and spread each with a little mayo; layer with slices of havarti. Toast until the cheese is melted and golden, about 1 minute. Ladle the soup into wide, shallow bowls and float 2 or 3 croutons on top of each serving.

PER SERVING 445 Cal., 39% (174 Cal.) from fat; 20 g protein; 19 g fat (11 g sat.); 49 g carbo (3 g fiber); 1,649 mg sodium; 43 mg chol.

Stop 2

PIER 46 SEAFOOD MARKET AND RESTAURANT

1131 Rossi Rd.
Templeton, CA

(805) 434-1950

pier46seafood.com

Templeton

Alums of the venerated wholesaler Central Coast Seafood, Eric Gonzales and Tony DeGarimore changed the entire dining dynamic in this wine- and food-centric region when they and their wives, Jennifer and Joanne, opened Pier 46 in 2008. (Just in time for the recession, Eric says to me, as I wrap myself around a glass of local McClean Viognier and a luscious platter of shrimp Louis.) Before that, retail fish was limited to tired supermarket offerings and the pent-up demand was tsunami-like in its intensity. Even hungry travelers without a local kitchen can share in the fish-forward freshness here via a wide-ranging and appealing menu of fish and shellfish salads, sandwiches, chowders, and platters—from Cal-centric fish tacos to crabcakes to gourmet quesadillas. Many choices and specials give a shout-out to the multicultural heritage and abundant garden bounty of this area; the salads are perky, the salsas crisp and clean, and there's no shortage of buttery goodness in the throwback favorite shrimp scampi. (Just give in to your inner '60s self.)

Crab Louis Salad

SERVES 4 ❈ 15 MINUTES

Again we visit iconic California fare, and life is eminently better for it. When I was a kid, the Dungeness crab disappeared for some years, and it wasn't until my teenage years that I tasted this sweet crustacean and learned to ignore my sore fingers in the quest for just one more morsel. Do not be tempted to drag this salad into the current century by pairing the crab with tender baby greens; the iceberg's—perhaps inelegant—crunch provides perfect counterpoint to the richness of the West Coast's (arguably) favorite shellfish.

1. **MAKE THE DRESSING:** In a small bowl, whisk together all the ingredients; taste for seasoning.

2. **MAKE THE SALAD:** Divide the lettuce among four plates, preferably chilled. Distribute the cucumber, carrot, and onion around the edges and drizzle the dressing generously back and forth over the salad. Arrange one-quarter of the avocado, one-quarter of the hard-cooked eggs, and one-quarter of the tomato slices around the sides. Mound the crab in the center, dividing it evenly among the salads. Serve with lemon wedges. Offer the remaining dressing on the side, for the gluttons (like me).

PER SERVING 468 Cal., 56% (260 Cal.) from fat; 31 g protein; 29 g fat (7.2 g sat.); 25 g carbo (5.3 g fiber); 885 mg sodium; 208 mg chol. GF/LC

Louis Dressing

½ cup plus 2 tbsp. mayonnaise

¼ cup crème fraîche or sour cream

¼ cup bottled cocktail sauce

2 tbsp. finely chopped green onion

⅛ tsp. fine sea salt, plus more to taste

⅛ tsp. white or black pepper, plus more to taste

Salad

½ head iceberg lettuce, limp outer leaves discarded, shredded (about 4 cups)

½ English cucumber, scrubbed and very thinly sliced

1 medium carrot, peeled and shaved lengthwise with a vegetable peeler

¼ cup slivered red onion

1 ripe Hass avocado, pitted, peeled, and sliced

2 hard-cooked eggs, sliced

2 tomatoes, sliced

1 lb. shelled cooked lump Dungeness crab

Lemon wedges, for serving

Artisan

PASO ROBLES

Nobody walks the sustainable/local walk
like chef Chris Kobayashi, who, with his
co-owner, brother Michael, put Paso on the
culinary map in 2006, long before it was
"discovered" by wine-tasting trippers in search
of excellent food. A fantastic bar and tables
overlooking the leafy square make it the place
to be for concerts on the park every Friday
evening in summer. 843 12th St.;
artisanpasorobles.com

Wine Tasting

PASO ROBLES

With superb views from the terrace, Lone
Madrone Winery has live music on spring-
summer-fall weekends (winemaker Neil Collins
also makes Tablas Creek's renowned wine).
Cass Winery was one of the first wineries to
offer food—excellent cheese plates and sandwiches under the oaks. Proulx Winery is the
passion of prolific consulting winemaker Kevin
Riley and wife Genoa (the land belongs to her
parents—her dad is artist Ken Fuller, whose
livestock paintings grace the tasting room). Lone
Madrone: 5800 Adelaida Rd.; Cass: 7350 Linne
Rd.; Proulx: 5424 Vineyard Dr.; pasowine.com

Famous Ahi Fish Tacos

MAKES 12 TACOS ✤ 20 MINUTES, PLUS 1¼ HOURS TO CHILL

Though only 26 miles from the Pacific, Pier 46 became the sole outpost of oceanic splendor in the midst of landlocked wine country. At this well-loved market/restaurant, the cool-crisp-spicy tacos are served with little mounds of squid salad and seaweed salad. If you have access to a Japanese market, you can easily re-create the presentation, but I like to eat these tacos right out of hand, just as tacos were meant to be eaten!

Cabbage Salad

3 tbsp. mayonnaise

2½ tbsp. sesame oil

1½ tsp. minced or finely grated fresh ginger

½ tsp. rice vinegar

¼ tsp. honey

¼ tsp. black sesame seeds (optional)

¼ tsp. fine sea salt

1 medium head napa cabbage, halved lengthwise, bottom third discarded, and slivered crosswise

¼ cup shredded red cabbage

4 green onions, light and dark green parts only, finely chopped

1 medium carrot, peeled, coarsely grated, and then chopped

Tuna

8 oz. sushi-quality center-cut ahi tuna

1 green onion, white and light green parts, minced

1 tsp. extra-virgin olive oil

½ tsp. sesame oil

¼ tsp. fine sea salt

12 small formed crunchy taco shells

Black sesame seeds, for garnish (optional)

1. **MAKE THE CABBAGE SALAD:** In a large bowl, whisk together the mayonnaise, oil, ginger, vinegar, honey, sesame seeds if using, and salt. Add the napa and red cabbages, green onions, and carrot and fold together until evenly coated. Cover and chill for 1 hour, so the flavors can marry.

2. **PREPARE THE TUNA:** Cut the tuna into ½-in. slices and freeze, uncovered, in a single layer on a small baking sheet for 20 minutes, to firm slightly. Cut the partially frozen tuna into neat ¼-in. dice and combine in a bowl with the green onion, olive and sesame oils, and salt. Cover and chill until serving time, up to 1 hour.

3. When ready to serve, scoop up about ⅓ cup of the cabbage salad with a slotted spoon, and place carefully in each taco shell, pressing in gently and evenly across the bottom. Top each with some of the tuna, dividing it evenly. Garnish with a sprinkle of sesame seeds if desired.

PER TACO 116 Cal., 48% (56 Cal.) from fat; 5.7 g protein; 6.4 g fat (1 g sat.); 9 g carbo (1.2 g fiber); 107 mg sodium; 9.5 mg chol. LC/LS

Cioppino with Toasted Garlic Bread

SERVES 4 ❋ 30 MINUTES

Cioppino, the classic California seafood-and-tomato stew, is iconic Fisherman's Wharf fare, with a place among San Francisco's most famous culinary contributions. Pier 46's version is tangy in all the right places and fits me like a glove. In my childhood, that fleeting time when food was served to me rather than prepared by me, this blushing, briny soup was one of my first love affairs.

Garlic Bread

2 tbsp. extra-virgin olive oil

1 tbsp. unsalted butter, melted

8 (½-in.-thick) slices rustic sourdough bread

3 garlic cloves, peeled and halved crosswise

Pepper

Soup Base

⅓ cup extra-virgin olive oil

3 ribs celery, finely chopped

1 medium white or yellow onion, finely chopped

1 tbsp. dried oregano, crumbled

3 bay leaves

½ tsp. pepper

3 garlic cloves, minced

½ lb. fresh fish (halibut and/or other firm white fish)

½ cup dry white wine

¼ cup white or red wine vinegar

¼ cup fish stock or 2 tsp. concentrated fish stock (optional)

1 (28-oz.) can crushed tomatoes

½ tsp. fine sea salt

8 live clams, in shells, scrubbed, and beards pulled off

8 live mussels, in shells, scrubbed, and beards pulled off

½ lb. medium shrimp, peeled and deveined, and/or small scallops

1. **MAKE THE GARLIC BREAD:** Preheat the oven to 350°. In a small bowl, combine the oil and butter. Place the bread slices on a baking sheet and brush both sides lightly with the oil mixture. Bake until golden, 10 to 15 minutes. Immediately rub one side of each slice firmly back and forth several times with the cut sides of the garlic cloves. Season with a little pepper.

2. **MAKE THE SOUP BASE:** In a large, heavy soup pot or dutch oven, warm the oil over medium-low heat. Add the celery and sauté for 2 minutes; add the onion, oregano, bay leaves, and pepper, and cook until onion is softened, stirring frequently, about 6 minutes more. Add the garlic and cook, stirring, for 30 seconds. Add half of the fish, the wine, vinegar, fish stock (if using), tomatoes, and salt. Increase the heat to medium-high and bring to a low simmer. Cook, stirring, for 1 minute, then reduce the heat to low, cover the pot, and let cook for 2 minutes.

3. Add the remaining fish along with the clams and mussels. Cook, stirring gently, for 6 minutes. Add the shrimp and/or scallops and cook for 2 to 4 minutes more, until the bivalves have all opened; discard any clams or mussels that have not opened after 10 minutes. Ladle into bowls, distributing the seafood as evenly as possible, and serve with slices of garlic bread.

PER SERVING 1,081 Cal., 29% (311 Cal.) from fat; 57 g protein; 36 g fat (7.1 g sat.); 132 g carbo (10 g fiber); 1,942 mg sodium; 122 mg chol.

15 Degrees C

TEMPLETON

With surprisingly few places to buy international (or even a broad selection of local) wines in this wine-country region, 15 Degrees C is a fortunate find. Choose from curated offerings—and the staff can explain them all—then grab snacks at the convivial square bar, or on the patio. Wine industry insiders flock here to try "the other guy's" vino. 624 S. Main St.; 15degreescwines.com

Stop 3

22317 El Camino Real
Santa Margarita, CA

(805) 438-4500

THE RANGE

Santa Margarita

Hardly your typical one-horse-town steakhouse, this chef-owned joint turns on the charm without even trying. Design and ambience are haute cowboy—think longhorns, cowhide, a riveted copper front door, and country-music album covers. Service is unpretentious but thoroughly professional—your server (likely chef and owner Jeff Jackson's wife, Lindsay) will know everything about the locally sourced meat, poultry, and produce on the menu, but won't overdo it on the passion (as sometimes happens in the northern wine regions). Depending on the season, choose from elk medallions with cherry bordelaise or beef carpaccio with capers, shaved parmesan, and micro greens—and do not dream of passing up the fried chicken if it's offered. The soundtrack spans Patsy Cline to Neko Case to Hank Williams, there's a patio with heaters, and a reasonably priced wine list that ranges from hyper-local to slightly farther afield—you are in wine country here. But this under-the-radar destination (shocker: no website) can stand with pride alongside any upscale big-city eatery. Note the "no reservations and no credit cards" policies; there's a bar serving great local wines across the street, plus an ATM. World's tiniest problems: solved.

Dragon's Breath

SERVES 6 TO 8 AS AN APPETIZER

20 MINUTES, PLUS 1 HOUR, 20 MINUTES TO STAND AND TO BAKE

Jeff Jackson doesn't pull any punches with his sophisticated menu, cash-only policy, and off-the-beaten-path location in the Old West–vibe-y town of Santa Margarita—and the same can be said for his signature appetizer. Although there's pepper "jam" and lots of lovely goat cheese from right around the corner, this dish is really all about the garlic. Thus the title, which I guess is referring to the kinda breath you'll have after you eat it. If you're a garlic hound, you've hit the jackpot. Not for first dates.

1. **MAKE THE PEPPER JAM:** Drain the peppers and slice into ¼-inch ribbons. In a bowl, combine the peppers and the remaining ingredients for the jam; let stand for at least 1 hour, for the flavors to marry. (Or chill up to 4 hours.)

2. **MAKE THE HERBED GOAT CHEESE:** In a bowl, combine the herbs, garlic, and chile flakes. Add the goat cheese and use a fork to blend to a smooth paste; add another tsp. or 2 of oil if necessary to make a whipped-cream-cheese–like consistency.

3. Preheat the oven to 375°. Make a layer of roasted garlic in a shallow, round gratin dish (or an 8-in. square baking dish). Scatter the pepper jam evenly over the garlic, then dollop the herbed goat cheese over the top; spread toward the edges slightly in an even layer. Bake until bubbling and slightly golden around the edges, 20 minutes, and serve with toasted baguette slices or crudités.

PER SERVING (WITHOUT BREAD OR CRUDITÉS) 238 Cal., 74% (177 Cal.) from fat; 8.9 g protein; 20 g fat (7.8 g sat.); 6.4 g carbo (1.3 g fiber); 346 mg sodium; 20 mg chol. LS/V

Pepper "Jam"

1 (12-oz.) jar fire-roasted red bell peppers

2 garlic cloves, minced

1½ tsp. extra-virgin olive oil

1 tbsp. balsamic vinegar

¼ tsp. fine sea salt

¼ tsp. pepper

2 to 3 drops hot sauce, such as Tabasco

Herbed Goat Cheese

1 tbsp. *each* minced fresh basil and minced fresh flat-leaf parsley

½ tsp. minced fresh rosemary

½ tsp. minced fresh thyme

4 garlic cloves, minced

⅛ tsp. red chile flakes, or to taste

12 oz. fresh goat cheese, softened and cut into 6 pieces

About 5 tsp. extra-virgin olive oil

20 Roasted Garlic cloves (page 166)

1 French or sourdough baguette, cut into ¼-in.-thick slices and toasted until golden, or assorted vegetable crudités, for serving

Lamb Chops with Potato–Goat Cheese Gratin

SERVES 4 �֎ 1³/₄ HOURS

Here is a primal, elemental dish that relies on excellent protein and yet boasts an elegant sensibility and restrained, refined flavors. This is not cowboy food. Lamb is not to everyone's taste for some reason, but I feel that finishing the pan juices with white wine, rather than red, results in a welcoming, bracing acidity, which also nicely balances the classic, consoling potato gratin.

8 small lamb loin chops (1³/₄ lbs. total)

Gratin

2 cups heavy cream

1 cup whole milk

4 garlic cloves, finely chopped

1 tsp. minced fresh rosemary

¹/₄ tsp. red chile flakes

³/₄ tsp. fine sea salt

¹/₄ tsp. white pepper, preferably freshly ground

1³/₄ lbs. Yukon Gold potatoes, washed, peeled, and rinsed quickly under running water

¹/₂ white or yellow onion, thinly sliced

5 oz. soft goat cheese, crumbled

Fine sea salt and black pepper

1 tbsp. extra-virgin olive oil

1 garlic clove, minced or pushed through a press

¹/₂ tsp. *each* minced fresh rosemary and minced fresh thyme

¹/₈ tsp. red chile flakes

¹/₄ cup medium-dry white wine, such as Chardonnay or Viognier

¹/₂ cup flavorful chicken broth, preferably homemade

3 tbsp. cold unsalted butter, cut into 3 pieces

1. Pat the chops dry with paper towels; let stand at room temperature while you make the gratin, about 45 minutes.

2. **MAKE THE GRATIN:** Preheat the oven to 400°. In a 2-qt. baking dish, combine the cream, milk, garlic, rosemary, chile flakes, salt, and white pepper. Slice the potatoes about ¹/₈ in. thick, preferably in a food processor fitted with the slicing blade, or with a mandoline (to make the process faster). Mix the potatoes and onion thoroughly with the cream mixture, to make sure they are evenly coated. Cover the dish with foil and place on a large, rimmed baking sheet to contain any boil-overs. Bake until the potatoes are tender when poked with the tip of a sharp knife, about 1 hour.

3. Uncover the dish and reduce the oven to 350°. Scatter the goat cheese evenly over the top and cook for about 25 minutes more, until the top is bubbling and very light golden brown. Turn off the oven, open the door slightly, and place four dinner plates and a serving platter inside along with the gratin, to warm. The gratin will firm up as it cools; reheat under a hot broiler for 1 to 2 minutes before serving if desired.

4. Season both sides of the lamb chops lightly with salt and black pepper. Place a large, heavy frying pan or sauté pan over medium-high heat and add the oil. When the oil is very hot, add the chops in a single layer, without crowding, and sauté for 2 minutes without moving them. Reduce the heat to medium-low, turn chops over with tongs and sauté for 4 minutes on the other side. Turn again, and cook until the temperature at the center reaches 115° on an instant-read thermometer (for medium-rare chops), 2 minutes more. Transfer the chops to the platter in the turned-off oven.

5. Pour off all but about 1 tsp. fat from the pan. Add the garlic, herbs, and chile flakes all at once and stir until fragrant, about 15 seconds. Add the wine and deglaze the pan, stirring, until the wine reduces by about half, about 30 seconds. Add the broth and again simmer to reduce by about half, 2 minutes. Remove the pan from the heat and add all the pieces of butter; swirl and stir constantly until the butter emulsifies into the sauce. Return the chops to the pan and turn the chops once or twice in the sauce, to coat and warm through (do not return to the heat, or the sauce may separate). Season with salt and pepper to taste, transfer the chops back to the warm platter, and serve with the gratin alongside.

PER SERVING 1,170 Cal., 70% (822 Cal.) from fat; 45 g protein; 92 g fat (51 g sat.); 41 g carbo (2.7 g fiber); 606 mg sodium; 327 mg chol. GF

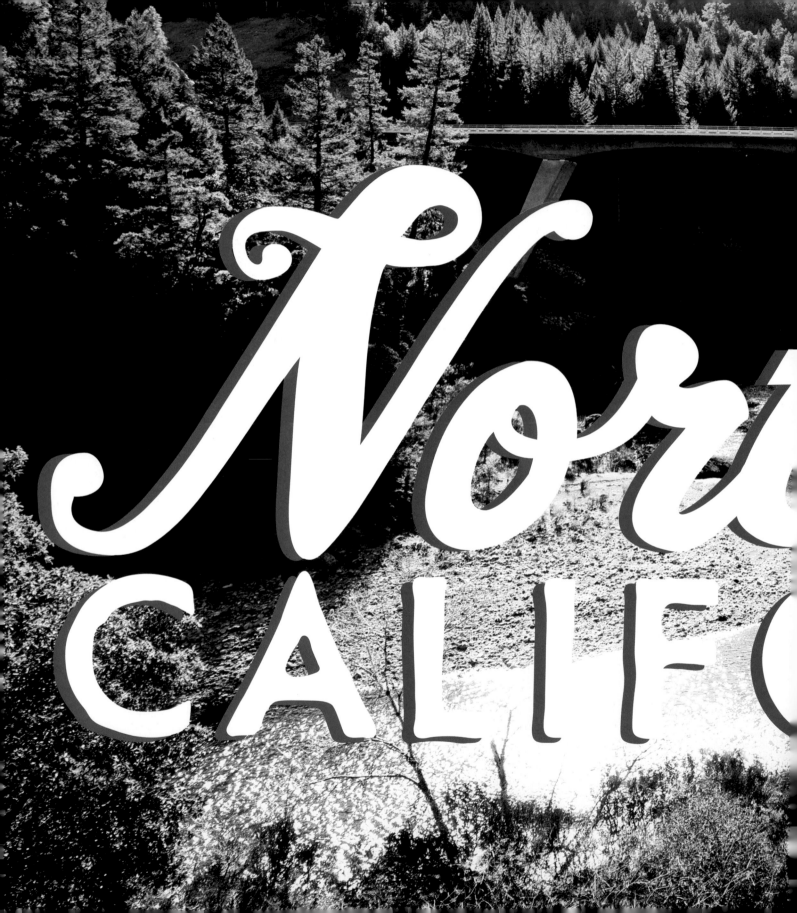

Route 4

Cambria *to* Old San Simeon *to* Big Sur

70 MILES

THIS ROUTE CONTINUES through what I'm incredibly lucky to call my own neck o' the woods, staying within sight of the Pacific throughout; it's one of the most iconic coastal routes of the world, IMHO.

Cambria is "for lovers" (and tourists), and though it has some very nice shops, galleries, and restaurants, the cutesy factor is a touch high for my taste (I prefer laid-back Cayucos, a few minutes south). North of Cambria, gaze east to spy over-the-top Hearst Castle, or stop to see the laziest sun-worshippers ever: massive sea lions that give new meaning to the word "beached." Zebras grazing alongside Hearst Ranch cattle are left over from Hearst Sr.'s schmancy game park.

The beach at *Old San Simeon* is a snapshot of the unspoiled coast that cries out for a swimming dog and a surfboard. Stop, get sand between your toes, and gaze at the horizon. Because after this, the drive will be equal parts life-altering and hair-raising (no wine, please).

After Ragged Point, the road begins to climb up and glide down, zig in and zag out, but there are plenty of pullouts for resting clenched knuckles, plus great photo ops. Below, surf crashes on rocks, above which a few intrepid souls have built houses that most of us will only ever dream of visiting (I always dream). There's no real "center" to *Big Sur*—it stretches along many miles of redwood-flanked road. But my heart belongs to Nepenthe and Esalen, two '50s- and '60s-era institutions that are no less fabulous for being a bit long in the tooth.

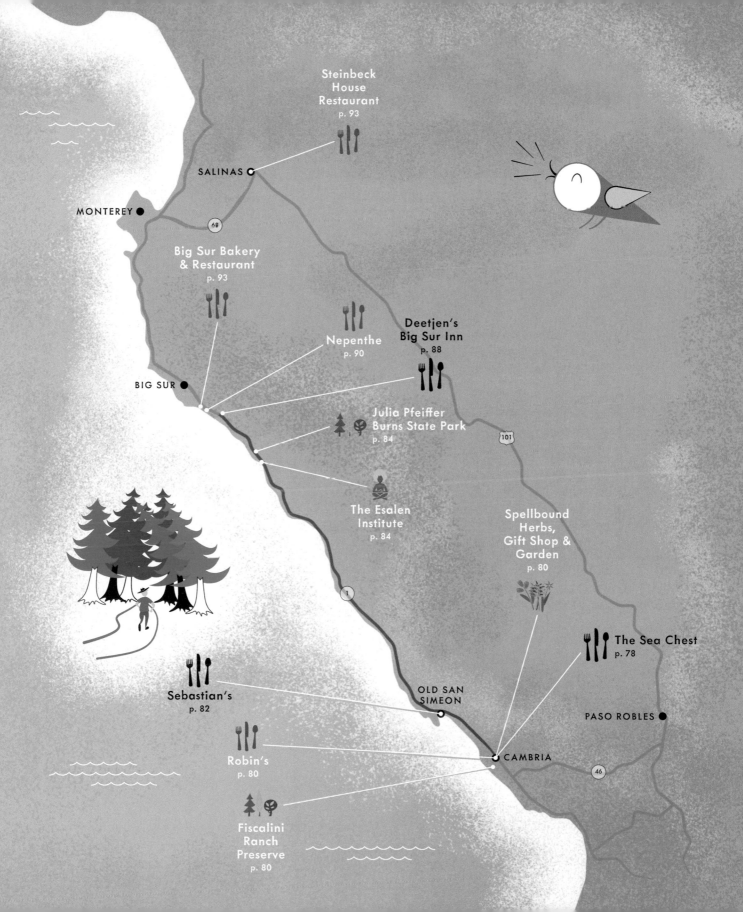

Steinbeck
House
Restaurant
p. 93

SALINAS

MONTEREY

68

Big Sur Bakery
& Restaurant
p. 93

Nepenthe
p. 90

Deetjen's
Big Sur Inn
p. 88

BIG SUR

Julia Pfeiffer
Burns State Park
p. 84

101

The Esalen
Institute
p. 84

Spellbound
Herbs,
Gift Shop &
Garden
p. 80

The Sea Chest
p. 78

1

Sebastian's
p. 82

OLD SAN
SIMEON

PASO ROBLES

Robin's
p. 80

CAMBRIA

46

Fiscalini
Ranch
Preserve
p. 80

Stop

1

THE SEA CHEST

Cambria

6216 Moonstone
Beach Dr.
Cambria, CA

(805) 927-4514

seachestrestaurant.
com

Like many residents on this idyllic stretch of coast, Jim and Karen Clarke migrated north from Orange County in search of unspoiled California. Not only did they find it—back in 1972—but the area is still remarkably pristine. That didn't stop their mom-'n'-pop seafood joint from becoming, and remaining, one of the most popular spots around. Oysters, clams, crab or shrimp Louis—simple beach food. For about a decade, Jim cooked while Karen researched recipes and made desserts. Then the menu started to grow; halibut was added at about the same time Hangtown Fry dropped off. It was time for some help. Busboy Steve Kniffen told Jim: "Train me as a chef and in a month you'll never need anyone else." A little arrogant, perhaps? That was in 1985, and Steve still mans the stove. Unquestionably, one of the high points of my whole journey was eating at the bar here and watching Steve work, while just outside the window, waves crashed onto the craggy rocks. Be prepared for a long but pleasant—and often boisterous—wait (wine and a deck chair are ideal).

Steamed Clams with White Wine and Green Onions

SERVES 4 ❧ 25 MINUTES

Around the world, wherever great clams are found, there is a tradition involving wine, fire, and quick cooking. In fact, many clam dishes vary little, because there's not too much you can do to a bucket of perfect clams without screwing them up. At The Sea Chest, possibly the most atmospheric little seafood joint for hundreds of miles around, you can drink in the up-close-and-personal view of the Pacific while you drink down the outrageous liquor left in the bowl after dispatching the bivalves.

4 lbs. live clams, such as Manila or littleneck, in shells, scrubbed

3 tbsp. extra-virgin olive oil

6 green onions, white and light green parts only, finely chopped

2 garlic cloves, minced

3 cups dry white wine

1 tbsp. unsalted butter

⅛ tsp. fine sea salt

¼ tsp. pepper

2 tbsp. finely chopped fresh flat-leaf parsley

Crusty bread, for serving

1. Discard any clams that are slightly open and do not close immediately when tapped with a finger. Place a very large sauté pan or a stock pot over medium heat and add the oil. Add the green onions and garlic and cook for 1 minute. Add the clams and white wine and cover the pan. Increase the heat to high. Bring to a boil; cook for 4 to 5 minutes, until each shell opens, stirring the shellfish once or twice. With a skimmer, lift out each clam as it opens and set aside on a platter. Discard any shellfish that have not opened after 5 minutes.

2. When all the clams have been transferred, simmer the wine and clam broth rapidly to reduce by about half, about 10 minutes. Return the clams to the pan, with all the juices from the platter, and add the butter, salt, and a few turns of the peppermill. Simmer for 1 minute, stirring occasionally with the skimmer, just until the clams have warmed through. Sprinkle with the parsley and ladle into bowls, giving everyone plenty of juice and some bread to soak it up.

PER SERVING (WITHOUT BREAD) 245 Cal., 74% (182 Cal.) from fat; 18 g protein; 15 g fat (3.5 g sat.); 10 g carbo (0.7 g fiber); 634 mg sodium; 53 mg chol. LC

Fiscalini Ranch Preserve

CAMBRIA

The trails through this preserve are the perfect prescription for bodies tired of riding in a car. Meandering through the Monterey pines and meadows, you'll come across few other souls. For entry points, see the map at visitcambriacalifornia.com/golocal/fiscaliniranch.html

Spellbound Herbs, Gift Shop & Garden

CAMBRIA

The cuteness factor is high here, but when your wish list includes potpourri, incense, aromatic soaps, candles, and lotions, or catnip for kitty, this is the place to stop. There are also bulk herbs and teas, plus a garden full of riotous abandon and actual faeries. 4101 Burton Dr.; spellboundherbs.com

Robin's

CAMBRIA

Robin and Shanny Covey started off with vegetarian and vegan fare at the forefront of their restaurant, but now convey a locally sourced and unsprayed omnivorous opus, with influences from Shanny's native Singapore and tasty points north-south-east-west. In a historic 1930s home complete with the original fireplace and expansive gardens, this is lovely Cambria's dining jewel. 4095 Burton Dr.; robinsrestaurant.com

Fried Calamari Steaks

SERVES 2 TO 4 ❊ 25 MINUTES

The concept of calamari as a "steak" (rather than rings) originated from a desire to fully utilize the massive sea animal known as the Humboldt squid, but prepping a steak from this leviathan is not for the faint of heart. Luckily, most good coast-adjacent fishmongers carry fresh or frozen, thoroughly pounded and cleaned steaks; this is a very, very good thing! Be sure to use two skillets, dividing the butter and oil between the pans, so you don't crowd the steaks. This recipe, a favorite at the Sea Chest, is easily doubled.

Two 6-oz. tenderized calamari steaks, about 1/3 in. thick

2 1/2 cups *panko* bread crumbs

2 large eggs

6 tbsp. extra-virgin olive oil

6 tbsp. unsalted butter

1 tbsp. finely chopped fresh flat-leaf parsley, for garnish

1 lemon, cut into 8 wedges, for serving

Rémoulade Sauce (page 205) or tartar sauce, for serving

1. Pound the calamari (unless you bought them already pounded): Cut each steak in half crosswise. Place a large sheet of plastic wrap on a work surface. Place a piece of calamari in the center and lay another sheet of plastic wrap on top. Using the flat side of a meat mallet, pound the calamari very lightly from the center outward, gently easing the calamari out to an even thickness of about 1/4 in. and about 5 by 3 in. in size. Repeat with the remaining pieces. Take care not to tear the delicate meat; this is not similar to pounding chicken.

2. Put the panko in a large, shallow bowl. In another large, shallow bowl, beat the eggs together with 1/4 cup water. Dip each steak first in the egg mixture, letting any excess drip away, and dredge in the panko, pressing gently to make sure all sides are coated lightly but evenly.

3. Add half the oil and half the butter to each of two large (12-in.) sauté pans. Heat over medium-high heat until sizzling. Place 2 steaks in each pan without overlapping, and cook without disturbing until golden brown on the bottom, about 1 1/2 minutes. With a metal spatula, turn and cook until the other sides are golden, about 1 1/2 minutes more. Drain on paper towels, then transfer the steaks to warmed dinner plates and scatter the parsley around the edges of the plates. Serve with the lemon wedges and rémoulade sauce alongside.

MAKE AHEAD: The steaks can be made through step 2 up to 4 hours in advance; chill the breaded steaks on a baking sheet, uncovered, until 5 minutes before you are ready to cook them.

PER SERVING (WITHOUT RÉMOULADE) 489 Cal., 75% (366 Cal.) from fat; 18 g protein; 42 g fat (15 g sat.); 12 g carbo (0.5 g fiber); 169 mg sodium; 323 mg chol. LC/LS

SEBASTIAN'S

Old San Simeon

442 SLO–
San Simeon Rd.
San Simeon, CA

(805) 927-3307

Sebastian's reminds me of Cher: They're both survivors. Since Old San Simeon's earliest incarnation around 1852 as a whaling industry hub, the town has gone through several boom-bust cycles, but there has always been a store in the building currently shared by Ian McPhee's packed eatery and the tasting room for Hearst Ranch Winery (as well as the post office). It's hard to believe this charming blocklong community once boasted two hotels, various saloons, a blacksmith, and a stage depot; now, Sebastian's and the tasting room are the only businesses in town (not counting the post office that's shared space with the store off and on for more than 100 years). Nearby, the large Spanish-style warehouses are empty, no longer filled with precious antiquities bound for the castle (visible way up in the hills to your east). I can't think of anything better than to sit at the edge of the deck in the sunshine, swinging my legs and gazing out at the historic bay, with a big juicy burger in one hand and an equally juicy glass of wine in the other.

Tri-Tip Sandwiches with Pickled Onions and BBQ Sauce

SERVES 8 ❖ 50 MINUTES

Tri-tip is a cut of beef (from the bottom sirloin, in case you are as meat-obsessed as I am) that until recently was rarely seen outside California. Indeed, its spiritual home is the Santa Maria region, not far from Old San Simeon, and Sebastian's. This radically satisfying cowboy-esque sandwich is a natural by-product of the spectacular wedge salad on page 86, in which Ian McPhee combines everything good about rustic California cuisine. That's if you find yourself with leftovers. (If in doubt, why not grill two 2-lb. tri-tips?)

1 (2-lb.) oak-grilled tri-tip (page 86)

8 French rolls, split

1/2 cup Garlic Butter (page 102) or unsalted butter, softened

About 1 1/4 cups sliced Quick Pickled Onions (page 243)

About 1 1/4 cups Ian's BBQ Sauce (page 86) or a smoky-sweet purchased BBQ sauce

1. Grill the tri-tip as directed on page 86. After meat rests 5 to 10 minutes, slice thinly.

2. Preheat the broiler. Toast the rolls cut side up until just barely golden, 1 to 1 1/2 minutes. Spread the bottom half of each roll with 1 tbsp. garlic butter, then pile on the sliced meat. Top each sandwich with some of the pickled onions and drizzle with BBQ sauce. Cover with the top of the roll.

PER SANDWICH 481 Cal., 40% (191 Cal.) from fat; 23 g protein; 22 g fat (11 g sat.); 49 g carbo (2.2 g fiber); 1,001 mg sodium; 86 mg chol. LC

On The Road

The Esalen Institute

BIG SUR

For years, this sprawling clifftop retreat was very difficult to visit, though controversial new policies now offer lots of ways to get in—for a price. Set among expansive vegetable and flower gardens in one of the most stunning spots along the California coast, this alternative-lifestyle haven offers workshops in yoga, meditation, and Gestalt psychology. My favorite: clothing-optional cliffside mineral baths and massage. If you aren't signed up for a workshop or retreat, the baths are open to the public only in the middle of the night, from 1 to 3 a.m. 55000 Hwy. 1; esalen.org

Julia Pfeiffer Burns State Park

BIG SUR

Arguably the most beautiful (and untouched) beach in California, this turquoise blue cove is off-limits to visitors, in order to protect the fragile environment. But you can get a great view of the beach—fed by an elegant waterfall—by walking the coastal trail. On the eastern side of Highway 1, several strenuous trails take you up toward Pfeiffer Ridge—and breathtaking views on a sunny day. Hwy. 1, about 3 mi. north of Esalen; parks.ca.gov/?page_id=578

Chicken Tortilla Soup with Lime *Crema*

SERVES 4 TO 6 �֎ 50 MINUTES

The flower- and cactus-dotted deck at Sebastian's is as bucolic a place as any I found along this entire spectacular coast. (And, lucky me, it's only a 35-minute drive from my home.) Just across the quiet street are the three warehouses that once contained massive swag from William Randolph Hearst's legendary European shopping trips. Art, tile, wood panels, and furniture were off-loaded from ships into the warehouses, before making their way up the hill to his castle, perched like a vision from Disneyland just above your lunch spot. Sebastian's very filling version of this classic Cal-Mex soup calls for puréeing half the soup, making it even more of a hearty meal. Grab a glass of Hearst Ranch Winery's Tempranillo to tame the soup's bite.

Soup

3 tbsp. canola or vegetable oil

6 small corn tortillas, cut into rough pieces, each about 1¼ in.

1 large yellow onion, chopped

3 garlic cloves, finely chopped

2 tbsp. chili powder

1 tbsp. ground cumin

2 fresh bay leaves or 1 dried leaf

½ tsp. fine sea salt, plus more to taste

¼ tsp. pepper, plus more to taste

1 qt. low-sodium chicken broth or homemade chicken stock

1 (14.5-oz.) can diced tomatoes with green chiles, or a 14-oz. can diced tomatoes mixed with a 4-oz. can chopped green chiles

1 (15-oz.) can black beans, rinsed and drained

1 lb. boneless, skinless chicken breasts, cut into ½-in. chunks

¼ cup roughly chopped cilantro

Lime Crema

Juice of 2 large limes

½ cup crème fraîche

Tortilla "Whiskers"

Canola or vegetable oil, for deep-frying

3 corn tortillas, sliced as thinly as possible (a paper cutter works well)

1. **START THE SOUP:** Place a soup pot or large dutch oven over medium heat and add the oil. Add the tortilla pieces to the hot oil and stir for 1 minute to warm. Add the onion, garlic, chili powder, cumin, bay leaves, salt, and pepper; stir to toast the spices and coat the tortilla pieces and onion. Cook, stirring occasionally, until the onion is translucent, 8 minutes.

2. Stir in the broth and diced tomatoes with chiles and bring to a boil. Simmer partially covered for 15 minutes, to blend the flavors. Remove from the heat.

3. Remove the bay leaves from the soup. In a blender, purée about half the soup, making sure to include plenty of the solids. Return the puréed mixture to the pot and add the black beans and chicken; return to a simmer and cook, partially covered, 5 minutes, or until the chicken is cooked through. Remove from the heat and stir in the cilantro; cover the pot and keep warm over very low heat.

4. **MAKE THE CREMA:** In a small bowl, whisk together the lime juice and crème fraîche.

5. In a heavy, deep saucepan or a deep-fryer, warm about 2 in. of oil to 350°, for frying the tortilla "whiskers." Add the slivered tortillas to the hot oil and fry, nudging occasionally with a skimmer, until golden brown and beautifully crisp, 2 minutes. Taste the soup for seasoning and adjust with salt and pepper. Ladle the soup into individual bowls and top each with a spoonful of the lime crema and a tangle of the tortilla whiskers.

PER SERVING 527 Cal., 42% (220 Cal.) from fat; 31 g protein; 25 g fat (6.7 g sat.); 47 g carbo (13 g fiber); 366 mg sodium; 75 mg chol.

BBQ Tri-Tip Wedge with Blue Cheese Dressing and Cherry Tomatoes

SERVES 4 TO 6 ❋ 1³⁄₄ HOURS

This outrageous, man-a-licious "salad" personifies all that is wonderful about California's sometimes healthy, sometimes decadent lifestyle. It is, technically, a salad, yes. There is super-crisp iceberg lettuce (which here belies its somewhat dicey reputation and shines bright), and a pungent, creamy dressing. Cherry tomatoes add festive color and pickled onions add bite. But the star of the salad is California's signature cut of smoky-sweet BBQ'ed meat, a tri-tip.

Ian's BBQ Sauce

2 tsp. canola or vegetable oil

½ small yellow onion, diced

1 garlic clove, minced

2 tsp. minced chipotle chile in *adobo* sauce, with sauce

½ cup ketchup

½ cup chili sauce, such as Heinz

¼ cup firmly packed brown sugar

¾ tsp. blackening spice mix

1½ tbsp. beef or chicken stock, or water

1½ tsp. apple cider vinegar

1½ tsp. lemon juice

½ tsp. liquid smoke (optional)

Blue Cheese Dressing

2 cups mayonnaise

1 cup buttermilk

1 tbsp. minced garlic

2 cups crumbled blue cheese (about 8 oz.)

¾ tsp. fine sea salt

Tri-Tip

1 (2-lb.) tri-tip roast, preferably pasture-raised, trimmed

1 tbsp. canola or vegetable oil

½ tsp. *each* fine sea salt and pepper

½ tsp. granulated garlic

Salad

1 large, firm head of iceberg lettuce, any discolored leaves peeled away

1 pt. red and/or yellow cherry tomatoes, halved

1 cup Quick Pickled Onions (page 243), for serving (optional)

1. **MAKE THE BBQ SAUCE:** In a heavy saucepan, warm the oil over medium heat. Add the onion and sauté until golden brown and slightly softened, about 5 minutes. Stir in the garlic and chipotle chile with adobo and sauté until aromatic, about 1 minute; do not let the garlic scorch. Stir in the remaining ingredients, and bring to a boil. Reduce the heat so the sauce is barely simmering. Partially cover the pan and simmer, stirring occasionally, for 1 hour. Remove from the heat.

2. **MAKE THE DRESSING:** In a small bowl, whisk together all the ingredients. Cover and chill for at least 1 hour, for the flavors to marry.

3. **GRILL THE TRI-TIP:** Remove the meat from the refrigerator and let stand for 30 minutes. Prepare a charcoal or gas grill for indirect medium heat (350° to 450°): *If using a charcoal grill*, set up a wood fire, ideally with seasoned oak (or soak oak chunks for 30 minutes, drain, and add to your charcoal). Leave an area clear for indirect heat and place a drip pan in the cleared area. *If using a gas grill*, soak oak wood chips for 30 minutes, drain, and wrap in foil. Turn all the burners to high, close the lid, and heat for 10 minutes. Then turn off one burner and lower heat to medium (350° to 450°) on the other burner(s). Place foil packet of wood chips directly on the heat element.

4. Rub the meat all over with oil, and rub in the salt, pepper, and garlic. Grill the meat over direct heat until it is well marked on all four sides, turning occasionally, about 10 minutes. Transfer to indirect heat and grill until done as desired, 20 to 30 minutes for medium-rare (130° to 135° on a meat thermometer). While the meat is cooking, baste it with the BBQ sauce every 5 to 10 minutes, turning the meat each time, and using all of the BBQ sauce. Transfer to a platter, tent loosely with foil, and let rest for 5 minutes.

5. **MAKE THE SALAD:** Prepare a large bowl of ice water. With a sharp knife, cut the iceberg into quarters or sixths, and immerse in the ice water, turning each wedge over a couple of times to be sure the ice water seeps in between the layers. Let soak for 5 minutes. Pull a wedge from the ice water and, holding it gently with the cut side down, shake energetically to rid it of as much water as possible. Repeat with the remaining wedges.

6. Place a wedge on each plate, cut side up. Drizzle each wedge generously with the blue cheese dressing and scatter the tomatoes and pickled onions over the top. Cut the grilled meat into 1-in. chunks and distribute on the plate around each wedge.

MAKE AHEAD: The BBQ sauce may be made up to 3 days ahead; cool to room temperature and chill until grilling time. The salad dressing may be kept, covered and chilled, up to 24 hours ahead.

PER SERVING 831 Cal., 58% (478 Cal.) from fat; 43 g protein; 53 g fat (16 g sat.); 50 g carbo (2.3 g fiber); 2,149 mg sodium; 146 mg chol.

Stop

3

DEETJEN'S BIG SUR INN

Big Sur

48865 Hwy. 1
Big Sur, CA

(831) 667-2378

deetjens.com

To me, this storied spot is one of the most iconic destinations along California's entire coast. Inaccessibility may play a part in its allure, but there is true magic in this restaurant, and in all of the somewhat ramshackle structures that shelter here under towering redwoods in the cleft of a canyon. Deetjen's evolved organically from a tent camp set up in the mid-'30s by Norwegian Helmuth Deetjen and his new bride, Helen, daughter of a land-owning, politically active California family. The couple began building Scandinavian-style cottages and feeding intrepid travelers in the late '30s, and very little has changed since. There are no marble bathrooms or fancy soaps—and the rustic style is invariably honest and welcoming. Excellent food draws visitors today just as it has since the earliest days, though the property is now owned and managed by a nonprofit set up after Grandpa Deetjen died in 1972. But don't for a moment imagine spartan simplicity: The antiques are real, fires crackle, and glasses sparkle. Before dining, hike up the hill behind the cabins to the "secret" bench ideally situated to showcase this dramatic coast.

Deetjen's Dip

SERVES 4, WITH TRADITIONAL BREAKFAST OR LUNCH ACCOMPANIMENTS ❖ 15 MINUTES

This famously rustic getaway is unpretentious in almost every way, and yet the food never feels dated or even a little bit rustic-funky. The Dip is perhaps Deetjen's most beloved dish, and it couldn't be easier to replicate at home. Serve it with home fries (page 90) or fruit, as they do at Deetjen's.

1. **MAKE THE HOLLANDAISE:** Place a double boiler insert or metal bowl over a saucepan of barely simmering water. Add the egg yolks and 1½ tbsp. water; whisk until pale yellow, slightly thickened, and foamy, about 1 minute. Add the melted butter in a thin stream, whisking constantly until the butter is absorbed and the sauce is thickened. Whisk in the lemon juice, salt, and cayenne. Taste and add more lemon juice if desired. Remove from the heat, cover, and keep warm.

2. Preheat the broiler. Cut the slices of turkey as needed so they will fit onto your English muffins without too much sticking out. Toast the muffins under the broiler, turning once, about 1 minute per side. Brush the cut sides with 1 tbsp. of the melted butter. In a cast-iron skillet or heavy frying pan, warm the remaining ½ tbsp. butter and the oil over medium-high heat. Sear the turkey breast pieces until caramelized outside and warmed through, 2 minutes, turning occasionally.

3. Place all 4 muffin bases on a work surface, cut sides up. Fit the turkey pieces in 1 or 2 layers on each, then top each with half a sliced avocado. Cover with the muffin top and press down to compact. Cut in half and skewer each with cocktail pick if you like. Serve ramekins of warm hollandaise on the side and encourage diners to dip each and every bite into the citrusy-sunny goodness.

PER SERVING 582 Cal., 67% (390 Cal.) from fat; 17 g protein; 44 g fat (20 g sat.); 340 g carbo (5.7 g fiber); 926 mg sodium; 196 mg chol.

Hollandaise

2 large egg yolks, preferably from pastured hens

½ cup unsalted butter, melted and kept warm

2 tsp. lemon juice, plus more to taste

½ tsp. fine sea salt

Pinch of cayenne

Sandwiches

4 (¼-in.-thick) slices best-quality smoked turkey breast from a deli (about 6 oz.), halved crosswise

4 English muffins, split

1½ tbsp. melted butter

2 tsp. olive oil

2 ripe Hass avocados, pitted, peeled, and sliced

Nepenthe

BIG SUR

This dreamy California legend is no less compelling today than when Liz and Dick briefly called it home, while filming *The Sandpiper*. With views to die for, a postmodern dining room with a central fireplace, endless outdoor seating (and warming firepits), and decent food of the seafood-and-burger genre, this is a place to settle in for the afternoon. Vacationers with cameras may now outnumber arty types, but it's still a Don't-Miss stop. 48510 Hwy. 1; nepenthebigsur.com

Herbed Home Fries

SERVES 4 TO 6 ✤ 30 MINUTES, PLUS AT LEAST 4 HOURS OR OVERNIGHT TO CHILL

There are two keys to crispness in home fries. The first is the chilling and drying-out period, and it's much easier on the cook first thing in the morning if the potatoes are already prepped to this point. But here comes the second key: The actual frying of the potatoes requires time and attention. You may feel the technique is labor-intensive, but this is the only way to create superlative home fries. Just get into a Zen rhythm while lovingly turning each potato. Imagine yourself in a hot tub at Esalen (page 84), just down the road from Deetjen's.

2½ lbs. red potatoes, each about 2 in.

2 tsp. fine sea salt

¼ tsp. pepper

1 cup loosely packed fresh flat-leaf parsley leaves and tender stems, finely chopped

1 tbsp. canola or vegetable oil

1 tbsp. extra-virgin olive oil

4 green onions, trimmed and finely chopped

1. In a large pot, cover the potatoes with cold water. Add 1 tsp. salt and bring to a boil over medium-high heat. Reduce the heat and let simmer until the potatoes are tender but not disintegrating, 15 to 18 minutes, depending on their size. Drain in a colander. When cool enough to handle, cut into bite-size pieces (in halves or in quarters, according to your bite size). Chill uncovered in a single layer on a baking sheet, for at least 4 hours and up to overnight, to dry slightly.

2. Preheat a very large cast-iron skillet or a griddle (or two large skillets) over medium-high heat. Cook in batches if necessary to avoid overcrowding. In a large bowl, combine the potatoes, 1 tsp. salt, the pepper, half the parsley, and the oils. Toss until lightly but completely coated with oil on all sides. Using tongs, place the potatoes in the skillet or on the griddle, starting in the top left corner and working clockwise. When the first side is deep golden brown, after about 3 to 4 minutes, begin rotating the pieces with your tongs in the order added. Don't worry if every single side does not get the crusty-brown treatment. When they are done to your liking, transfer the potatoes to a warm serving platter and scatter with the remaining ½ cup parsley and the green onions. If cooking in two batches, keep the first warm in a low (200°) oven while you cook the second, but optimum crispness will be achieved only if the potatoes are served right away.

PER SERVING 216 Cal., 20% (44 Cal.) from fat; 4.8 g protein; 5.1 g fat (1 g sat.); 38 g carbo (4 g fiber); 93 mg sodium; 0 mg chol. GF/LC/LS/VG

Pan-Fried Zucchini-Feta Cakes with Raita

MAKES ABOUT 16 SMALL CAKES; SERVES 8 ❈ 30 MINUTES, PLUS AT LEAST 1 HOUR TO CHILL

This dish is a unique mash-up of styles—
Is it Greek? Is it Indian?—in which the elegance
and tastiness factors exemplify the fabulous
abilities of California's chefs to pull from the best
culinary traditions of the global lexicon.
It's versatile enough to make a nice appetizer
or lunch dish, and I would also add it to a
breakfast buffet with fresh-squeezed citrus juices,
sparkling wine from California's Central Coast,
and mounds of lovingly crisped smoked bacon.

Raita

½ English cucumber,
shredded on the large holes
of a box grater

1 cup plain yogurt

⅓ cup finely chopped
red onion

1 tbsp. finely chopped cilantro

1 tbsp. finely chopped fresh
mint leaves

1 tbsp. Meyer lemon juice,
or 1½ tsp. lemon juice from
a standard lemon

½ tsp. fine sea salt

⅛ tsp. pepper

⅛ tsp. cayenne

Zucchini Cakes

1½ lbs. green zucchini,
shredded on the large holes of
a box grater (about 3 zucchini)

2 tsp. kosher salt

1¾ cups *panko* bread crumbs

3 large eggs, lightly beaten

8 oz. feta cheese, crumbled

2 tbsp. finely chopped fresh
flat-leaf parsley leaves

½ tsp. pepper

About 3 tbsp. canola or
vegetable oil

1½ cups mixed or
micro greens

1. **MAKE THE RAITA:** Wrap the shredded cucumber in a double layer of paper towels—or a clean kitchen towel—and squeeze firmly to remove the excess water. In a medium bowl, blend the cucumber together with the remaining ingredients. Cover with plastic wrap and chill for at least 1 hour, for the flavors to marry, and up to 4 hours.

2. **MAKE THE ZUCCHINI CAKES:** In a colander, toss the zucchini with the salt and let stand for 15 minutes. Using your hands, squeeze as much water as you possibly can out of the zucchini, a handful at a time. Spread on a double layer of paper towels and blot with more paper towels. In a large bowl, toss the zucchini with the panko, eggs, feta, parsley, and pepper, tossing well to be sure the mixture is evenly blended.

3. Preheat the oven to the lowest setting (about 200°). In a large cast-iron skillet, heat the oil over medium-high heat until very hot. Use a ¼-cup dry measure to scoop up the mixture and form into slightly flattened 2½-in. patties. Pan-fry the cakes in batches until golden brown and crisp on one side, about 2 minutes. Turn over with a metal spatula and cook until browned on the other side and cooked through, about 2 minutes more. Keep the first batch of cakes warm in the oven on a platter or baking sheet while you finish cooking the second batch. Add a bit more oil to the skillet if necessary. Serve warm, with some of the greens on top and the raita on the side.

PER SERVING 219 Cal., 61% (133 Cal.) from fat; 11 g protein; 15 g fat (6 g sat.); 12 g carbo (1.6 g fiber); 604 mg sodium; 109 mg chol. LC/V

Deetjen's attained icon status on my list of destinations when I was 12 years old. It's even more enticing now.

Big Sur Bakery & Restaurant

BIG SUR

"Come to your senses and slow down," advises this tiny, widely respected eatery. A wood-fired oven informs the dinner menu in the converted 1936 ranch-style house, and you'll find some of the best bread outside San Francisco, plus expertly prepped and sauced meat, fish, and poultry, and ethereal pizzas with a California twist. The next morning—if you're staying nearby—grab a steaming cup of coffee and one (or three!) of the many creative and mouthwatering pastries, but be prepared to wait. 47540 Hwy. 1; bigsurbakery.com

Steinbeck House Restaurant

SALINAS

The food's not really the draw in this 1897 Queen Anne house, birthplace and boyhood home of John Steinbeck, which opened as a restaurant in 1974. You're here for the history, and there's plenty of it (including the pinafore uniforms of the octogenarian servers). Tea and scones or quiche would be an excellent option. 132 Central Ave.; steinbeckhouse.com

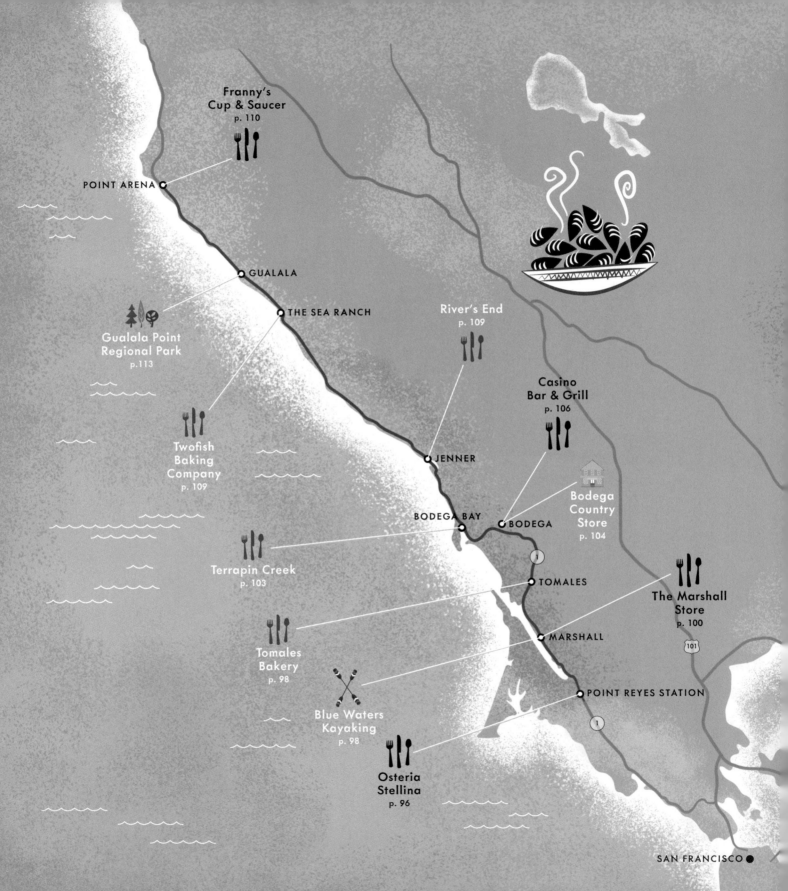

Franny's
Cup & Saucer
p. 110

POINT ARENA

GUALALA

Gualala Point
Regional Park
p.113

THE SEA RANCH

River's End
p. 109

Casino
Bar & Grill
p. 106

Twofish
Baking
Company
p. 109

JENNER

Bodega
Country
Store
p. 104

BODEGA BAY

BODEGA

Terrapin Creek
p. 103

TOMALES

The Marshall
Store
p. 100

MARSHALL

101

Tomales Bakery
p. 98

POINT REYES STATION

Blue Waters
Kayaking
p. 98

1

Osteria
Stellina
p. 96

SAN FRANCISCO

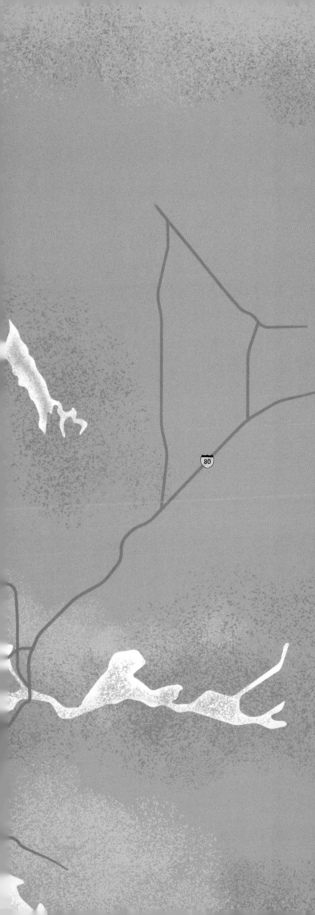

Route 5

Point Reyes Station *to* **Marshall**
to **Bodega** *to* **Point Arena**

94 MILES

JUMPING AHEAD, I AVOID the dense urban jewel of San Francisco, reserving it for another time. Northern Californians will tell you this drive—north of the city, beginning at the southern tip of Tomales Bay—is the state's most stunning coastal route. This SoCal native may differ, but not loudly.

For generations, this pastoral landscape has supplied San Francisco's cavorting gourmands with oysters, clams, and dairy products; luckily, a good percentage of the goodies have stayed right here, to be served in excellent restaurants and sold at farmers' markets (okay, populated by city weekenders). *Point Reyes Station* has a polished, earthy chic vibe—you'll likely spot bearded scruffsters, sleek moms, and skinny-jeaned techies in earnest conversation.

Heading north, savor the long, slow drive up the east side of narrow Tomales Bay, a miracle of nature called home by a gazillion generations of oysters. Halfway up the bay, blink-and-you-miss-it *Marshall*—long under-claiming a population of 50 human souls—cantilevers out over the peaceful estuary. Freshwater is scarce here, so development is, thankfully, limited.

Angling inland, the road skirts *Bodega* town on its way up to more soigné and photo-ready Bodega Bay, but don't be tempted to pass Bodega by (Hitchcock fans and collectors of kitsch will thank me). Above Bodega Bay, you enter a spare, otherworldly landscape of rocky promontories, alarming precipices, and curling mists. Take plenty of rest stops to drink it in, but save the drinking for later. Little *Point Arena*, with its magnificent lighthouse, loudly celebrates its enduring counterculture identity; in the summer it teems with tourists, but wintertime residents exchange the same $20 bill for months.

OSTERIA STELLINA

Point Reyes Station

11285 Hwy. 1
Point Reyes Station,
CA

(415) 663-9988

osteriastellina.com

Christian Caiazzo started cooking as a teenager—flipping burgers and grilling steak in country club kitchens—before moving on to some far more prestigious stoves, like Union Square Cafe in New York City and San Francisco's Postrio (in its early-'90s heyday). Then in 2001, life brought Christian to Point Reyes Station. As a green-market shopper for Hudson Valley produce in New York, he had been well aware of the stellar possibilities offered by a rich agricultural region, and West Marin County boasts arguably some of the best and widest range of foodstuffs in the United States, "rivaled only, perhaps, by Orcas Island," says Christian. But the lack of eateries offering local food floored him. After stints at Cowgirl Creamery and a coffee bar, he opened Osteria Stellina in 2008 ("midwinter, and just in time for the recession," he says). A flower-, art-, and light-filled room where local ranchers and farmers populate menu and tables alike, the chef executes Christian's brand of lush-'n'-local magical minimalism. New: a general store and bottle shop next door, offering transportable local bounty.

Grilled Asparagus with Meyer Lemon Aioli

SERVES 4 AS AN APPETIZER ❈ 25 MINUTES

Local Zuckerman Family Farms is renowned for its amazing and sustainably grown asparagus. With perfection like that, there's no need to do much. But this aioli is so worth the mild effort involved—it's a sunny expression of the goodness of garlic and fragrant Meyer lemon.

1. **MAKE THE AIOLI:** In a food processor, combine the egg, garlic, vinegar, mustard, and salt. Process until evenly blended. With the motor running, drizzle in the olive and canola oils very, very slowly at first, adding slightly faster after the first ¼ cup has been emulsified. Add 1 tsp. of the lemon juice and the pepper; pulse two or three times. Taste for seasoning and add another ½ tsp. lemon juice and/or pinch of pepper, if desired. Transfer to a bowl and stir in the lemon zest. (The aioli will improve and mellow if allowed to rest for 24 hours; cover and chill, then return to cool room temperature before serving. It will keep for up to 5 days.)

2. Snap off the bottom ends of the asparagus about 1 to 1½ in. above the base (where they break easily). Peel the next 2 in. with a vegetable peeler, peeling up toward the tip. Bring a large, wide pot of lightly salted water to a boil, and fill a large, wide bowl with ice water. Ease the asparagus into the boiling water and cook for 1 minute. Using tongs, transfer the spears to the ice water to stop the cooking. Drain briefly on a kitchen towel.

3. Prepare a charcoal or gas grill for medium-high heat (about 450°). Brush the cooking grate clean and grill the asparagus perpendicular to the bars of the grate, turning to char them evenly, until beautifully grill-marked, 3 to 5 minutes. Transfer the asparagus to a platter and immediately toss with the lemon juice, to stop discoloration. Serve with a pot of the aioli on the side. Bliss.

Lemon Aioli

1 large egg, at room temperature

1 large garlic clove, minced

½ tsp. white wine vinegar

½ tsp. Dijon mustard

¼ tsp. fine sea salt

¼ cup extra-virgin olive oil

¼ cup canola oil

1½ to 2 tsp. Meyer lemon juice

⅛ tsp. white pepper, preferably freshly ground, plus more to taste

2 tsp. finely grated Meyer lemon zest

1 lb. super-fresh medium-size asparagus, preferably from the farmers' market

Fine sea salt

1 tbsp. lemon juice

PER SERVING 277 Cal., 92% (256 Cal.) from fat; 3 g protein; 29 g fat (3.4 g sat.); 3.5 g carbo (1.4 g fiber); 152 mg sodium; 53 mg chol. GF/LS/V

On The Road

Blue Waters Kayaking

MARSHALL

There is perhaps no better way to experience the stunningly beautiful waters of Tomales Bay than from a kayak. Choose from morning paddles, sunset tours, or a full day delving into inlets and outcrops. Personal best: a quiet moonrise reflected in the dark and crystalline waters. 19225 Shoreline Hwy.; bluewaterskayaking.com

Tomales Bakery

TOMALES

The tiny town of Tomales may seem too small for a bakery of this caliber, but behind the charmingly unassuming farm-community façade, there are a lot of Bay Area refugees who have helped put this place on the map. From sensational sticky buns to savory pizzas and focaccia, it's one place that's worth seeking out. Super-popular with bikers of the spandex—not black leather—variety. 27000 Hwy. 1; (707) 878-2429

Seared Prawns with Pan-Fried Endive and Parsnip Purée

SERVES 4 ❖ 25 MINUTES, PLUS 40 MINUTES TO POACH

At Osteria Stellina, the prawns might arrive with a mound of *fregola sarda*, a Sardinian pasta similar to Israeli couscous, which could happily be added to this inspired dish. The sweet prawns and rich root vegetable purée are beautifully offset by the slightly smoky bitterness of the endive. If you use the (sublime!) head-on live spot prawns, they will squirm a bit when they hit the pan; please don't be squeamish: This is the literal definition of "fresh." (Peel the prawns as you eat; supply finger bowls for an added level of fancy.) If you like, you can use all parsnip or all rutabaga; butternut squash may even be substituted in a pinch.

Parsnip and Rutabaga Purée

1 lb. parsnips, peeled and cut into 1-in. chunks

1 lb. rutabaga, peeled and cut into 1-in. chunks

½ cup unsalted butter, cut into chunks

2 tbsp. whole milk

½ tsp. fine sea salt

¼ tsp. pepper

1 Belgian endive, quartered lengthwise through the core

1 radicchio di Treviso, quartered lengthwise through the core

2 tbsp. extra-virgin olive oil, plus more for brushing the vegetables

Fine sea salt and pepper

2 tbsp. unsalted butter

8 extra-large head-on live prawns, such as Santa Barbara spot prawns (about 4 oz. each), or 20 smaller head-on prawns or shrimp

1. **MAKE THE PURÉE:** In a medium heavy-bottomed saucepan, combine the parsnips, rutabaga, butter, milk, salt, pepper, and 2 tbsp. water. Bring the liquid to a boil, then reduce the heat so the liquid is just barely simmering; cover the pan and poach the vegetables until very tender, about 40 minutes. Using a slotted spoon, transfer the vegetables to a food processor; add half the liquid from the pan. Purée until very smooth, adding additional liquid from the pan as needed to achieve a silky, puddinglike consistency. Discard any unused liquid from the pan and return the vegetables to the pan; cover, and keep warm.

2. Brush the endive and radicchio quarters with a little oil and season lightly with salt and pepper.

3. Place a large, heavy-bottomed sauté pan or frying pan over medium-high heat and add 1 tbsp. oil and 1 tbsp. butter. Season the prawns lightly with salt and pepper. When the butter foam has subsided, add half the prawns and sauté until no longer pink, 30 to 60 seconds on each side, depending on their size. (Do not overcook these precious shellfish!) Transfer to a platter, discard the oil mixture and quickly wipe out the pan with a paper towel. Add the remaining oil and butter and, when the butter foam subsides, flash-fry the remaining prawns in the same way. Transfer to the platter. Wipe out the pan, and, still over medium-high heat, pan-fry the endive and radicchio quarters all at once, turning occasionally, until wilted and golden, 1½ to 3 minutes.

4. Spoon a mound of the warm purée onto each plate, and place one-fourth of the prawns on top of the purée. On each plate, lean 1 endive and 1 radicchio quarter up against the prawns.

PER SERVING 491 Cal., 72% (355 Cal.) from fat; 5.7 g protein; 41 g fat (19 g sat.); 31 g carbo (8.9 g fiber); 256 mg sodium; 95 mg chol. GF/LC/LS

THE MARSHALL STORE

Marshall

19225 Hwy. 1
Marshall, CA

(415) 663-1339

themarshallstore.com

Tomales Bay is as rich in oysters as it is in history, and the family behind The Marshall Store is woven deep into the fabric of this very special estuary. This bare-bones-on-the-inside spot—with its breathtaking waterside dining—is owned by Heidi and Shannon Gregory along with their dad, Tod Friend (who also owns Tomales Bay Oyster Company, supplier of all the oysters here), and caterer Kim Labao. Ducks will be duckin' and divin' mere feet away from your perch above the tranquil, sparkling water, as you tuck into impeccably prepared shellfish, perfumed by the hard-working little smokehouse next door to the main building (which first opened in 1926 as a general store). My contacts in the area call this the "best on the bay," and it is refreshingly free of attitude (but do beware summer weekends, when the hordes from San Francisco descend on every oyster joint along this "strip"). Your experience here will also be radically affected by the weather: If it's too cold to sit outside, hang out at the stand-up-only bar that shares space with the shucking station.

Dungeness Crab Sandwiches with Rémoulade

SERVES 4 ❖ 20 MINUTES

Here is California's version of a Down East Maine lobster roll! If you can't find—or afford—Dungeness crab for these bright and fragrant sandwiches, blue crab (from the East and Gulf Coasts) may be substituted. However, if you are tempted to substitute a bottled tartar sauce for the chunky-fresh goodness of the addictive rémoulade, you will have my sympathy but certainly not my understanding. There are times when shortcuts can be taken. This is not one of them.

1. **MAKE THE RÉMOULADE:** In a medium bowl, whisk together the mayonnaise and vinegar; fold in the pickled onions, cornichons, capers, dill, paprika, cayenne, salt, and pepper. Taste for seasoning.

2. **MAKE THE VINAIGRETTE:** In a small bowl, whisk together all the ingredients thoroughly; if making ahead of time, whisk again just before serving.

3. Preheat the broiler and assemble the remaining ingredients. Toast the rolls, cut sides up, until not quite turning color (you just want them warm and slightly crisp). Spread the base and top of each roll generously with rémoulade. Build the sandwiches on the roll bases in the following order, dividing the ingredients evenly: an even layer of crab, sliced cucumber, then daikon radish sprouts. Drizzle each with about 1 tsp. of the vinaigrette, then layer with the tomatoes and romaine leaves and top with the other half of the roll. Press down gently, and cut in half. Skewer each half with cocktail picks, if desired.

MAKE AHEAD: The rémoulade and vinaigrette can be kept, covered and chilled, 1 day.

PER SANDWICH 727 Cal., 39% (284 Cal.) from fat; 37 g protein; 32 g fat (4.8 g sat.); 77 g carbo (3.8 g fiber); 1,739 mg sodium; 99 mg chol.

Rémoulade

1 cup mayonnaise

1½ tbsp. tarragon vinegar

1 tbsp. finely chopped cocktail onions

2 cornichons, finely chopped

1 tbsp. capers, drained and roughly chopped

1½ tsp. finely chopped fresh dill

¼ tsp. Hungarian sweet paprika

⅛ tsp. cayenne

¼ tsp. *each* fine sea salt and pepper

Vinaigrette

3 tsp. extra-virgin olive oil

1 tsp. white wine vinegar

¼ tsp. Dijon mustard

⅛ tsp. salt

Pinch of pepper

4 bread rolls (such as Acme Deli Rolls)

1 lb. Dungeness shelled cooked crab

Half a European cucumber, thinly sliced

1 cup daikon radish sprouts

2 small ripe tomatoes, thinly sliced

1 head romaine lettuce, inner heart only

BBQ Oysters with Garlic Butter and House Sauce

MAKES 24 OYSTERS ❖ 15 MINUTES, PLUS 1 HOUR TO CHILL

There are two choices for enjoying the outrageous "shell likker" that results from the brief time these oysters spend over hot coals, when the garlic butter gets all sexy with BBQ sauce and the natural oyster juices: A. Have plenty of crusty bread on hand to sop it up, or B. Make like a hedonist (i.e., me) and simply slurp the likker from the shell after you've downed the sublime oyster. This recipe works best with medium Pacific oysters; tiny ones won't hold enough yummy juices.

Garlic Butter

3/4 cup (6 oz.) unsalted butter, softened

3 garlic cloves, minced

1 1/2 tbsp. roughly chopped fresh flat-leaf parsley

1 1/2 tbsp. minced red onion

1/4 tsp. *each* fine sea salt and pepper

The Marshall Store BBQ Sauce

1/3 cup ketchup

2 to 3 tbsp. chipotle hot sauce, or sauce from a can of chipotle chiles in *adobo*, to taste

1 garlic clove, minced

2 tsp. prepared horseradish

Juice of 1 large, juicy lime

1/4 tsp. fine sea salt

24 medium raw Pacific oysters, shucked and on the half-shell

Crusty bread, for serving

1. **MAKE THE GARLIC BUTTER:** In a bowl, blend all the ingredients with a fork. Scoop out into the center of an 8-in. sheet of plastic wrap and form into a 7-in. log, using the plastic wrap to shape. Wrap the log with the plastic and twist the ends to seal. Chill for at least 1 hour to set.

2. **MAKE THE BBQ SAUCE:** In a bowl, whisk together all the ingredients. (Chipotle chiles are very hot; adjust the quantity according to taste.)

3. Prepare a charcoal or gas grill for medium heat (350° to 450°). Place a large grilling basket on the cooking grate. Have ready a large platter or plates for serving the oysters. Remove the garlic butter from the refrigerator, and unwrap. Arrange the oysters on the grilling basket and top each with about 1/2 tbsp. of the garlic butter. Close the lid and grill until the butter has melted, the juices are sizzling slightly around the edges of the shells, and the oysters are only just firm (do not overcook, or they will be tough). This will take 4 to 6 minutes, depending on the size of your oysters. With tongs, transfer the oysters to a perfectly flat platter or plates, and top each oyster with a tsp. of the BBQ sauce. Serve with small forks and crusty bread.

MAKE AHEAD: The garlic butter can be kept, refrigerated, up to 1 week, and frozen up to 1 month.

PER OYSTER 98 Cal., 62% (61 Cal.) from fat; 4.9 g protein; 6.9 g fat (3.9 g sat.); 3.8 g carbo (0.1 g fiber); 138 mg sodium; 40 mg chol.

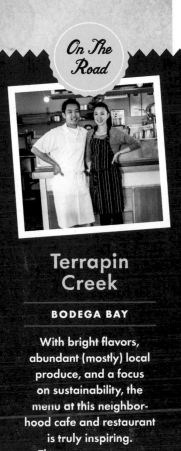

Terrapin Creek

BODEGA BAY

With bright flavors, abundant (mostly) local produce, and a focus on sustainability, the menu at this neighborhood cafe and restaurant is truly inspiring. The young owners—Andrew Truong and Liya Lin, who originally hail from New York and Georgia—worked in San Francisco as a sous chef at Bacar (Andrew) and as a cook at Michael Mina (Liya). Located in what is arguably a touristy town, the mini-mall spot serves dinner Thursday through Monday. 1580 Eastshore Rd.; terrapincreekcafe.com

Bodega Country Store

BODEGA

At first glance, this ramshackle clapboard building, which features fun and tacky memorabilia from *The Birds*, might appear to be pure tourist trap, but don't forget, you're in West Sonoma County. This means the crab rolls, salmon chowder, and more are big-city sophisticated. Be sure to pick up a life-size cutout of Mister Hitchcock himself. 17190 Bodega Hwy.; bodegastore.com

Grilled Fish Tacos with Chile-Lime Slaw and Avocado-Tomatillo Salsa

SERVES 2 TO 4 ❈ 35 MINUTES, PLUS 1 HOUR TO CHILL AND ROAST

Fish tacos are so popular in California that countless establishments are devoted to them. South of the border, fish tacos are a staple in every small town within a stone's throw of the sea. But the idea that really good fish tacos are fast street food is a misconception. The slaw must be impeccably cool and crisp, the fish quality beyond suspicion, and the spices pungent. When you experience the sublime marriage of all the carefully cultivated elements folded up into a tiny corn tortilla, you will know in your heart that the journey was worth every step. At The Marshall Store, they do it the old-fashioned way: right. You can too.

Slaw

2 1/2 cups *each* shredded red cabbage and shredded green cabbage (each about 1/4 of a medium cabbage)

1 cup cilantro, roughly chopped

1/2 jalapeño chile, stemmed, seeded, and minced

Juice of 3 large limes

1/2 tsp. fine sea salt

1/4 tsp. pepper

Avocado-Tomatillo Salsa

1 lb. tomatillos, peeled and quartered

1/4 yellow onion, sliced

1 jalapeño chile, stemmed, halved, and seeded

1 ripe avocado, pitted and peeled

1 cup cilantro leaves and tender stems

1/2 tsp. fine sea salt

1/4 tsp. pepper

Fish

1 1/2 tsp. *each* ground coriander, ground cumin, and Hungarian sweet paprika

1 lb. rock cod fillets, cut into 1 1/2-in. chunks

1/4 tsp. *each* fine sea salt and pepper

2 tsp. canola or vegetable oil

Eight 6-in. corn tortillas, homemade (page 15) or purchased

1 shallot, finely chopped

1 jalapeño chile, stemmed, seeded, and minced

Cilantro leaves, for garnish

Lime wedges

1. **MAKE THE SLAW:** In a bowl, toss together all the ingredients. Chill for at least 30 minutes and up to 2 hours, tossing occasionally.

2. **MAKE THE SALSA:** Preheat the oven to 425°. In a small roasting pan, toss the tomatillos, onion, and jalapeño together. Roast until browned in places and tender, about 25 minutes. Cool to room temperature and chill until close to serving time. In a blender, combine the roasted tomatillo mixture, avocado, cilantro, salt, and pepper. Blend until smooth. Taste for seasoning.

3. **GRILL THE FISH:** Prepare a charcoal or gas grill for medium-high heat (about 450°). In a small, dry cast-iron skillet over medium heat, combine and toast the coriander and cumin until aromatic, about 20 seconds; combine with the paprika. Season the fish with salt and pepper and coat with the dry spice rub, distributing it evenly. Brush the cooking grate clean and coat the fish on both sides with canola oil. Place the fish in a fish basket or on an oiled grilling grid on the grill and cook without moving for 2 minutes. Begin turning the fish with a metal spatula, in the order added to the grill, and cook until firm and golden, about 2 minutes more. Transfer to a platter. (Alternatively, you can cook the fish in an oiled, well-seasoned cast-iron skillet or grill pan over medium-high heat.)

4. Warm the skillet over medium-high heat. Working with a tortilla at a time, dip it briefly into a shallow bowl of water. Transfer to the hot skillet and cook until water evaporates from first side and tortilla is browned in places, about 30 seconds. Flip and cook until dry, about 15 seconds more. Wrap the tortillas in a clean kitchen towel to keep warm. Repeat with the remaining tortillas. Flake some fish onto each tortilla, then top with slaw and salsa. Scatter a little shallot and jalapeño over the top, and garnish with cilantro leaves. Serve with lime wedges.

PER 2-TACO SERVING 585 Cal., 43% (249 Cal.) from fat; 28 g protein; 29 g fat (2.6 g sat.); 62 g carbo (12 g fiber); 816 mg sodium; 37 mg chol. GF

Stop 3

CASINO BAR & GRILL

Bodega

17000 Bodega Hwy.
Bodega, CA

(707) 876-3185

You may experience a small crisis of confidence when you pass through the door from Bodega's funky main street to the dark, unprepossessing interior (think: dive) of this landmark roadhouse. Persevere. On the left, the main bar—manned by a hefty chap who doesn't see much need for a corkscrew—serves locals, bikers, and hipsters alike. But the smaller bar at the back is where magic happens: the food. The two are independently managed (and cash-only), so you'll have to pay for drinks and food separately, but it's really not a hardship. Evelyn Casini has owned the place since 1949 (she and her husband, Art, bought it from his brother, who'd first opened it in 1939). For the first 50 years or so, Evelyn didn't see much point in paying a bartender, but recently she's relented, showing up just to chat once or twice a night. Several different chefs rotate through the closet-size kitchen (check tonight's menu on Facebook). On the night I was there, chef Mark Malicki was working happy alchemy with the greatest ingredients West Marin and Sonoma County have to offer—and that's saying a mouthful.

Lemon Tart with Crème Fraîche and Honey

SERVES 4

25 MINUTES, PLUS 2¼ HOURS TO CHILL AND BAKE

Lucky for me, on the night I visited Casino,
I got to savor one of chef Mark Malicki's
little individual tartlets. With a tender shortbread
crust, tart lemon curd, and honeyed
crème fraîche, this is a dessert fit for the gods.

1. **MAKE THE CURD:** In the top of a double boiler over medium heat, whisk together the lemon zest, juice, sugar, eggs, and egg yolks. Cook until thickened, stirring all the time, 8 to 10 minutes; do not allow to boil. Add the butter a piece at a time, stirring constantly, until it is absorbed. Remove from the heat. Scrape into a bowl and place plastic wrap directly on the surface to prevent a skin from forming. Cool to room temperature and chill at least 2 hours or up to overnight.

2. **MEANWHILE, MAKE THE CRUST:** Pulse the flour, butter, and salt in a food processor until the mixture resembles coarse meal. Add the ice water, 1 tbsp. at a time, pulsing just until the dry ingredients are moistened. Shape the dough into a flat rectangle; wrap in plastic wrap and refrigerate at least 1 hour.

3. Preheat the oven to 425°. Roll out the dough into a 16- by 7-in. rectangle that is ⅛ in. thick. Fit into an ungreased 14- by 4-in. rectangular tart pan with a removable bottom. Prick the bottom and sides with a fork. Line the shell with foil and fill with pie weights. Bake for 15 minutes. Remove the pie weights and foil and bake 10 to 15 minutes longer or until golden brown. Cool completely on a rack.

4. With a rubber spatula, work the lemon curd through a strainer into a bowl. Spoon the curd into the tart shell, spreading it evenly. Cut the tart into 4 pieces. Top each piece with a dollop of crème fraiche and a drizzle of honey.

Lemon Curd

Grated zest of
1 organic lemon

½ cup lemon juice

½ cup sugar

2 large eggs

2 large egg yolks

½ cup salted butter,
cut into 8 pieces

Crust

1 cup all-purpose
flour

⅓ cup cold unsalted
butter, cut into
pieces

¼ tsp. fine sea salt

3 to 4 tbsp. ice
water

½ cup crème fraîche

2 tbsp. local honey

PER SERVING 763 Cal., 63% (484 Cal.) from fat; 9.3 g protein; 54 g fat (33 g sat.); 62 g carbo (1.1 g fiber); 302 mg sodium; 337 mg chol. LS/V

Farm Hen Cassoulet

SERVES 4 TO 6 ❖ ABOUT 3¾ HOURS, PLUS OVERNIGHT TO SOAK AND COOK

This recipe includes a simple confit of chicken—a gentle cooking method that's traditional in France. Confit yields incredibly moist meat and deep flavor (keep the blended confit oil refrigerated for up to two weeks, and use it in salad dressings and/or sautés). There is poetic justice to eating cassoulet in a roadhouse in rural California that one family has owned since 1939. In France, that would be precisely the sort of place where cassoulet has been on the menu for generations. Only here, the clientele leans toward Silicon Valley insiders rather than local peasants.

Chicken Confit

4 chicken legs with thighs, preferably from pasture-raised chickens

Fine sea salt

10 black peppercorns

10 peeled garlic cloves

About 2½ cups canola or vegetable oil

About 2½ cups extra-virgin olive oil

1 lb. slab bacon, cut into ⅓-in. cubes

1 large white or yellow onion, roughly chopped

3 medium carrots, peeled and roughly chopped

1 lb. Tarbais or other white beans, such as cannellini, soaked in water overnight

1 cup dry white wine (optional)

2 bay leaves

Fried Bread Crumbs

1 tbsp. leftover confit oil (from chicken confit, above)

1 cup fresh bread crumbs

1 garlic clove, minced

¼ tsp. *each* fine sea salt and pepper

¼ cup finely chopped fresh flat-leaf parsley

1 cup crème fraîche

1. **MAKE THE CHICKEN CONFIT:** Preheat the oven to 300°. Rinse the chicken in cold water and dry with paper towels thoroughly (this will reduce popping moisture in the hot oil). Season generously with salt. Place the chicken, peppercorns, and garlic in a large dutch oven or cast-iron and enamel pot; add enough of the combined oils to cover by about half an inch. Cover the pot and bake until tender but not falling apart, about 2½ hours. Check occasionally: The oil should tremble, but never come to a real simmer; reduce the oven temperature as necessary.

2. Increase the oven temperature to 325°. Lift the chicken from the pot, and drain off the confit oil (reserve for frying bread crumbs). In the same pot, spread the bacon in an even layer. Add just enough water to barely cover the bacon, and place the pot over medium-high heat (this helps the bacon plump up nicely). When the water has evaporated and the bacon begins to sizzle, about 10 minutes, reduce the heat to low and cook, stirring occasionally, until the bacon pieces are browned on all sides. With a slotted spoon, transfer the bacon to a plate. Increase the heat to medium-high and add the onion and carrots; cook until tender and evenly browned, about 8 minutes. Return the bacon to the pot and add the chicken and the drained beans. Add the white wine (if using), 1 tsp. salt, and enough cold water to cover the ingredients by about half an inch; tuck the bay leaves below the surface. Bring to a simmer over medium-low heat.

3. Partially cover the pot and put in the oven; cook until the beans are tender at the center but not falling apart. This will take anywhere from 50 minutes to 2 hours, depending on the freshness of the beans. Check occasionally and add a bit more water and/or wine if the beans are too dry—you never know how much they will soak up.

4. **MAKE THE BREAD CRUMBS:** In a small skillet, warm the oil over medium heat. Add the bread crumbs and stir to coat evenly with the oil. Cook until golden brown, stirring frequently, 2 to 3 minutes. Stir in the garlic, salt, and pepper, and remove from the heat.

5. Divide the warm cassoulet among shallow bowls, topping each one with parsley, fried bread crumbs, and a dollop of crème fraîche.

PER SERVING 997 Cal., 66% (661 Cal.) from fat; 42 g protein; 74 g fat (27 g sat.); 33 g carbo (5.6 g fiber); 1,523 mg sodium; 194 mg chol.

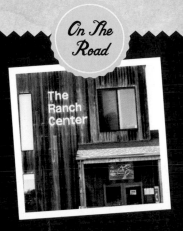

Twofish Baking Company

THE SEA RANCH

Opinions may differ on the sprawling, ticky-tacky community of The Sea Ranch— a diametric opposite to nearby laid-back Gualala—but no one can fault a bakery/ coffee shop with this level of commitment to quality baking. Über-popular morning buns are made with flaky, croissant-like dough and spicy cinnamon sugar, tied up in a knot you'll want to remain permanently attached to. Devoted repeat weekenders outnumber travelers and the vibe is super-friendly. 35590 Verdant View; twofishbaking.com

River's End

JENNER

The website for this restaurant is ILoveSunsets. com, and indeed, sunset is a fine time to find yourself on this secluded, dramatic promon- tory. My anti-tourist-trap radar often puts me off an eatery that's all about the view, but not here. Order up well-crafted, impec- cable Sonoma/Mendo produce, and take it all, deliciously, in. Including the view. 11048 Hwy. 1; ilovesunsets.com

213 Main St.
Point Arena, CA

(707) 882-2500

frannyscupandsaucer.
com

FRANNY'S CUP & SAUCER

Point Arena

The Burkey women are bakers. This teensy shop front, with a bakery inside but no table service, has been in the Burkey family since 1997. For the first eight years, it was called Point Arena Bakery, and little Franny worked the counter for her mom, Barbara (she later called this "forced labor"). Franny, as kids do, grew up and briefly drifted away, to work in other food-related businesses. Then Franny came home, took over the bakery, and changed the name and the entire feeling of the place, but Barbara still helps out. Do they ever clash, these two generations who work so closely together? "We're both alphas," says Barbara, "and things can get a little crunchy, but our realms don't really overlap." Sweet. And speaking of sweet: Every single place you look, there is sugar in some form—or something equally delicate and bewitching, like Japanese lunchboxes or beautiful jewelry from India. It's a little girl's dream, all pink and pretty and fluffy and delightful. Don't miss the Raspberry Violet Rhapsody truffles—one of 14 types of truffles. Oh My.

Chocolate-Filled Doughnut Muffins

MAKES 12 MUFFINS (OR 6 JUMBO MUFFINS)
20 MINUTES, PLUS 30 MINUTES TO BAKE AND COOL

I was hooked the moment I saw the sugar-crusted dome of Barbara and Franny's monster doughnut muffins. Then I discovered the secret chocolate center—meltdown! You can use a small ice cream scoop to fill the muffins with ganache and spoon leftover ganache, warmed, over ice cream.

1. **MAKE THE GANACHE:** In a saucepan, warm the cream over low heat just until hot. Remove from the heat and add the chocolate; cover and let stand for 3 minutes. Add the salt and stir with a whisk until combined and the chocolate is melted and smooth. Transfer to a bowl and let cool until firm (about 2 hours in the refrigerator).

2. **MAKE THE MUFFIN BATTER:** Preheat the oven to 350°. Line a standard 12-cup muffin pan (or 6-cup jumbo muffin pan) with paper liners, then spray the top surface with cooking spray. In a bowl, whisk together the flour, sugar, baking powder, baking soda, salt, cardamom, and orange zest. In another bowl, combine the butter, buttermilk, eggs, and vanilla. Whisk until blended. Add to the dry ingredients and stir and fold together just until combined. The batter will be thick and a little shaggy.

3. Spoon about 3 tbsp. batter into each (standard size) cup, to come just over halfway up the cup. Scoop up 1¹/2 tsp. of ganache and place on the batter in the center of each muffin. Top with about 2 tbsp. of the remaining batter, dividing it evenly and making sure to fully enclose the ganache with batter. Bake for about 20 minutes or until golden brown and firm to the touch. Cool in the pan for 5 minutes, then remove the muffins.

4. **MAKE THE CINNAMON SUGAR:** Combine the sugar, cinnamon, and cloves in a bowl. Put the melted butter in a second bowl. Dip each muffin top in the melted butter and then into the cinnamon sugar mixture.

Ganache Filling

½ cup heavy cream

4 oz. semisweet dark chocolate, roughly chopped

Tiny pinch of Maldon sea salt or *fleur de sel*

Muffins

Cooking-oil spray

2 cups all-purpose flour

1 cup sugar

2½ tsp. baking powder

½ tsp. baking soda

½ tsp. fine sea salt

⅛ tsp. ground cardamom

Finely grated zest of ½ orange

½ cup unsalted butter, melted

½ cup plus 2 tbsp. buttermilk

2 large eggs

1 tsp. vanilla extract

Cinnamon Sugar

½ cup sugar

1 tbsp. ground cinnamon

⅛ tsp. ground cloves

¼ cup unsalted butter, melted, for brushing

PER MUFFIN 375 Cal., 46% (171 Cal.) from fat; 4.6 g protein; 19 g fat (12 g sat.); 49 g carbo (1.6 g fiber); 257 mg sodium; 80 mg chol. LS/V

Bacon, Roasted Tomato, and Pesto Slippers

MAKES 4 TURNOVERS ❋ 15 MINUTES, PLUS 1¼ HOURS TO ROAST AND BAKE

Walking into this jewel-like confectionery in the tiny town of Point Arena is like entering a fairy tale. One that stars these mind-boggling turnovers. It's worth seeking out puff pastry made with real butter for these gems (Dufour is an excellent brand, available at well-stocked markets).

Chile-Spiked Bacon

4 slices thick-cut bacon, halved crosswise

2 tbsp. brown sugar

⅛ tsp. red chile flakes

Roasted Tomatoes

1 cup grape tomatoes

2 tsp. extra-virgin olive oil

Fine sea salt and pepper

Pesto

1 garlic clove

4 walnut halves

4 oz. fresh basil leaves

⅓ cup extra-virgin olive oil

½ cup grated asiago cheese

¼ tsp. *each* fine sea salt and pepper

½ cup ricotta, strained through a cheesecloth-lined sieve

2 Roasted Garlic cloves (page 166)

3 tbsp. grated asiago

¼ cup *each* shredded mozzarella and provolone

14-oz. package frozen puff pastry made with real butter, thawed

1 large egg, beaten

Fine sea salt and pepper

¼ tsp. red chile flakes

1. **MAKE THE BACON:** Preheat the oven to 375°. Lay the bacon in a single layer on a baking sheet lined with foil or parchment paper. Coat each piece of bacon with a thin layer of brown sugar and sprinkle with some chile flakes. Bake until crispy and browned; baking time will depend on the thickness of the bacon, about 17 minutes. Gently pry the bacon from the foil and let cool on a rack, to prevent sticking, until ready to use.

2. **ROAST THE TOMATOES:** Increase the oven temperature to 400° and line a rimmed baking sheet with parchment paper. Toss the tomatoes, oil, and a little salt and pepper together on the baking sheet. Bake for 30 minutes, or until the tomatoes are collapsed and browned. Set the tomatoes aside.

3. **MAKE THE PESTO:** In the bowl of a food processor, pulse the garlic until finely chopped. Add the walnuts and basil. With the food processor on, add the oil slowly in a thin stream. Process until the basil is finely chopped. Add the asiago, salt, and pepper. Process to combine the cheese, then transfer to a small bowl.

4. Increase the oven temperature to 450°. Line the baking sheet with a new piece of parchment if necessary. In a small bowl, whisk together the ricotta, roasted garlic, and 1 tbsp. of the asiago. In another small bowl, toss together the mozzarella and provolone.

5. Unfold the pastry on a lightly floured work surface; the pastry will be approximately 14 by 9 in. Roll it lightly and trim the edges to create a 10-in. square. Cut into four 5-in. squares and transfer to the parchment-lined baking sheet.

6. On each square, spread 1 tsp. of the pesto in a diagonal line from one corner to the opposite corner. Place 1 tbsp. of the ricotta mixture in the middle of the square. Place one-fourth of the roasted tomatoes along the diagonal smear of pesto and on top of the ricotta, and press down gently. Top the tomato with 2 pieces of bacon, overlapping, and put one-fourth of the mozzarella mixture on top of the bacon on each turnover. Fold up the two opposing corners of dough that are not covered by ingredients, and pinch together to make a tidy open-ended "slipper." Secure with a toothpick. Repeat to make 3 more slippers.

7. Whisk the egg with 1 tsp. water and ¼ tsp. salt. With a pastry brush, brush the surface of each slipper lightly with the egg wash. Sprinkle each slipper with 1½ tsp. of the remaining grated asiago, a little salt and pepper, and a pinch of chile flakes. Transfer to the oven and bake until golden brown and cooked on the bottom, 16 to 19 minutes. Cool on a rack and serve warm or at room temperature.

PER TURNOVER 877 Cal., 68% (595 Cal.) from fat; 24 g protein; 67 g fat (19 g sat.); 46 g carbo (3.4 g fiber); 1,229 mg sodium; 102 mg chol.

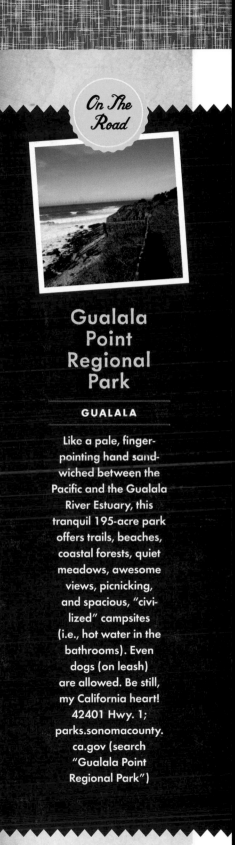

Gualala Point Regional Park

GUALALA

Like a pale, finger-pointing hand sandwiched between the Pacific and the Gualala River Estuary, this tranquil 195-acre park offers trails, beaches, coastal forests, quiet meadows, awesome views, picnicking, and spacious, "civilized" campsites (i.e., hot water in the bathrooms). Even dogs (on leash) are allowed. Be still, my California heart! 42401 Hwy. 1; parks.sonomacounty.ca.gov (search "Gualala Point Regional Park")

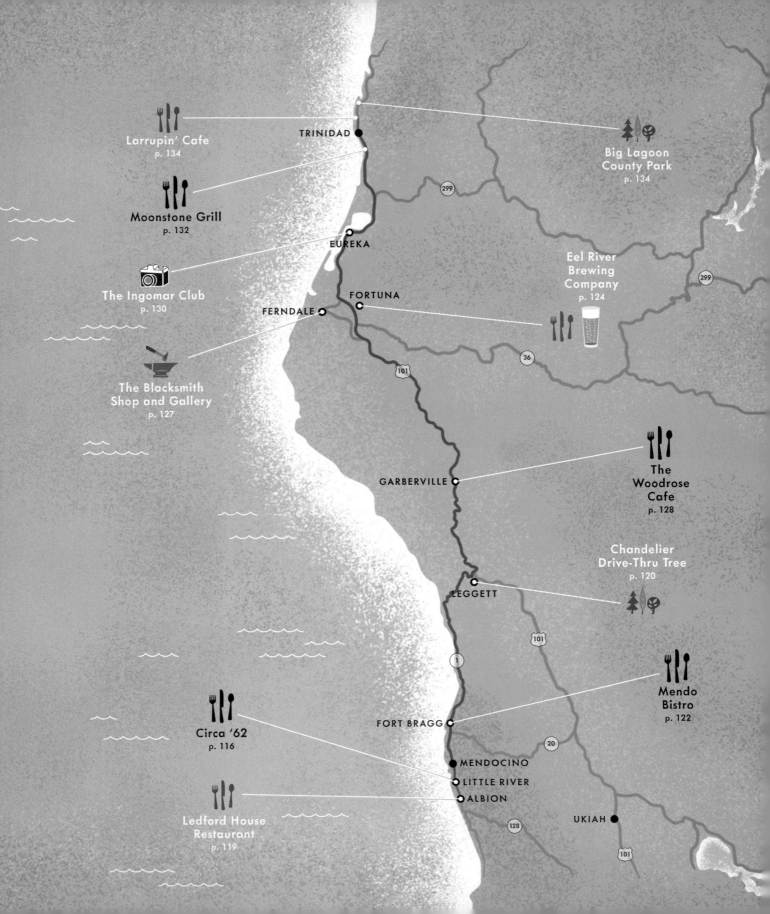

Larrupin' Cafe
p. 134

Moonstone Grill
p. 132

The Ingomar Club
p. 130

The Blacksmith
Shop and Gallery
p. 127

Circa '62
p. 116

Ledford House
Restaurant
p. 119

TRINIDAD

EUREKA

FERNDALE

FORTUNA

GARBERVILLE

LEGGETT

FORT BRAGG

MENDOCINO
LITTLE RIVER
ALBION

UKIAH

Big Lagoon
County Park
p. 134

Eel River
Brewing
Company
p. 124

The Woodrose
Cafe
p. 128

Chandelier
Drive-Thru Tree
p. 120

Mendo
Bistro
p. 122

299

299

36

101

101

1

101

20

128

101

Route 6

Little River *to* Fort Bragg
to Garberville *to* Trinidad

168 MILES

REDDING

36

RED BLUFF

5

LITTLE RIVER IS A SMALL, flower-decked cliffside community with no obvious center. The big draw hereabouts is breathtaking Mendocino, a few miles north—a mysteriously New England–esque gem of a town that's been featured in many a movie and TV show; when the sun shines on the white-painted clapboard homes and shop fronts, you'll feel like a star. If you can find a parking place.

Not far north, *Fort Bragg* is another cup of tea—as short on charm as Mendocino is long. The original fort was established by Anglos in the midst of an Indian reservation, which later morphed into a lumber town. The majestic old building that once housed the lumber company store—now home to Mendo Bistro—still rises like a glittering phoenix above the ever-so-slowly gentrifying town.

As you head north, grassy promontories jut out into the Pacific, and Monterey pines embrace lonely homes and deep coves. Away from it all—but with the views of a lifetime. You're meandering toward that game-changing moment when Highway 1 (aka Shoreline Highway) ceases to exist, turning east to leave the ocean behind and head up into redwood country. As you wind toward 101 ("489 turns!"), watch the vegetation change dramatically: from manzanita and fir to the beloved redwood trees that fueled generations of bank accounts and woodstoves.

The quirky town of *Garberville* conjures alternative lifestyles and old-school lumberjacks in equal part; it marks the southern entrance to the Avenue of the Giants. From here through the Victorian-style confections of Eureka, you will never be out of sight or influence of these striking, iconic trees. In tiny, semirural *Trinidad*, just north of Eureka but a world away, you'll feel the strong tribal influence that (for once) blended happily with the interests of waterfront commerce.

CIRCA '62

Little River

7051 N. Hwy. 1
Little River, CA

(707) 937-5525

schoolhousecreek.com

Cozy, interconnecting rooms, a fireplace, 150-year-old wooden floors, burnished and coffered ceilings, and a spectacular view of the Mendocino coast: These are all just accessories to the fantasy of your best-breakfast dreams. Kevin and Sandy VanderBes are refugees from the world of really *big* hotels, and it's clear they never had a problem with the concept of hospitality, just the scale. The couple, and their like-minded staff, seem to thrive on creating radically special moments for their guests. A few years ago, when they took over this historic blue-clapboard inn—its several buildings including a restaurant in what was once the Ledford farmhouse, a wedding gift from a father to his daughter circa 1862—they turned a tarnished south-of-Mendocino jewel into a warm, woodsy, and welcoming spot. It boasts such excellence as "bacon dipped in crack" (i.e., Roundman's bacon from Fort Bragg), a hash-brown waffle that's unbelievably crisp, and huevos rancheros that make all others cringe at the comparison. All this, plus the adorable local critters—rabbits, squirrels, chipmunks, various birds—snacking on kitchen contributions just outside the window.

Hash-Brown Waffles

SERVES 4 ❖ 15 MINUTES, PLUS 12 MINUTES TO COOK

This ethereally crisp "waffle" is an art form well worth mastering. Most of the time, you get a beautiful, golden waffle print; sometimes you have to work for it. This recipe is designed for a 4-waffle Belgian waffle iron. Each waffle will eventually accommodate 1 packed cup of potato; just keep spreading and pushing.

2 lbs. Idaho or russet potatoes

Cooking-oil spray

4 tbsp. canola or peanut oil

1 tsp. fine sea salt

½ tsp. pepper

Boysenberry or maple syrup or Poached Eggs (page 118)

1. Preheat your Belgian waffle iron (if the waffle iron has settings, set to medium-high). Just before you plan to cook the hash browns, peel the potatoes and, using the large holes of a box grater, grate into a large bowl. Put the shredded potatoes in a colander and give them a quick rinse, removing some but not all of the starch. Spread a clean kitchen towel over a work surface and transfer the shredded potatoes to the center of the towel. Fold the short ends of the towel together, overlapping, to fully enclose the potatoes and then twist from both ends of the towel, twisting and squeezing as hard as possible to remove as much water as you can.

2. When the waffle iron is ready, spray the grids with cooking spray. Firmly pack shredded potatoes into a 1-cup measure and pile them into the center of one of the grids of the iron. Spread the potatoes to an even thickness, drizzle about 1 tbsp. of the oil over the potatoes and season with salt and pepper. Repeat with the remaining 3 cups of potatoes in the remaining 3 waffle iron grids. Spray the top grids with cooking spray and close the waffle iron (this may take some effort). If the iron does not lock (or does not have a lock), weight it down with a heavy cast-iron skillet and continue to squeeze the iron shut until you can lock it. Set a timer for 12 minutes. Have some coffee—you deserve it.

3. Once the timer goes off, open the waffle iron. Use a butter knife to gently dislodge and lift the waffles out of the iron, one by one. Serve immediately on warm plates with plenty of syrup, or topped with poached eggs.

PER SERVING (WAFFLES ONLY) 310 Cal., 41% (128 Cal.) from fat; 3.7 g protein; 14 g fat (1.1 g sat.); 43 g carbo (3.9 g fiber); 391 mg sodium; 0 mg chol. GF/LC/LS/VG

This st
my kitch
agree
or mild.
punch,
contribu
to spicy f
of chipo
in

Ranchero

¼ cup extra-

1 small yellow
chopped

½ *each* small
red bell pepp
seeded, and
(or use 1 who
bell pepper)

3 garlic clove

½ tsp. sugar

½ tsp. fine s
to taste

1 (14.5-oz.) c
tomatoes (in
roughly chop

½ (7-oz.) ca
adobo sauce
whole with t

½ tsp. smok
more to taste

½ tsp. dried
crumbled, pl

Chandelier Drive-Thru Tree

LEGGETT

I would never condone cutting a big chunk out of a magnificent tree today (many so treated have now fallen dead), but this tree stands as testament to older, more cavalier times. As such, it is an honor to drive or walk through (I defy anyone to do so without putting the resulting images on Instagram). 67402 Drive-Thru Tree Rd.; drivethrutree.com

Almond Flour Pancakes with Buttermilk Syrup

MAKES ABOUT 12 PANCAKES; SERVES 4 ❖ 30 MINUTES, PLUS 1 HOUR TO CHILL

In the winter, these delish pancakes are served with caramelized pears. Yum. In summer, they are graced with a sunny dollop of lemon curd, such as the one on page 229, and fat, juicy berries. The lovely nutty flavor and open crumb structure of these cakes trump any other pancake I've ever encountered. Don't skip this amazing, easy-to-prepare syrup. It will totally bust open your established breakfast paradigms.

Batter

2 large eggs

3/4 cup sweetened vanilla almond milk

1 tsp. best-quality vanilla extract

1 1/2 cups almond meal or almond flour, such as Bob's Red Mill

1/4 cup all-purpose flour

1 tsp. baking powder

1/4 tsp. fine sea salt

Buttermilk Syrup

3/4 cup sugar

1/2 cup buttermilk

1 tsp. finely grated lemon zest

1 cup unsalted butter

2-in. piece of a cinnamon stick

1 tsp. baking soda

1/4 tsp. fine sea salt

1 tsp. best-quality vanilla extract

Melted butter or cooking-oil spray

1. **MAKE THE BATTER:** In a large bowl, energetically whisk the eggs, almond milk, and vanilla. Whisk in the almond meal, flour, baking powder, and salt until smooth. Chill for 1 hour.

2. **MAKE THE SYRUP:** In a small saucepan, combine the sugar, buttermilk, and lemon zest. Place over medium heat and stir until the sugar dissolves and the mixture is steaming, about 3 minutes. Remove from the heat. In a tall, heavy saucepan, combine the butter and cinnamon stick over medium heat. Cook until the butter has melted, the foam subsides, and the butter begins to turn brown (but not black) and smell nutty, about 9 minutes. Remove from the heat. Immediately begin to slowly and carefully whisk the warm buttermilk mixture into the browned butter. The butter will boil up, foam, and release a lot of steam, so be careful! Whisk in the baking soda and salt. Let cool for 5 minutes, stirring frequently; add the vanilla. Remove the cinnamon stick and save for another use if desired. Use syrup immediately, while still warm, or reheat very gently; do not allow to boil.

3. Preheat the oven to lowest heat. Preheat a nonstick or well-seasoned cast-iron griddle to medium-high heat, until a drop of water flicked onto the surface evaporates instantly. Brush the griddle with a little melted butter. Spoon a scant 1/4 cup of the batter onto the griddle per pancake. When the pancakes have begun to bubble in the center and a few of the bubbles have popped (the undersides will be golden), use a nonstick spatula to flip them to the other side. Cook for 1 minute more, then transfer to a platter in the oven while you cook the remaining pancakes. Serve immediately on warmed plates, with warm buttermilk syrup.

MAKE AHEAD: The buttermilk syrup can be stored in the refrigerator in an airtight container for up to 2 weeks; reheat it over low heat to warm.

PER SERVING 942 Cal., 72% (677 Cal.) from fat; 15 g protein; 76 g fat (35 g sat.); 57 g carbo (5 g fiber); 768 mg sodium; 244 mg chol. V

2

MENDO BISTRO

Fort Bragg

301 N. Main St.
Fort Bragg, CA

(707) 964-4974

mendobistro.com

Up until 2002, Fort Bragg was a lumber company–dominated town, so this small city is playing a bit of catch-up when it comes to commerce and tourism. Mendo Bistro occupies the mezzanine position within a vast, cathedral-like atrium that once made up the old Company Store—you can imagine folks from the boonies gazing slack-jawed at all the fabulous merchandise in this grand setting. The ground-floor-center position—visible from the tables above—is home to a hip bar-and-brunch space called Barbelow, and music wafts up to diners at the top of the grand, gracious staircase. Husband-and-wife team Nick Petti and Jaimi Parsons (who own both bistro and bar) come from a musical background, but decided in 1999 that their culinary passions were more important, and opened their restaurant in this unique space. Nick is a dedicated forager, and he brings this sensibility to the menu, sourcing seafood mostly from Fort Bragg boats, offering a Mendocino County–centric wine list, and curing his own meats.

Wild Mushroom Risotto

SERVES 4 TO 6 ❋ 1 HOUR

Risotto can be as bland as baby food or as spectacular and flavorful as a starch dish can get. This one falls, happily, into the latter category. The difference, as with any risotto, is the addition of wine, aromatic vegetables, and patience. Don't try to rush the risotto; great minds have established the 18-minute guideline for cooking risotto, and who are we to argue? (Many of these people have long, sharp knives.) The variety of mushrooms suggested here is a loose guideline; substitute whatever wild and interesting domestic 'shrooms you are able to source in your area.

6 tbsp. unsalted butter

4 tbsp. extra-virgin olive oil

1 lb. cremini mushrooms, stalks trimmed and thickly sliced

14 oz. shiitake mushrooms, stems discarded, thickly sliced

1 1/2 tsp. fine sea salt

1 tsp. pepper

1/2 cup finely chopped shallots or red onions

3 garlic cloves, minced

1 1/2 cups Arborio rice

1 1/4 cups dry white wine

4 2/3 cups vegetable broth, warmed

1/4 cup heavy cream (optional)

1/4 cup grated parmigiano-reggiano or grana padano

Pinch of ground nutmeg

2 tbsp. finely chopped fresh flat-leaf parsley

1. In a large saucepan, melt 3 tbsp. butter with 2 tbsp. olive oil over medium-low heat. Add the mushrooms and season generously with 1 tsp. salt and 1/2 tsp. pepper; sauté until tender and juicy, about 10 minutes. Transfer the mushrooms to a bowl.

2. In the same pan, again over medium-low heat, combine the remaining 3 tbsp. butter and 2 tbsp. oil; when melted, sauté the shallots until translucent, about 5 minutes. Add the garlic and rice and stir until the rice is just glazed; do not allow the garlic to burn. Add the wine and simmer until almost evaporated, about 4 minutes. Add the warm broth, 1/2 cup at a time, stirring until it is absorbed before adding the next 1/2 cup. It should take about 20 minutes to gradually add all the broth.

3. When the rice is creamy but there is still a little bite left at the center of each grain, stir in the cream, if desired, and the cheese. Remove from the heat and stir in the reserved mushrooms with all their accumulated juices, the remaining 1/2 tsp. salt and 1/2 tsp. pepper, the nutmeg, and the parsley.

PER SERVING 348 Cal., 57% (198 Cal.) from fat; 6.9 g protein; 23 g fat (9.7 g sat.); 32 g carbo (2.3 g fiber); 857 mg sodium; 35 mg chol. LC/V/GF

Eel River
Brewing
Company

FORTUNA

People come for the exotic, certified organic brews— of course, my vote goes to California Blonde Ale—but the (beer-friendly) food is great too. Cheeses are local, tortillas are hand-made, and stout-smoked spareribs are out of this world. A shaded garden with horseshoe pits is a nice alternative to the clubby sports-bar vibe. 1777 Alamar Way; eelriverbrewing.com

Figs are one fruit that simply can't be forced into any other season but their own; when the moment arrives, grasp it with both hands and your heart!

Fall Salad with Warm Figs, Hazelnuts, and Pomegranate Vinaigrette

SERVES 4 ✥ 20 MINUTES

Most of the denizens of old Fort Bragg, like those in all remote communities where one company was king, did their shopping in the big Company Store, which sold everything from cereal to diapers to kit houses. When the industry was a lucrative one, a company store often stood out as the fanciest building in town—that's the case for the space occupied by Mendo Bistro, with its soaring ceilings and vast atrium. The menu pays fond homage to the goodness of this now heavily settled stretch of the Lost Coast.

Pomegranate Vinaigrette

3 tbsp. pomegranate juice

1½ tbsp. lemon juice

1½ tsp. orange juice

1 tbsp. honey

1 tsp. rice vinegar

2 tbsp. extra-virgin olive oil

2 tbsp. canola or vegetable oil

¼ tsp. fine sea salt, plus more to taste

⅛ tsp. pepper, plus more to taste

Ricotta Toasts

½ cup ricotta

¼ tsp. fine sea salt

⅛ tsp. pepper

8 (½-in.-thick) slices French baguette

2 green onions, white and light green parts only, thinly sliced

½ tsp. paprika

2 tsp. canola or vegetable oil

8 fresh figs, stemmed and halved lengthwise

¼ cup hazelnuts, coarsely chopped

4 cups (4 oz.) mixed greens

1. **MAKE THE VINAIGRETTE:** In a small bowl, combine the pomegranate juice, lemon juice, orange juice, honey, and rice vinegar. Slowly drizzle in both oils, whisking constantly, until creamy. Taste for seasoning and adjust with salt and pepper.

2. **MAKE THE RICOTTA TOASTS:** Preheat the oven to 400°. In a bowl, combine the ricotta, salt, and pepper. Stir until thoroughly blended. Place the baguette slices on a baking sheet and toast until pale golden brown, about 8 minutes. Let cool slightly, then spread a thick layer of ricotta over each piece of toast. Sprinkle with green onions and garnish with paprika.

3. Place a heavy frying pan or cast-iron skillet over medium heat and add the canola oil. When the pan is hot, add the figs, cut side down, and sear for 1 to 2 minutes, until golden brown and crusty, but not blackened.

4. In a small frying pan over medium-high heat, toast the nuts until they turn a light golden brown, about 3 minutes. Add the greens to a mixing bowl with 1/4 cup of the vinaigrette and toss gently but thoroughly. Divide among four plates and top with the toasted nuts. Arrange 4 fig halves around each plate and top with 2 ricotta toasts. Pass the remaining vinaigrette alongside.

PER SERVING 537 Cal., 43% (232 Cal.) from fat; 14 g protein; 26 g fat (5 g sat.); 67 g carbo (6.4 g fiber); 662 mg sodium; 16 mg chol. V

Grilled Local Lingcod
with Brown Butter Hollandaise

SERVES 4 ❖ 20 MINUTES

Hollandaise is a justifiably popular sauce that's excellent with fish and seafood—perhaps that explains its huge popularity along the Pacific Coast. This variation is made with browned butter instead of the usual melted butter. When cooked until nut brown, butter takes on an extra richness and complexity that turns this sauce into a grown-up version of the classic sauce. The blender technique here is actually easier for the home chef to reproduce. (Blender hollandaise takes me back to my college years!) If you only try one hollandaise in this book—and I urge you to make them all!—this is the one. Impeccably fresh and preferably locally and sustainably fished cod or other white fish is a given, right?

Hollandaise

2 large egg yolks, preferably from pastured hens

3 tbsp. lemon juice

1/2 cup best-quality unsalted butter

1 tbsp. capers

4 skinless fillets of lingcod, black cod, halibut, or other firm-fleshed white fish (about 7 oz. each)

Canola or vegetable oil, for brushing

1/2 tsp. *each* fine sea salt and pepper

Finely chopped fresh flat-leaf parsley leaves, for garnish

1. **MAKE THE HOLLANDAISE:** If you plan to make the hollandaise ahead of time (up to 30 minutes only), place a double boiler insert or heatproof bowl over a pot of (but not touching) gently simmering water. In a blender, combine the egg yolks, lemon juice, and 2 tbsp. water.

2. In a small saucepan, melt the butter over medium-low heat. Swirl the butter occasionally until the foam subsides, 2 to 3 minutes, then continue cooking, watching constantly, until golden and nutty brown but not burned, 1 to 2 minutes more. Watch carefully! Immediately remove from the heat and let the butter cool for 2 minutes. Turn on the blender and slowly pour the hot butter into the yolk-lemon mixture; it will thicken slightly. As soon as all the butter is absorbed, scrape the hollandaise into the top of the double boiler and remove it from the heat (or, if serving immediately, scrape it into a warm bowl). Fold in the capers. The sauce may be held in the double boiler over hot but not simmering water for up to 30 minutes, while you grill the fish.

3. Pat the fish dry with paper towels. Lightly brush both sides of the fish with oil and season both sides with just a touch of salt and pepper. Let the fish stand at room temperature while you preheat a grill. Prepare a charcoal or gas grill for high heat (450° to 550°; or preheat a ridged grill pan). Gently place the fish on the hottest part of the cooking grate (or the grill pan) and grill without moving for 3 minutes, then turn it over with a metal spatula and cook until the flesh is opaque in the center but still moist, about 2 minutes more. Transfer the fish to warm plates, drizzle with generous spoonfuls of hollandaise, and garnish with parsley.

PER SERVING 434 Cal., 63% (274 Cal.) from fat; 37 g protein; 31 g fat (16 g sat.); 1.6 g carbo (0.2 g fiber); 378 mg sodium; 269 mg chol. GF/LC/LS

The Blacksmith Shop and Gallery

FERNDALE

Ferndale may be a little gimmicky, but these two gorgeous store-fronts are more art gallery than blacksmith's shop. Hand-forged fireplace tools, cutlery, knobs, bottle openers, and hooks (in all price ranges) will vie for your attention; limited online presence means you should give in to the urge to buy. I did. 455 and 491 Main St.; ferndale blacksmith.com

THE WOODROSE CAFE

Garberville

911 Redwood Dr.
Garberville, CA

(707) 923-3191

thewoodrosecafe.com

When the building that now houses The Woodrose Cafe went up in 1950 as an establishment called Bud's Café, the influence of the local lumber industry on Garberville was massive. From the '60s through 1977, the cafe was known as Herb's. (This coincides with the time period of Ken Kesey's iconic book *Sometimes a Great Notion* and the film of the same name starring Henry Fonda and Paul Newman—about a stubborn family of lumberjacks, set in a fictional town much like Garberville—a must-read/rent before or during your road trip, IMHO.) Then the place became The Woodrose and began serving healthy, earth-nurturing food with an emphasis on organic, way before it became a hip identity for an eatery. That same vision continues today under four new owners (one of whom, Laurel, has literally been eating at The Woodrose her entire life).

Rasta Ranchero

SERVES 4 ❖ 50 MINUTES

Don't worry, be happy, mon. The lumberjack sensibility that once dominated Garberville has been joined by a relaxed, Rasta-esque attitude, as the agriculturally dominant crop has moved slowly away from hardwood toward a more mellow cultivar. Witness: You can get a side of Niman Ranch bacon with this colorful and politically correct breakfast (it's vegan and gluten-free). Ideally, make sure all the ingredients are organic, from the veggies to the spices.

Ranchero Sauce

1 tbsp. extra-virgin olive oil

1/2 small yellow onion, finely chopped

1/4 *each* green and red bell pepper, finely chopped

1 (14.5-oz.) can diced tomatoes (including liquid)

1/2 cup tomato juice

1/2 cup (4 oz.) fresh store-bought salsa

1 1/2 tsp. ground chipotle chile

1 1/2 tsp. ground cumin

3/4 tsp. fine sea salt

1/4 tsp. pepper

14-oz. block extra-firm organic tofu

Cooking-oil spray

1/2 tsp. fine sea salt

1/4 tsp. pepper

Eight 6-in. corn tortillas, homemade (page 15) or purchased, warmed

1 large or 2 small ripe organic avocados, pitted, peeled, and sliced

1 cup black olives, pitted and thickly sliced

2 organic green onions, thinly sliced

Cilantro leaves, roughly torn, for garnish

1. **MAKE THE RANCHERO SAUCE:** In a large, heavy saucepan, warm the oil over medium-low heat. Add the onion and bell peppers and sauté until softened, stirring frequently, about 8 minutes. Stir in the tomatoes, tomato juice, salsa, and all the spices and bring to a simmer. Partially cover the pan and simmer, stirring occasionally, for 25 minutes or until thickened and the flavors develop. Remove from the heat.

2. Meanwhile, place the block of tofu between paper towels and weight it down with a heavy skillet or plate. Let stand at least 15 minutes to remove any excess liquid. Slice the tofu into 8 cutlets.

3. Place a large cast-iron skillet or nonstick frying pan over medium-high heat. Coat the tofu cutlets with cooking spray and season with salt and pepper. Pan-fry the cutlets until golden brown, about 3 minutes; turn carefully and fry the other side until golden.

4. Place 2 warm tortillas on each plate, overlapping, and top each portion with 2 tofu cutlets. Spoon a generous amount of ranchero sauce over the cutlets, and top with sliced avocado, olives, and green onions. Sprinkle with the cilantro.

PER SERVING 623 Cal., 51% (320 Cal.) from fat; 19 g protein; 36 g fat (3.8 g sat.); 62 g carbo (12 g fiber); 1,513 mg sodium; 0 mg chol. VG/GF

On The Road

The Ingomar Club

EUREKA

The once-rich lumber industry here provided funding for some off-the-charts Victorian homes, many of which have been preserved, but this one takes the cake. In fact, it looks much like a cake. Unless you know a member of the (somewhat controversial) private club—membership is limited to men, though ladies are tolerated on special occasions—you'll have to gawk at the exterior only. 143 M St.; ingomar.org

Anywhere men and women work hard in the outdoors, there's a need for hearty breakfasts—and this jewel goes to show they can honor all dietary preferences.

Eggs Woodrose

SERVES 4 ❖ 25 MINUTES

In the slightly '60s-throwback, frontierlike town of Garberville, breakfast is a crucial part of the day. This may be related to all the hard-workin' men and women in the timber business or it may be the other local industry, which involves a more tender plant variety with many magical properties, some of them medicinal. At Woodrose Cafe, eggs Woodrose is served with home-fried organic potatoes and a gluten-free cheese sauce; those who eschew meat can replace the ham with a pile of freshly steamed organic baby spinach, and for a completely gluten-free dish, skip the English muffin.

Cheese Sauce

About 2 cups organic whole milk

1/2 tsp. fine sea salt

1/2 tsp. organic paprika

1/4 tsp. organic celery salt

1/2 tsp. *each* organic garlic powder and organic onion powder

1/4 tsp. ground white pepper

1/4 cup canola oil

1/4 cup gluten-free flour, such as Cup4Cup

3/4 cup grated extra-sharp white cheddar cheese

1/4 cup freshly grated parmesan cheese

4 slices Niman Ranch or other best-quality ham, halved crosswise

4 sprouted-whole-wheat English muffins, split

1 tsp. white vinegar

8 pasture-raised organic eggs

1 tbsp. finely snipped fresh chives

1. **MAKE THE CHEESE SAUCE:** In a double boiler set over gently simmering water, combine 2 cups milk, the salt, and spices. Warm until a "skin" of seasoning forms on the surface, about 4 minutes. In a small bowl, whisk together the oil and flour with a fork, to create a smooth paste. Slowly add to the milk mixture and warm through, whisking, but do not bring to a boil; the sauce will thicken quickly. Stir in the cheeses until melted and smooth, and remove from the heat. Adjust the texture with a little additional milk, if necessary. The sauce should be smooth and rich but not gloppy.

2. Preheat the broiler to high heat. Broil the ham slices just until slightly sizzling; at the same time, toast the muffins on both sides until light golden brown. Turn off the broiler and leave the ham and muffins in the oven with the door ajar. In a wide saucepan, bring 3 in. of water to a very gentle simmer and add the vinegar. Crack the eggs 1 at a time just above the surface of the water. Cover the pan and cook for 3 minutes, or until whites are just set.

3. **ASSEMBLE THE PLATES:** Place a split toasted muffin on each of four plates, and top each half with a slice of ham. With a slotted spoon, remove the eggs from the poaching water; rest the spoon on a folded paper towel for a moment to remove excess water before placing 1 egg atop the ham on each muffin half. Spoon some of the cheese sauce over all and scatter with the chives.

MAKE AHEAD: The cheese sauce may be held over warm but not hot water in the double boiler for up to 1 hour, covered; do not bring to a boil.

PER SERVING 739 Cal., 56% (415 Cal.) from fat; 52 g protein; 46 g fat (17 g sat.); 42 g carbo (4.6 g fiber); 1,409 mg sodium; 499 mg chol.

Stop 4

100 Moonstone
Beach Rd.
Trinidad, CA

(707) 677-1616

moonstonegrill.com

MOONSTONE GRILL

Trinidad

I've found that most "all about the view" eateries tend to offer lackluster food and service. Here's the sublime exception. Great food (mostly local), wine (from all over), and chilled adult beverages are taken very, very seriously at Moonstone. There's not another building in sight as I perch at the bar, drinking in the sight of the Pacific at its confluence with the Little River; heading west, the next stop is Maui, but I wouldn't dream of being anywhere else.

When Sam Merryman began building at this secluded spot on Moonstone Beach in 1964, he wasn't sure if he was building a home or a restaurant. (Then the permits came in.) Thirty-five years later, his place, Merryman's, was still going strong, but it was time for Sam to take it easy. Two local restaurateurs, Chris Smith and Bill Chino, took over the reins and made only a few cosmetic changes (aside from the renaming). "It's still all about the view," says Chris. What stands today is an urbane and sophisticated spot where conviviality reigns inside and most of the artwork is outside the huge windows. Around sunset, we're talking Masterpiece Theatre.

Braised Beef Short Ribs

SERVES 4 TO 6 ❈ 30 MINUTES, PLUS 6 HOURS
TO BAKE AND COOL (AND OVERNIGHT IF DESIRED)

Braising the ribs a day ahead, then chilling overnight is the way to go with this decadent dish: You can remove any accumulated white fat, and the meat will slice nicely. Serve over soft, creamy polenta.

1. Preheat the oven to 275°. Brush the short ribs all over with 3 tbsp. of the oil, and season with salt and pepper. Let stand at room temperature for 30 minutes.

2. In a large, heavy saucepan, combine the celery, onion, carrot, garlic, thyme, bay leaf, and red wine. Bring to a boil over medium-high heat, then reduce the heat slightly and simmer, uncovered, until the wine is reduced by half, about 10 minutes. Add the consommé and simmer for 5 minutes more. Remove from the heat.

3. Warm a large, heavy frying pan over medium-high heat. When the pan is very hot, sear the short ribs without moving for 2 minutes, until golden brown. Turn over and sear on the other side, about 2 minutes more. Transfer the ribs to a roasting pan, and add the braising liquid and vegetables. Cover the pan tightly with foil and bake for 5 hours, turning over halfway through; the meat should be very tender. Remove from the oven and cool to room temperature.

4. Remove the ribs and pull into chunks. Strain the braising liquid through a fine-mesh strainer into a bowl. In a frying pan over medium-high heat, warm the remaining 1 tbsp. oil. Add the rib meat and sear for 1½ minutes, then turn and sear the other side. Add the braising liquid and bring to a simmer. Simmer until thickened, about 10 minutes. Transfer the meat to warm bowls. Increase the heat under the frying pan and boil the liquid briskly for 5 minutes more, until reduced by half. Remove from the heat and gradually whisk in the cold butter until it's absorbed and emulsified. Adjust the seasoning with salt and pepper. Spoon the sauce over the ribs.

Ribs

2¾ lbs. boneless beef short ribs, cut from the chuck

4 tbsp. canola or grapeseed oil

1½ tsp. fine sea salt, plus more to taste

1 tsp. pepper, plus more to taste

Braising Liquid

4 stalks celery, finely chopped

½ white onion, finely chopped

1 carrot, finely chopped

2 garlic cloves, smashed

1 thyme sprig

1 bay leaf

1 cup dry red wine, such as Cabernet

2 cups (one 15-oz. can) beef consommé or beef broth

3 tbsp. unsalted butter, cold, cut into small pieces

PER SERVING 459 Cal., 55% (253 Cal.) from fat; 45 g protein; 28 g fat (9.2 g sat.); 3.7 g carbo (0.6 g fiber); 984 mg sodium; 132 mg chol. LC

Big Lagoon County Park

TRINIDAD

The sand spit separating the 3-mile-long lagoon from the Pacific is home to agates and moonstones, plus seals, sea lions, otters, terns, puffins, osprey, and blue herons. Prospect for solitude on the beach—it's big enough—or go canoeing, kayaking, or rowboating. There's safe swimming in the protected waters of the lagoon. Big Lagoon Park Rd.; redwoods.info (search "Big Lagoon County Park")

Larrupin' Cafe

TRINIDAD

For a small town, Trinidad has some amazing restaurants! Here's another: top-notch protein from land and sea, accompanied by not-your-typical-small-town veggies, and outstanding wild rice. The upstairs/downstairs dining room is art-filled and colorful, and the wine list can hold its own with those of my hometown in wine country. 1658 Patrick's Point Dr.; larrupin.com

Ancho Chile Chocolate Torte
with Cinnamon Cream

SERVES 8 TO 10 ❈ 40 MINUTES, PLUS 6¼ HOURS TO BAKE AND CHILL

The smoky-hot aroma of chile is mysterious and fleeting in this dense and decadent chocolate cake. Close your eyes, and dream of sitting at the most romantic table on the north coast of California while you watch the sunset.

Torte

1 cup granulated sugar

1 whole dried ancho chile, stemmed and coarsely chopped

6 oz. bittersweet chocolate, roughly chopped

7 oz. unsweetened chocolate, roughly chopped

1 cup plus 2 tbsp. (9 oz. total) unsalted butter, cut into 18 pieces, at room temperature

6 large eggs

Ganache

1 whole dried ancho chile, stemmed and coarsely chopped

3/4 cup heavy cream

6 oz. bittersweet chocolate, finely chopped

Cinnamon Cream

1 cup heavy cream

2 tbsp. powdered sugar

1/2 tsp. ground cinnamon

1. **MAKE THE TORTE:** In a heavy saucepan, combine 3/4 cup water, 1/2 cup granulated sugar, and the chile. Place over medium-high heat and bring to a boil, stirring all the time. As soon as the sugar has fully dissolved, remove from the heat and let stand, covered, for 1 hour.

2. Preheat the oven to 350°. Into the oven put a roasting pan that is 1 in. or so wider and higher than a 10-in. nonstick cake pan or 10-in. springform pan. Butter the cake pan and line the bottom with a circle of parchment paper. Butter the top of the parchment and dust the pan with flour, shaking out the excess.

3. Pour the chile-sugar mixture through a fine-mesh sieve set over a bowl and discard the solids. Return the chile-sugar mixture to the saucepan and bring to a boil. Remove from heat, add the chocolates, and stir until completely melted and smooth. Add the butter and stir until completely incorporated; set aside.

4. To prepare a water bath, bring a teakettle of water to a boil. Meanwhile, with a handheld mixer or in the bowl of a stand mixer, combine the eggs and remaining 1/2 cup sugar. Beat on high speed for about 3 minutes, until pale and fluffy; do not overbeat. Stir one-quarter of the chocolate mixture into the egg mixture, until smooth. Gently fold in the remaining chocolate mixture, until the two are only just barely combined; the mixture will be like a light, fluffy pudding.

5. Scoop the batter into the prepared cake pan. Place the cake pan into the roasting pan in the oven. Carefully pour the boiling water around the edges of the roasting pan; it should reach about halfway up the sides of the cake pan. Bake the cake until firm around the edges but still a little jiggly in the center, 45 to 50 minutes. Remove from the oven and let cool to room temperature. Invert the cake onto a flat serving plate. Cover with plastic wrap and chill for at least 4 hours, or overnight.

6. **MAKE THE GANACHE:** In a heavy saucepan, combine the chile and cream. Place over medium-high heat and bring to a boil; do not let it boil over. Remove from the heat and let stand, covered, for 20 minutes. Strain the chile and seeds from the cream, and discard. In a double boiler over gently simmering water, melt the chocolate, stirring occasionally. Pour the chile-infused cream into the chocolate, stirring until the chocolate is smooth. Remove from the heat and let cool for 10 minutes.

7. Just before serving, make the cinnamon cream: Put the cream, powdered sugar, and cinnamon in the bowl for a handheld mixer or a stand mixer, and whip on medium-high speed until soft peaks form. To serve, remove the cake from the refrigerator and remove the plastic wrap. Pour the ganache over the top, starting in the center and easing it out to and over the edges with a metal icing or offset spatula. Cut into wedges and top each with a dollop of cinnamon whipped cream.

PER SERVING 754 Cal., 75% (566 Cal.) from fat; 11 g protein; 63 g fat (37 g sat.); 45 g carbo (5.3 g fiber); 67 mg sodium; 239 mg chol. LS/V

NEW SAMMY'S COWBOY BISTRO

Talent, OR

2210 S. Pacific Hwy.
Talent, OR

(541) 535-2779

Hugging a quiet stretch of highway between Talent and Ashland, the concrete building housing New Sammy's resembles a low-slung after-hours club, devoid of windows or much in the way of a door. But once you find your way inside, the rewards are myriad and unquestionably worth the journey. A warren of small, cozy rooms is decorated in farmhouse style with plenty of glittering crystal, good linens, and mementos of a life well-lived, much of it in Europe, and much centered on the wonderful world of wine. Pastoral oils celebrate livestock and the rural life, yet the menu of Charlene Rollins—respected ex–Chez Panisse and ex–Boonville Hotel (Mendocino County) chef—is, not surprisingly, as intriguing and well-informed as might be found in any food-centric metropolis. "Sammy," it transpires, was a name often seen in the Rollins family. So when Vernon—the wine expert in the family—and Charlene welcomed their newborn son, Sammy, he became the "New Sammy" celebrated in the restaurant's name. Find a hotel nearby and let yourself be coddled by these two relaxed but exacting professionals.

COWBOY
BISTRO

Truffled Cheese Tortelli

SERVES 4 ❈ 1 HOUR, PLUS 1³/4 HOURS TO CHILL AND ROAST

These big truffle-scented packages could feel overly rich, if not for Charlene's deft hand with goodness from the garden, resulting in a brightly balanced, veggie- and flavor-packed plate instead.

1. **MAKE THE TORTELLI:** In a bowl, stir together the cheeses, egg, salt, and pepper. Place 2 won ton wrappers on a dry work surface. Spoon 2 tsp. of filling in the center of each wrapper and brush two adjacent edges lightly with water. Fold the wrapper over the filling to make a triangle. Press the mound of filling down gently and the edges of the wrappers together, easing out any air. Brush one outer corner with water, then fold together with the other outer corner and press together to seal. Repeat, making a total of 20 tortelli. Place them on a baking sheet lined with parchment paper, cover with plastic wrap, and chill 1 to 6 hours.

2. **MAKE THE SQUASH AND BROCCOLI:** Preheat the oven to 350°. In a roasting pan, toss the squash with 1 tbsp. oil and ¹/4 tsp. *each* salt and pepper. Roast for 20 minutes, stirring once or twice. Toss the broccoli with the remaining 1 tbsp. oil and ¹/8 tsp. each salt and pepper. Add to the squash and roast until tender and slightly golden, 18 minutes more. Set aside.

3. Bring a large pot of salted water to a boil. Meanwhile, in a large frying pan, melt the butter over medium-low heat. Add the garlic and sage to the pan and cook gently until the garlic is softened and golden, about 2 minutes. Add the roasted vegetables and toss to coat with the garlic butter. Cover and keep warm until using.

4. When the water comes to a boil, lower to a simmer and add all the tortelli, stirring after 30 seconds to keep any from sticking to the bottom. Cook until tender, about 2 minutes. Remove with a slotted spoon and transfer to the pan with the vegetables. Toss together and divide among four bowls. Top each with parmigiano, fleur de sel, and pepitas.

PER SERVING 456 Cal., 58% (264 Cal.) from fat; 16 g protein; 30 g fat (15 g sat.); 33 g carbo (3 g fiber); 602 mg sodium; 114 mg chol. LC/V

Tortelli

¹/3 cup (2¹/2 oz.) fresh goat cheese, softened

¹/3 cup (2¹/2 oz.) ricotta

¹/3 cup (1 oz.) grated parmigiano-reggiano

¹/3 cup (³/4 oz.) grated truffled pecorino

1 large egg, beaten

¹/4 tsp. *each* fine sea salt and pepper

20 won ton or gyoza wrappers (each 3¹/2-in. sq.), thawed if frozen

Squash and Broccoli

12 oz. butternut squash, peeled and cut into ³/4-in. cubes

2 tbsp. extra-virgin olive oil

Fine sea salt and pepper

1 cup broccoli florets

4 tbsp. unsalted butter

2 garlic cloves, minced

12 leaves fresh sage, finely chopped

¹/4 cup grated parmigiano-reggiano, for serving

Fleur de sel, for serving

2 tbsp. pumpkin seeds (*pepitas*), toasted, for serving

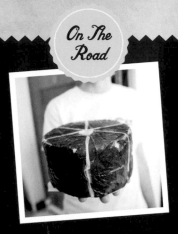

Rogue Creamery

CENTRAL POINT

The Northwest has been dairy country ever since settlers on the Oregon Trail made butter by hanging milk pails from their traveling bovines. This heavenly spot offers cutely named and delicious cheeses with a sense of place—like Roguella mozzarella—and eccentric snacks (milk chocolate blue cheese truffles). Excellent picnic fare—and the company ships.
311 N. Front St.; roguecreamery.com

Jacksonville Inn

JACKSONVILLE

A true gem in this old mining town—a Historic Landmark District—the inn, with a 2,000-bottle wine list, has been called the most romantic inn in Oregon. In fine weather, the tree-dotted patio is prime real estate, while indoors, old bricks and rustic details belie the sophistication of this multistar spot.
175 E. California St.; jacksonvilleinn.com

Parmesan Flan

SERVES 8 ❈ 25 MINUTES, PLUS 2 HOURS TO BAKE AND COOL

At this delightfully quirky, deeply artistic restaurant, the creamy-cheesy flan is often served with a mix of sautéed broccoli, roasted purple potatoes, gold and chioggia beets, and radicchio—all cut into bite-size pieces—with white beans, capers, and shallots. Toss the prepared vegetables with three-quarters of the vinaigrette, then divide among plates. Make a hole in the middle of each pile of vegetables and turn the flans out into the spaces. Push the vegetables up against the side of each flan and drizzle with a little of the remaining vinaigrette. The flans can be made with domestic parmesan cheese but will be vastly more complex in flavor with imported aged parmigiano-reggiano.

Flan

2 cups half-and-half

3½ oz. imported parmigiano-reggiano cheese, cut into ½-in. cubes, plus extra grated cheese, for serving

6 oz. fresh goat cheese, softened

2 large egg yolks

4 large whole eggs

½ tsp. fine sea salt

¼ tsp. white pepper

Cooking-oil spray

Vinaigrette

3 tbsp. lemon juice

1 small garlic clove, minced

1 small shallot, finely chopped

2 anchovies, minced

¼ tsp. fine sea salt

⅛ tsp. black pepper

½ cup plus 1 tbsp. extra-virgin olive oil

Mixed baby lettuces

2 tbsp. snipped chives

1. **MAKE THE FLAN:** In a small saucepan, combine the half-and-half and parmigiano cubes. Over medium-low heat, bring the mixture just up to a simmer, stirring occasionally, then remove from the heat and let stand, covered, for 1 hour.

2. Preheat the oven to 325°. In the bowl of a mixer fitted with the paddle attachment, combine the goat cheese, egg yolks, and whole eggs. Set to low speed and beat until the eggs are blended with the cheese, scraping down the sides once. Meanwhile, strain the warm half-and-half mixture through a fine sieve, scraping and pressing down. With the paddle still turning at low speed, slowly pour the warm mixture into the goat cheese mixture. Season with salt and white pepper, and strain through the fine sieve into a large glass pitcher.

3. Bring a teakettle of water to a boil. Coat eight 6-oz. custard cups with cooking spray. Place in a deep metal roasting pan and divide the custard among them. To make a water bath, carefully pour the boiling water around the edges of the roasting pan, to come about two-thirds of the way up the sides of the ramekins.

4. Cover the whole pan with foil and bake for 25 minutes, until the custards are firmly set around the edges and only slightly jiggly in the center. Remove the ramekins from the water bath and let cool on a rack for 30 minutes.

5. **MAKE THE VINAIGRETTE:** In a bowl, whisk together the lemon juice, garlic, shallot, anchovies, salt, and black pepper. Slowly whisk in the oil in a thin stream, whisking until creamy.

6. Arrange a bed of lettuces on each serving plate. Run a thin knife around the edge of each ramekin to release the custard, then turn each one out onto the lettuces and spoon vinaigrette over the top. Scatter with a little extra grated cheese and a pinch of chives.

MAKE AHEAD: Custards may be made through step 4 and cooled to room temperature, covered, and chilled overnight. Return to full room temperature before serving.

PER SERVING 373 Cal., 81% (303 Cal.) from fat; 14 g protein; 34 g fat (14 g sat.); 3.9 g carbo (0.1 g fiber); 364 mg sodium; 301 mg chol. GF/LC/V

Stop 2 🍴

1270 Front St.
Crescent City, CA

(707) 464-1076

VITA CUCINA

Crescent City, CA

Devon and Michelle Morgante—both alums of the Culinary Institute of America in Hyde Park, New York—met in the kitchen of a restaurant in Sonoma County. The restaurant closed, and Michelle's mom, Sherri, who was working in Antarctica, suggested they apply for food-service positions at the National Science Foundation's station at the bottom of the world. An interview in New Zealand and four months of waiting, immunizations, and myriad X-rays followed. (Medical facilities are limited on the station, and health-related evacuations are unpopular with the management.) Two seasons on the ice came next, and when the couple boarded the first flight out after the second year's transportation-free winter months, Michelle was seven months pregnant. Sensing that it was time to settle down, they gravitated toward one of the few remaining non-destination coastal towns in California, Crescent City. Reentering "civilian" life with new jobs, car, house, and baby required serious mental adjustment. With the help of Michelle's sister, Yvette, and their mom, Vita Cucina grew organically out of a bimonthly cooking class gig at a kitchen-gadget store into today's simple, open-plan bakery and restaurant. It's highly valued by devoted locals, who had been desperate for the well-crafted food made with love.

Homemade Granola

MAKES 2 QUARTS ❖ 10 MINUTES, PLUS 30 MINUTES TO BAKE

There is no reason not to make your own granola. The ingredients are fresher and crunchier and you can balance the flavors to your own personal taste. See this inspiring recipe as a rough guideline, and experiment to find out how you like it best; add dried cherries, golden raisins, dried blueberries ... any of your favorite dried fruit. This is a great breakfast for the morning after a heavy dinner—you'll be raring to go!

2½ cups extra-thick rolled oats, such as Bob's Red Mill

1 cup shredded sweetened coconut

½ cup sliced almonds

½ cup walnut pieces

½ cup pecans, chopped

½ cup unsalted sunflower seeds

½ cup sesame seeds

½ cup wheat germ

½ cup safflower oil

½ cup honey

½ cup *each* dried cranberries and dried currants

Fresh fruit, such as bananas or mixed berries, cut into bite-size pieces

Milk or plain yogurt

1. Preheat the oven to 325°. In a large bowl, combine the oats, coconut, almonds, walnuts, pecans, sunflower seeds, sesame seeds, and wheat germ; mix together well.

2. In a small saucepan, combine the oil and honey. Warm over medium-low heat until the honey flows freely and blends evenly with the oil. Pour the honey mixture over the dry ingredients and mix thoroughly. Divide the mixture between two large rimmed baking sheets, spreading into an even layer. Bake until crumbly and golden, stirring occasionally so the mixture browns evenly and rotating the pans halfway through baking, about 30 minutes.

3. Stir in the dried cranberries and currants and enjoy warm from the oven, or place in an airtight container. Serve in a bowl with fruit and milk as desired.

MAKE AHEAD: The granola keeps in an airtight container up to 10 days.

PER ½-CUP SERVING (GRANOLA ONLY) 327 Cal., 58% (191 Cal.) from fat; 6.3 g protein; 21 g fat (3.5 g sat.); 32 g carbo (4.5 g fiber); 19 mg sodium; 0 mg chol. LC/LS/V

Brandy Peak Distillery

BROOKINGS

This family-owned micro distillery creates earthy concoctions that consistently win awards. Aged pear brandy and blackberry liqueur offer imbibers the chance to consume quintessential Oregon fruit all year long, and with a kick. Do you know how perfectly ripe fruit becomes a heady bevvy? No? Go ahead, take the tour! 18526 Tetley Rd.; brandypeak.com

101 Hawaiian B.B.Q.

CRESCENT CITY

Short on atmosphere but way long on flavor, this unlikely spot (close to Vita Cucina), in a soul-free mini-mall, will wow your palate with crowd-pleasers like kalua pork and chicken or shrimp tempura, plus more esoteric island fare like Loco Moco. Portions are humongous, so consider sharing. 1270 Front St.; 101hawaiianbbq.com

Homemade Focaccia

MAKES 1 FOCACCIA; TEN 3- BY 5-IN. PIECES �֎ 20 MINUTES, PLUS 2½ HOURS AND OVERNIGHT TO RISE AND BAKE

Don't be put off by the night-before start on this recipe; you will be making your own focaccia once a week when you see how simple—and rewarding—it is. Devon and Michelle Morgante manage to raise two adorable children while they bring previously unheard-of baked sweet and savory goodies to a bland strip mall in their small community.

Sponge

1¼ cups bread flour

¼ tsp. active dry yeast

Dough

3¾ cups bread flour

1 tsp. active dry yeast

2¼ tsp. fine sea salt

Oil for bowl, pan, and glazing top

Rosemary leaves and coarse sea salt, for sprinkling (optional)

1. **MAKE THE SPONGE:** In the bowl of a stand mixer, combine the flour, yeast, and 1½ cups warm (about 110°) water and whisk with a fork until blended. Cover loosely with plastic wrap and let stand overnight at room temperature.

2. **THE NEXT DAY, MAKE THE DOUGH:** Fit the mixer with the paddle attachment. Add the flour, yeast, fine sea salt, and 1 cup plus 2 tbsp. warm (about 110°) water to the sponge. Mix on low speed, scraping down the sides once, until the dough is blended together. Continue to beat on medium-low speed for 8 minutes, until elastic; the dough will be very sticky. Turn out into a lightly oiled bowl, then drizzle the dough with oil to coat it lightly. Cover the bowl loosely with plastic wrap and let stand at room temperature for 1 to 1½ hours or until doubled in bulk.

3. Preheat the oven to 400°. Turn the dough out onto an oiled 10- by 15-in. pan. Gently press out the dough with your fingertips toward the edges of the pan. Invert a second pan on top to cover (but not touch dough). Let rise about 1 hour or until dough rises above the pan edges and looks pillowy. Lightly brush dough with additional oil; dimple with fingertips. Sprinkle with some of the coarse sea salt and top with rosemary, if desired.

4. Bake until golden all over, beginning to brown on the edges, and the internal temperature reaches 190° to 200° on an instant-read thermometer, about 30 minutes. Remove from the pan and cool on a rack.

PER 3- BY 5-IN. PIECE 107 Cal., 7% (8 Cal.) from fat; 3.5 g protein; 0.9 g fat (0.1 g sat.); 21 g carbo (0.8 g fiber); 191 mg sodium; 0 mg chol. LC/LS/V

Open-Face Veggie Sandwiches

SERVES 4 ❖ 35 MINUTES, PLUS 25 MINUTES TO ROAST

With their passion for authenticity and high-quality ingredients, the Morgantes needed nothing more than word of mouth to quickly make them the top lunch spot in Crescent City. At Vita Cucina, this perennially popular sandwich is spread with roasted garlic aioli, rather than mayonnaise. If you have any roasted garlic on hand (doesn't everyone?), thoroughly whisk 1 or 2 tsp. into the mayonnaise we've called for here.

⅓ cup balsamic vinegar

¼ cup extra-virgin olive oil

1 tsp. *each* fine sea salt and pepper

1 medium eggplant (about 1 lb.), peeled and cut lengthwise (not into rounds) into ½-in.-thick slices

1 medium red onion, cut into ¼-in.-thick slices

¼ cup mayonnaise

¼ cup fresh pesto, purchased or homemade

Four 5- by 3-in. pieces focaccia, homemade (page 148) or purchased

2 fire-roasted red bell peppers, drained well and cut into thick strips

1 cup feta cheese, crumbled

1. Preheat the oven to 400°. In a large bowl, whisk together the vinegar, oil, salt, and pepper. Add the eggplant and onion slices and toss until evenly coated. Lay the eggplant slices out flat on one side of a large, rimmed baking sheet, and pile the onion slices on the other side. Roast for 25 minutes, turning once. Remove from the oven and let cool, leaving the oven on if you plan to finish the sandwiches right away.

2. Spread 1 tbsp. mayonnaise and 1 tbsp. pesto on top of each piece of focaccia. Top each focaccia piece in the following order, dividing everything evenly: onion, eggplant, bell peppers, and feta.

3. Place the sandwiches on the baking sheet, return to the hot oven, and toast until warmed through (the feta will not melt), 5 to 8 minutes.

PER SANDWICH 624 Cal., 49% (305 Cal.) from fat; 15 g protein; 35 g fat (9.3 g sat.); 63 g carbo (6.9 g fiber); 1,632 mg sodium; 38 mg chol. V

Gold Beach Books

GOLD BEACH

Don't let the wonderful world of books become digital-only: Support indie bookstores like this incredible gem! Right beside U.S. 101, countless stacks of curated content and rare books await you—and the helpful, knowledgeable staff will make you swoon. They don't make 'em like this anymore. 29707 Ellensburg Ave.; oregoncoastbooks.com

Stop 3

517 Jefferson St.
Port Orford, OR

(541) 366-2200

redfishportorford.com

REDFISH

Port Orford, OR

Redfish commands a truly majestic point just south of the fishing town of Port Orford; when you sit in the airy, soaring room, taking in the view and surrounded by art and impeccable design details, it's not surprising to learn that the owner, Chris Hawthorne, has been an artist all his life. In fact, everyone in his family is an artist. "We bought the site intending to build an art gallery," he says, "but a gallery doesn't need a view like this." The restaurant occupies the southern spot on the property, and across a plant-filled courtyard and sculpture garden is a large gallery housing 16 artists, 8 of whom are related to Chris. Of course, in 2010, everyone told Chris he was crazy to become a first-time restaurateur. "But business is business," he says. As a successful artist living in Port Orford since 1975, he hoped a "fresh approach"— plus the amazing bounty of the southern Oregon Coast—would garner success. He was right: The wine list wins awards every year, and I believe the food is on a par with Portland's, in a prettier setting.

Redfish Sea Bass Ceviche

SERVES 4 AS AN APPETIZER ❖ 25 MINUTES, PLUS 6 HOURS TO CHILL

At Redfish, the chef offers a daily ceviche selection, ranging from shrimp to octopus to conch. This is one of those dishes that depend 100 percent on the quality of the fish. Okay— best-quality citrus, perky young garlic, and crisp-happy cilantro make a difference too. Serve these with sweet-salty plantain chips or a bowl of tortilla chips for scooping up every last morsel.

1. Working over a glass or ceramic bowl to catch the juice, cut down on either side of the membranes of the oranges to release each pith-free segment. Cut into 1/4-in. dice; you should have about 1/4 cup of juice. Cut the sea bass into similar-size dice.

2. Add the orange and its juice, sea bass, and all remaining ingredients, except the oil, to the bowl. Fold gently and cover with plastic wrap. Chill for at least 6 and up to 8 hours, stirring the ingredients every 2 or 3 hours.

3. When ready to serve, divide the ceviche among small, shallow bowls, glasses, or cups. Drizzle each portion with a touch of extra-virgin olive oil and serve at once.

2 oranges, peel and bitter white pith completely removed with a sharp knife

16 oz. impeccably fresh sea bass, very cold

1/2 cup peeled and julienned jicama

1/4 cup minced red onion

1/4 cup roughly chopped cilantro

1 tbsp. minced garlic

4 tsp. lemon juice

2 tbsp. lime juice

1 tsp. fine sea salt

4 drops hot sauce, such as Tabasco

Best-quality extra-virgin olive oil, for drizzling

PER SERVING 165 Cal., 15% (25 Cal.) from fat; 22 g protein; 2.8 g fat (0.6 g sat.); 11 g carbo (2.5 g fiber); 462 mg sodium; 46 mg chol. GF

Tu Tu' Tun Lodge

NEAR GOLD BEACH

If you can swing the expense (quite reasonable in winter), do stay at this pristine, ultra-comfortable, and slightly exclusive lodge, a 15-minute drive up the Rogue River from town. If not, take advantage of the lodge's dinner, open to a very few nonguests, strictly by reservation. Gifted chef Scott Guynn is garden-driven and creates exquisite and tasty communal-table tableaux in a stunning setting. 96550 N. Bank Rogue River Rd.; tututun.com

Talk about a room with a view! This place is a veritable feast for all the senses!

Lamb Burgers with Tapenade

SERVES 6 ❈ 35 MINUTES, PLUS 1 HOUR TO CHILL

At Redfish, the lamb burger is a mixture of ground lamb shoulder and leg of lamb that is topped with a thick grilled slice of vine-ripe tomato and a tapenade of Lucques, picholine, and kalamata olives. Here, we've simplified slightly. Use a light hand when forming the burgers, to keep them from becoming tough. If taleggio is unavailable, substitute another flavorful triple-crème cheese, like robiola or St. André. Brie may have the correct consistency, but the flavor is too mild to stand up to the lamb.

Burgers

2 tbsp. extra-virgin olive oil, plus extra for brushing

1 small yellow onion, finely chopped

3/4 tsp. fine sea salt, plus more to taste

1/2 tsp. pepper, plus more to taste

2 lbs. coarsely ground lamb

Citrus-Honey Vinaigrette

1 1/2 tbsp. white wine vinegar

2 tsp. honey

1 tsp. Dijon mustard

1/2 tsp. fine sea salt

1/4 tsp. pepper

1 tsp. finely grated orange zest

1 tbsp. orange juice

4 tbsp. extra-virgin olive oil

6 oz. taleggio cheese, cut into 6 squares, slightly softened

6 cups mixed baby greens, washed and dried

6 ciabatta rolls, split

1/4 cup best-quality purchased olive tapenade

1/4 cup mayonnaise

6 to 12 slices juicy, ripe tomatoes, preferably heirloom

1. **MAKE THE BURGERS:** Place a frying pan over medium-low heat and add the oil. When it is warm, add the onion and cook, stirring occasionally, until very soft, about 6 minutes. Transfer to a large bowl and let cool for 5 minutes. Add the salt, plenty of pepper, and the lamb. Using a fork, blend the ingredients. Then, using (clean) hands, form the mixture into 6 loose, even patties. Flatten slightly so they are about 3/4 in. thick. Chill for at least 1 hour.

2. **MAKE THE VINAIGRETTE:** In a large bowl, whisk together all the ingredients until smooth.

3. Remove the burgers from the fridge. Prepare a charcoal or gas grill (or a ridged cast-iron grill pan) for medium-high heat (about 450°). When the cooking grate (or grill pan) is very hot, brush one side of the burgers lightly with oil and season generously with salt and pepper. Place the burgers on the grill, oiled side down, and cook for 3 minutes. Oil and season the top sides, then turn over, top with a square of cheese, and loosely tent with foil. Cook for 3 to 7 minutes more, to your desired doneness (130° to 135°, for medium-rare); the cheese should be soft and drippy. While the burgers are cooking, toss the greens in the bowl with the vinaigrette.

4. Let the burgers rest for 3 to 5 minutes, while you toast the ciabatta rolls on the grill. Grill, cut side down, for 1 to 2 minutes, until golden.

5. In a small bowl, stir together the tapenade and mayo. Spread the tapenade mixture on the bottom of each roll, and place a cheese-topped burger on the tapenade. Top with a slice or two of tomato, then cover with a roll top. Serve the salad alongside.

MAKE AHEAD: The burgers can be made through step 1 and kept, chilled, up to 4 hours.

PER SERVING 746 Cal., 59% (443 Cal.) from fat; 39 g protein; 50 g fat (18 g sat.); 36 g carbo (2.4 g fiber); 878 mg sodium; 113 mg chol.

Route 8

Coos Bay *to* Newport *to* Otis

130 MILES

HEADING NORTH FROM PORT ORFORD, the road angles inland, bisecting pastures and cranberry bogs; the beach, when you do reach it, is flat and deep. Just south of *Coos Bay*, the small town of Bandon wears its historic architecture proudly; fill up on small-town charm and shop-ortunities here, because Coos Bay is, and has long been, an industrial center for the region's still-ubiquitous timber industry.

On the way up toward Florence, you'll pass many miles of spectacular rolling dunes—though you may have to traverse a small forest to reach them (not in the slightest a hardship). Here, Oregon's cherished beach-access laws can truly be appreciated: Every mile of beach in the state is open to the public.

Approaching the city of *Newport*, you will cross the Yaquina Bay Bridge, an imposing, art deco/Depression-era engineering feat that soars high over the bay, dropping you off in the (self-proclaimed) Dungeness Crab Capital of the World. While Coos Bay is all about timber, Newport is all about seafood. Busy port, tourist destination, and real town with a resource-based economy: Newport can lay claim to all those descriptors. One-street Nye Beach lies north of the harbor, with my kinds of eclectic boutiques, galleries, and lovely old-fashioned beach houses.

North of Newport, the dunes are gone, and beaches are deep and wide with sandstone bluffs. Seafood foraging is super-popular here; rent a crab ring, or pick up a bucket and spade (be sure to buy a license and stay within the daily limit for your chosen shellfish). If you prefer to catch wildlife with your eyes, the refuge at Siletz Bay offers an astounding parade of herons, hawks, pelicans, and other splendid coastal birds. *Otis*? Well, there's not much to it except the Otis Cafe and a post office. Send a postcard—remember those?

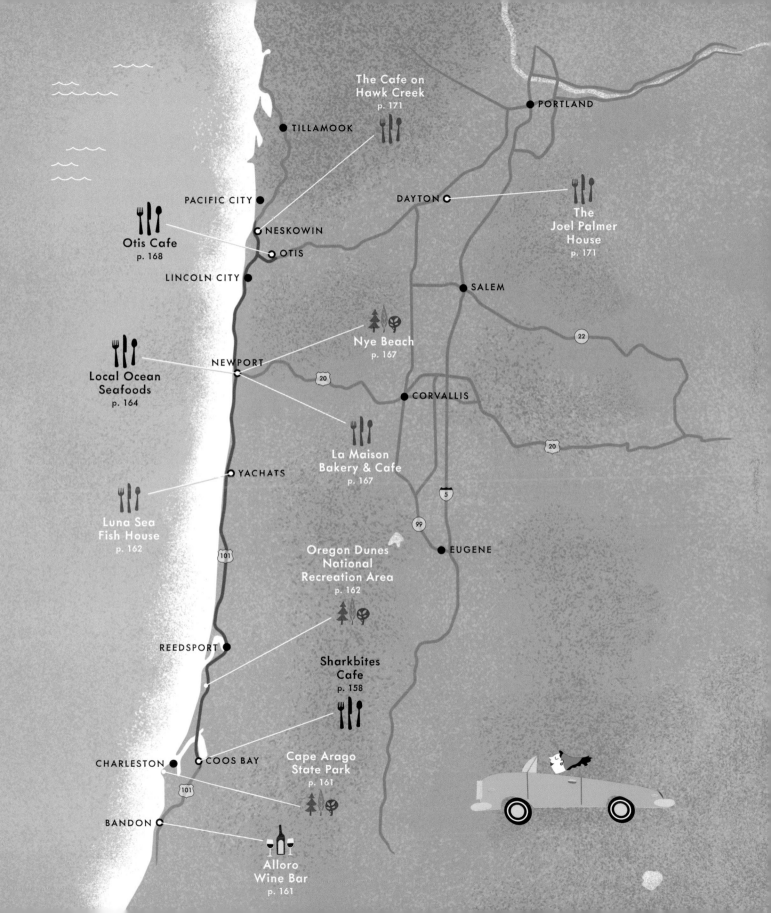

The Cafe on
Hawk Creek
p. 171

PORTLAND

TILLAMOOK

PACIFIC CITY

DAYTON

The Joel
Palmer
House
p. 171

Otis Cafe
p. 168

NESKOWIN

OTIS

LINCOLN CITY

SALEM

Nye Beach
p. 167

Local Ocean
Seafoods
p. 164

NEWPORT

22

20

CORVALLIS

La Maison
Bakery & Cafe
p. 167

YACHATS

Luna Sea
Fish House
p. 162

5

101

99

Oregon Dunes
National
Recreation Area
p. 162

EUGENE

REEDSPORT

Sharkbites
Cafe
p. 158

CHARLESTON

COOS BAY

Cape Arago
State Park
p. 161

101

BANDON

Alloro
Wine Bar
p. 161

SHARKBITES CAFE

Coos Bay

240 S. Broadway
Coos Bay, OR

(541) 269-7475

sharkbitescafe.com

Sharkbites Cafe occupies center stage on a funky Gold Rush–esque Main Street boasting a cutesy factor of zero. Coos Bay is a working port and makes no claim to be anything else—it's a real town with busy folks who work hard and expect great food and atmosphere afterward. Okay, maybe tourists do tend to drift through on their way to other, more picture-perfect spots along this photographer's dream of a coastline. The unconventional cafe here had me—surprise, surprise—at "there's a bar" (which includes exotic dry sodas from Seattle). But, oh, there's so much more! Live music and other happenings season the week, and the large open space hosts a surf shop toward the rear. Decor runs the gamut from a giant stuffed marlin over the bar to vintage wooden surfboards and an entire wall of burlap coffee sacks. There's a definite new-millennium mom-'n'-pop vibe happening here, with adorable Lia Menten pouring water, supervising the room, and happy to share the story of how she and husband Brian fell into restaurant ownership/management, when all they really intended to do was sell surf and beach gear.

Dungeness Crabcakes

MAKES ABOUT 15 CRABCAKES ❖ 35 MINUTES, PLUS 2 HOURS TO CHILL

A good crabcake recipe is like a little black dress: Just knowing you have it gives you confidence. Brian and Lia started their restaurant with no professional training, so their crabcakes are the result of love, sweat, and tears. This version may not be exactly the same as the one you'll encounter at Sharkbites—Brian and Lia treat that recipe as a state secret—but it's a damned fine version nonetheless.

1 lb. shelled cooked lump Dungeness crab

1 whole egg, lightly beaten

¼ cup mayonnaise

1 tbsp. Dijon mustard

2 tbsp. minced white onion

1 tbsp. minced red bell pepper

2 tsp. finely chopped fresh dill

½ tsp. fine sea salt

¼ tsp. pepper

1¼ cups *panko* bread crumbs

2 tbsp. unsalted butter

2 tbsp. canola or vegetable oil

Lemon wedges, for serving

1. In a colander, press the crab firmly to remove as much liquid as possible without breaking up the crabmeat too much.

2. In a bowl, thoroughly combine the egg, mayonnaise, mustard, onion, bell pepper, dill, salt, and pepper. Fold in the crab and half of the panko, breaking up the crab a little but leaving some small lumps intact. Place the remaining panko on a plate. Scoop up ¼ cup of the crab mixture and form a small patty. Place on the panko, then use a spatula to turn over; coat the other side. Pat the panko gently around the sides. Transfer to a nonstick baking sheet and make the remaining crabcakes in the same way. Cover with plastic wrap and chill for at least 2 hours.

3. Preheat the oven to the lowest setting (about 200°) and place a small baking sheet on an oven rack. In a large nonstick frying pan, warm 1 tbsp. butter and 1 tbsp. oil over medium-low heat. When the foam subsides, gently slide half of the crabcakes into the pan. Cook the first side until golden brown, 5 to 6 minutes. Turn and brown on the other side, 4 to 5 minutes more. Keep the first batch of cakes warm in the oven. Wipe out the pan with a paper towel and repeat to make the second batch of crabcakes. Serve with lemon wedges.

MAKE AHEAD: The crabcakes can be made through step 2 and kept, covered and chilled, up to 4 hours.

PER CRABCAKE 87 Cal., 48% (42 Cal.) from fat; 7.6 g protein; 4.7 g fat (1.2 g sat.); 3.3 g carbo (0.1 g fiber); 240 mg sodium; 41 mg chol. LC

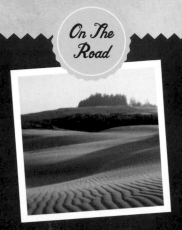

Oregon Dunes National Recreation Area

NEAR REEDSPORT

Seen the rocks? Now it's time to take in the ever-shifting, soft-contoured sand dunes. The dunes are home to some unfortunate OHV/ATV action, but you can avoid it by sticking to day-use areas, such as John Dellenback Dunes Trail (2.7 miles one way). Canoeing and horseback riding (Florence has good options) are other less intrusive choices. Trailhead: Eel Creek Campground, 10 miles south of Reedsport on U.S. 101. Recreation Area Visitor Center: 855 Hwy. Ave., Reedsport; fs.usda.gov (search for "Oregon Dunes day use")

Luna Sea Fish House

YACHATS

Though virtually everything comes with chips, and the menu is full of seafood-shack standards, this is not your typical waterfront tourist joint. Most of the menu's fish is caught by the owner, and other ingredients are fresh and local. Send home goodies from the smokehouse too. 153 N.W. U.S. 101; lunaseafishhouse.com

O.K, beef burgers are pretty good, but this juicy burger is an equal-opportunity employer and just as tasty!

Dakine Black Bean Burgers

SERVES 4 ❖ 1 HOUR, PLUS 2 HOURS TO CHILL

The Hawaiian pidgin term *dakine* is variously defined, as "a good thing" or, according to Sharkbites owner Brian, "something cool." And this burger is. Maybe it's just me, but there's something thoroughly right about an eatery with a full bar and an excellent black bean burger. Coos Bay is the largest community on Oregon's coast, and that may be why it can support a happening, eclectic establishment like Sharkbites.

Burgers

2 (15-oz.) cans black beans, drained and rinsed

1 green bell pepper, stemmed, seeded, and roughly chopped

1/2 white onion, roughly chopped

6 garlic cloves

2 eggs, lightly beaten

1 tbsp. Thai chili sauce or Sriracha

2 tsp. ground cumin

1 tsp. mild or hot chili powder

Kosher salt and pepper

1 1/2 cups *panko* bread crumbs

Canola oil, for brushing

4 large slices Monterey jack cheese (6 oz. total)

Chipotle Mayo

1/3 cup mayonnaise

1 tsp. minced canned chipotle chiles in *adobo*, with adobo sauce to taste

1/2 tsp. lime juice

4 soft rolls or buns, split and toasted

1 large ripe avocado, pitted, peeled, and sliced

1 large ripe red or yellow tomato, thickly sliced

2/3 cup shredded iceberg lettuce

1 cup Caramelized Onions (page 42) or 1 medium onion, sliced and grilled until tender and golden

1. **MAKE THE BURGERS:** With a sturdy fork or potato masher, mash the beans in a bowl into a thick paste. In a food processor, pulse the bell pepper, onion, and garlic until very finely chopped—almost pulverized. Add the vegetables to the bowl of beans along with the eggs, chili sauce, cumin, chili powder, and 1 tsp. salt and stir to combine. Mix in the panko until the mixture is sticky and holds together. Divide the mixture into 4 patties about 1 in. thick, and put on a plate or platter. Cover with plastic wrap and chill for at least 2 hours.

2. **MAKE THE CHIPOTLE MAYO:** In a small bowl, whisk together the mayonnaise, chipotle, and lime juice. Taste for seasoning and adjust with adobo sauce if desired. Chill until ready to use.

3. Prepare a charcoal or gas grill (or a well-seasoned grill pan) for medium-high heat (about 450°). Lightly oil both sides of the burgers and season with salt and pepper. Grill, with the lid closed, until browned in places, 3 to 4 minutes. Turn over and top with the cheese. Close the grill lid and cook until the cheese has melted, about 3 minutes more. (If using a grill pan, cover with foil to melt the cheese.)

4. Spread the cut side of the bottom half of each roll with a little chipotle mayo, then layer on the lettuce and tomato. Top with a burger, the caramelized onions, a few slices of avocado, and the top half of the bun.

MAKE AHEAD: Patties can be made through step 1 and kept, covered and chilled, up to 4 hours.

PER BURGER 830 Cal., 47% (389 Cal.) from fat; 30 g protein; 43 g fat (13 g sat.); 81 g carbo (13 g fiber); 1,577 mg sodium; 151 mg chol. V

Stop 2

213 S.E. Bay Blvd.
Newport, OR

(541) 574-7959

localocean.net

LOCAL OCEAN SEAFOODS

Newport

Some restaurants are proud to state, "We use local and sustainable ingredients whenever possible." Local Ocean is not one of them—here, local catch is all there is. This place walks the local walk so seriously that you are unlikely to consume any fish on the premises that was not brought into the dock just across the street; plus, the eatery shares space with a seafood market. Owner Laura Anderson is a third-gen fisherperson, and very active in the sustainability movement on the Oregon Coast; chef Charlie Branford believes so strongly in the freshness of his product that he refuses to cook any of it beyond medium-rare. Folks just can't seem to get enough of the creatively prepared oysters, rockfish, fresh and smoked salmon, clams, crab, and all the other swimmers. This adds up to a very busy restaurant, so get there early and even then be prepared to wait—especially on weekends. The view of busy Yaquina Bay harbor is up close and personal, and there are plenty of brews to be had just down the road at Rogue Ales.

Shrimp and Spicy Noodle Salad

SERVES 4 ❖ 30 MINUTES

Newport, Oregon, has a little identity problem, but that doesn't bother me in the slightest. This town isn't sure whether it's a tourist destination, a potential retirement spot, or a working harbor. No town supported only by a working harbor would be able to host an eatery of Local Ocean's caliber—which is an excellent thing for visitors. In addition to that, the ability to stroll a few blocks after lunch and see oceans of pink shrimp being offloaded from a fishing boat makes the experience almost as sweet as the toothsome little shrimp themselves.

1. **MAKE THE SPICY SAUCE:** In a large frying or sauté pan, stir together the vinegar and brown sugar until the sugar dissolves, about 3 minutes. Whisk in the remaining sauce ingredients.

2. Soak the fresh noodles according to the package instructions; drain well and set aside. Place the celery, carrot, bell pepper, zucchini, mushrooms, cabbage, and onion in a large heatproof bowl (big enough to accommodate the noodles and shrimp).

3. Bring the sauce to a gentle simmer and add the noodles. Simmer until the sauce thickens slightly, about 5 minutes. Immediately pour the sauce and noodles into the bowl with the vegetables and toss to coat everything. Add the shrimp, green onions, and about three-quarters of the cilantro, and toss. Divide the salad among four plates and garnish with the remaining cilantro.

*If fresh yakisoba noodles are unavailable, cook spaghetti or linguine in boiling salted water until barely al dente, about three-quarters of the suggested cooking time. Drain well, add to the sauce in step 3, and finish cooking as the sauce thickens.

PER SERVING 734 Cal., 17% (124 Cal.) from fat; 42 g protein; 14 g fat (13 g sat.); 113 g carbo (7.2 g fiber); 581 mg sodium; 295 mg chol.

Spicy Sauce

1⅓ cups apple cider vinegar

¾ cup brown sugar

3 tbsp. Asian chili garlic paste

3 tbsp. black bean garlic sauce

2 tbsp. sesame oil

12 oz. fresh yakisoba noodles*

2 stalks celery, cut into ½-in. matchsticks

1 medium carrot, peeled and cut into ½-in. matchsticks

1 red bell pepper, stemmed, seeded, and cut into ½-in. matchsticks

1 medium zucchini, cut into ½-in. matchsticks

4 oz. mushrooms, trimmed of woody stems, and quartered

¼ head cabbage, shredded

½ red onion, cut into ½-in. matchsticks

1 lb. cooked pink or bay shrimp, cut into bite-size pieces if large

3 green onions, trimmed and thinly sliced

Leaves from 1 small bunch cilantro, finely chopped

Stop 3

OTIS CAFE

Otis

1259 Salmon
River Hwy.
Otis, OR

(541) 994-2813

otiscafe.com

Otis, Oregon, spans fewer than 200 acres, but its cafe's culinary profile looms almost as large as the portions. The gift certificates read: "Welcome to the Otis Cafe! Worth the weight/wait!!" German potatoes, sourdough pancakes, and molasses bread are all stellar standouts, but with only four booths, two small tables, and seven extremely cozy counter stools, the cafe is likely to leave you waiting for a while. No worries: You could maybe do a little anticipatory aerobics. Or read the local paper and watch the cars go by. The town sits at an important junction: Turn east on the Salmon River Highway (aka State 18), and you travel inland via the idyllic wine country around McMinnville toward Portland. Head north on the Oregon Coast Highway (aka U.S. 101) and you are embarking on the less-traveled coastal and woodland routes of northern Oregon.

Once at my table, waitress Linda Owings shepherds me through the ordering process, and I learn that she's been working here for 30 years—sadly for customers, she'll soon be stepping down to concentrate on her grandkids. The current owner, Jeff England (his co-owner is wife Lynne), was home-schooled with Linda's kids. There's a hearty German vibe here, although the original owner, Virginia Morgan, who developed most of the recipes, wasn't German.

Molasses Bread

MAKES ONE 2-LB. LOAF ❖ 5 MINUTES, PLUS 1¼ HOURS TO BAKE AND COOL

At the Otis Cafe, this famous bread is made with a sourdough starter that's been alive and kicking for more than 20 years—but that's a little bit difficult to reproduce in a home kitchen! Here, I've provided a quick-and-easy version that will have your breakfast guests swooning when they slather it with sweet butter and berry preserves, preferably from Oregon.

Oil or butter, for preparing the pan

2 cups all-purpose flour

1 cup whole-wheat flour

1 tsp. fine sea salt

1 tsp. baking soda

1²/₃ cups buttermilk

1 large egg, lightly beaten

½ cup blackstrap molasses

1. Heat the oven to 325°. Grease a 4- by 8-in. or a 5- by 9-in. loaf pan.

2. In a large bowl, mix together the dry ingredients. In a glass measuring pitcher or medium bowl, whisk together the buttermilk, egg, and molasses. Pour the buttermilk mixture into the dry ingredients and stir together with a fork just enough to combine.

3. Pour the batter into the loaf pan. Bake until firm and a toothpick inserted in the center comes out clean, about 1 hour. Cool on a rack for 15 minutes. Run a small offset spatula around the edge of the loaf, and turn out the loaf. Excellent warm or at room temperature.

PER SLICE (16 PER LOAF) 124 Cal., 8% (10 Cal.) from fat; 3.8 g protein; 1.1 g fat (0.3 g sat.); 25 g carbo (1.3 g fiber); 210 mg sodium; 14 mg chol. LC/LS/V

German Potatoes with Cheddar and Green Onions

SERVES 4 TO 6 ❀ 35 MINUTES, PLUS 1 HOUR, 50 MINUTES TO BAKE AND CHILL

The historic and much-loved Otis Cafe is, literally, the biggest draw in Otis, Oregon. (Okay, there is a little post office.) On Linda's sage advice, I order the quarter-portion of these outrageous German potatoes; this "minimal" portion could easily have satisfied two of me. Worth the weight, indeed. The yumminess of this dish is directly dependent upon your chosen seasoning salt.

3 large Idaho or russet potatoes (2½ lbs. total)

3 tbsp. canola or vegetable oil

1 medium yellow onion, finely chopped

4 green onions, trimmed and coarsely chopped

1½ tsp. Otis Seasoning Salt*, or your favorite seasoning salt

8 oz. white cheddar cheese, coarsely grated (about 2 cups)

1. Preheat the oven to 425°. Wash the potatoes, pat dry with paper towels, and pierce all over several times with the tip of a knife. Place the potatoes directly on the top oven rack and bake until just tender when pricked with the point of a small knife or toothpick, 35 to 45 minutes. Cool to room temperature, then chill for at least 1 hour, and preferably overnight.

2. Place a large nonstick frying pan over medium heat and add 1 tbsp. of the oil. When the oil is hot, sauté the onion until tender, stirring occasionally, 5 to 6 minutes. Transfer the onion to a small bowl to cool, about 5 minutes; fold in the green onions. Wipe out the pan with a paper towel.

3. Peel the potatoes and grate them on the large holes of a box grater; toss the grated potatoes with 1 tsp. seasoning salt. Warm the frying pan over medium-high heat and add 1 tbsp. of oil. When it is hot, add the potatoes and spread them quickly into an even layer. Season evenly with 1/4 tsp. seasoning salt. Use a wide, flat spatula to press the potatoes down firmly. Continue cooking, pressing down with the spatula occasionally, for about 7 minutes, or until the bottom is golden brown and crisp (reduce the heat slightly if the potatoes begin to scorch).

4. Place a large plate over the top of the frying pan and hold it very securely with one hand. With an oven mitt on the other hand and a very firm grip on the handle of the pan, quickly invert the potatoes onto the plate. Add the remaining tbsp. of oil to the pan and slide the potatoes back into the pan with the cooked side on top. Sprinkle with the remaining 1/4 tsp. seasoning salt. Continue cooking, pressing down with the spatula occasionally, until golden brown and crisp, 5 to 6 minutes more. Remove from the heat.

5. Preheat the broiler. Carefully invert the potato cake onto a rimmed baking sheet. Top the potatoes with the onion mixture and cover with the grated cheese. Broil until the cheese is melted, 1½ minutes.

*Otis Cafe's proprietary seasoning salt is available via phone (see page 168), or email otiscafe@live.com. The cafe ships lots of this tasty secret seasoning, especially over the holidays.

PER SERVING 362 Cal., 48% (173 Cal.) from fat; 13 g protein; 19 g fat (8.7 g sat.); 36 g carbo (3.5 g fiber); 252 mg sodium; 41 mg chol. GF/LS/V

The Joel Palmer House

DAYTON

Four generations of mushroom and truffle foragers—Joseph Czarnecki opened Joe's Tavern in Reading, PA, in 1916—stand behind this fine-dining destination in Willamette Valley wine country (the wine list is huge). Current-generation Czarnecki chef Christopher gives free rein to his playful nature in the sophisticated, fungus-centric, and wine-conscious tasting menu. 600 Ferry St.; joelpalmerhouse.com

The Cafe on Hawk Creek

NESKOWIN

Because Neskowin is famous for Proposal Rock (just what it sounds like), many patrons at the cafe are either about to be, or just got, engaged (though locals love the perfect-crust pizza, sunny deck, and cozy little bar—serving regional brews—too). At breakfast, sip world-class coffee with your crispy beer-batter pancakes. Yowza! 4505 Salem Ave.; (503) 392-3838

Route 9

Pacific City *to* Manzanita *to* Cannon Beach *to* Astoria

91 MILES

OREGON'S NORTHWEST COAST is within weekending distance of Portland, so the traditional timber and fishing industries that dominate the southern coast, while still in evidence, tend to be overshadowed by the tourist and retirement economies.

Windswept and unspoiled *Pacific City* feels far off the beaten track. Everywhere in Oregon, beach access is fully democratic; a horseback ride along a beach shared with surfers and PC's famous dory-boat fisherpeople is just one of the unique beach opportunities you wouldn't find in California.

Just north, dramatic Cape Kiwanda is battered by some of the state's wildest surf, and the large and small basalt plugs known as sea stacks loom offshore as you continue the drive. The road veers inland through the Siuslaw National Forest, but if there's time, head west to Cape Lookout and then north on Three Capes Scenic Loop, along Netarts Bay.

Tillamook is rather industrial, but since the predominant industries are cheese and smoked foods, I'm willing to overlook this. One-street-long *Manzanita* is charming in a cedar-shake and locals'-bar kind of way, far preferable to the artsy, polished-whalebone aesthetic of *Cannon Beach*, seemingly attached by an umbilical cord to the suburbs of Portlandia. At Cannon Beach, you encounter the last of three officially named Haystack Rocks along the coast. From here, the road dips inland of Ecola State Park, and then it's a straight shot, past no-need-to-stop Coney Island–esque Seaside, into the historic and well-preserved architectural gem of *Astoria*, the oldest city west of the Rockies. Perched prominently on a small spit at the mouth of the mighty Columbia River, the small, friendly city may sorely tempt you to up and move here.

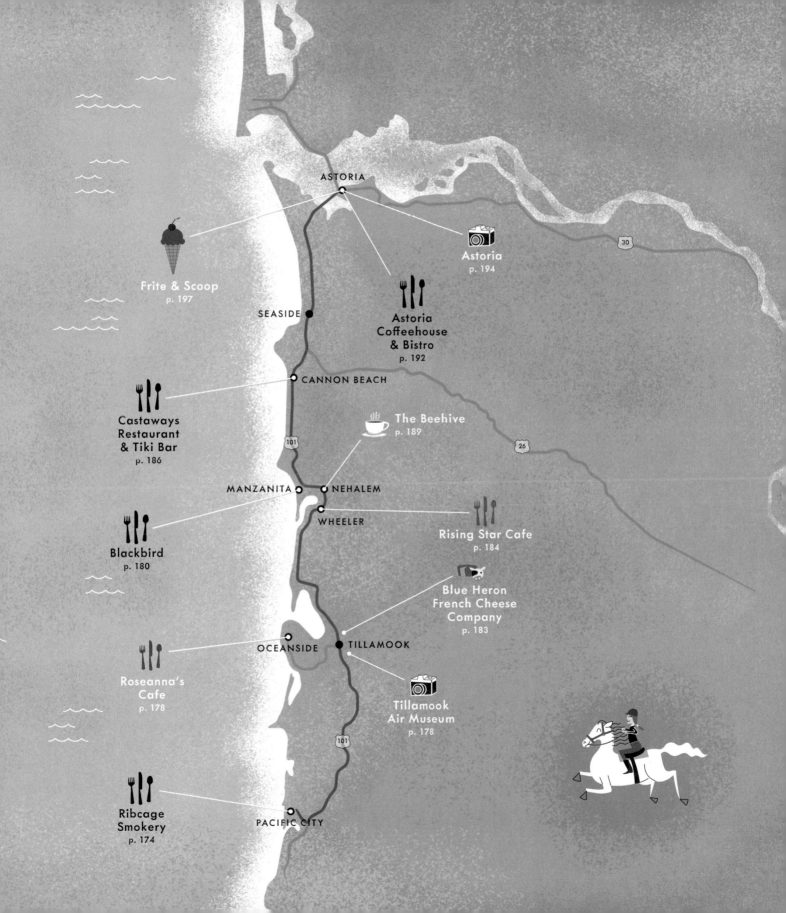

ASTORIA

Astoria
p. 194

Frite & Scoop
p. 197

Astoria
Coffeehouse
& Bistro
p. 192

SEASIDE

CANNON BEACH

Castaways
Restaurant
& Tiki Bar
p. 186

The Beehive
p. 189

101

MANZANITA   NEHALEM

WHEELER

Blackbird
p. 180

Rising Star Cafe
p. 184

Blue Heron
French Cheese
Company
p. 183

OCEANSIDE   TILLAMOOK

Roseanna's
Cafe
p. 178

Tillamook
Air Museum
p. 178

101

Ribcage
Smokery
p. 174

PACIFIC CITY

30

26

RIBCAGE SMOKERY

Pacific City

Much to my great dismay, the Ribcage has closed since I did my drive, but I feel very lucky to have gathered these delicious recipes so we can continue to eat the restaurant's incredible food. The Ribcage was a labor of love by two passionate dreamers—Sean and his wife, Chenin—who embrace each incarnation of their journey with laughs, wine, and introspection. This made them the perfect hosts. Sean was the long-haired pit master with a wicked sense of humor: Thursday was "Nice Rack!" night at the Ribcage Smokery, and Reuben pizza was a favorite. The lovely, always-smiling Chenin was named for a wine and raised by winemakers (duh), and the two were married at Groth Vineyards in Napa, so marinating started early. Their fascination with smoking—and the restaurant business—came later, after a job-mandated move to Oregon. (They stumbled upon Pacific City while looking for beer and a beach, both of which are in good supply.) I look forward to the Carltons' next chapter, and hope it includes more tasty stuff. Meanwhile, whip up some of Sean's goodness in your own kitchen!

Chinese Chicken Salad

SERVES 4 ❖ 30 MINUTES

The menu at the Ribcage was loosely targeted at rabid smoky-meat aficionados, but happily, also included lighter choices like this deeply flavorful take on a chow mein–diner classic. After all, although I may often appear to be trying, (wo)man cannot live on red meat alone. If you use breast meat for this salad, cut the cooking time in half.

1. **MAKE THE VINAIGRETTE AND STIR-FRY SAUCE:** In a large salad bowl, whisk the ingredients for the vinaigrette until smooth and creamy. In a small bowl, whisk the ingredients for the stir-fry sauce. Set aside.

2. Preheat a large wok or large cast-iron skillet (ideally 14 in.) over high heat. Add the greens to the bowl with the vinaigrette and toss until lightly coated. Divide the greens among four plates.

3. In the wok, warm the oil over high heat. When it is very hot, add the chicken and toss to coat with the oil. Spread into an even layer and let cook undisturbed for 1 minute; stir and turn over, then let cook for 1 minute more. Add the garlic and green onions, and stir for 30 seconds. Add the stir-fry sauce and toss to blend, and cook for 2 minutes more, or until the chicken is done and the sauce has thickened slightly.

4. Divide the chicken among the plates, placing it atop the greens. Add the carrots and tortilla strips to the hot wok and stir-fry until the tortillas are slightly golden brown, about 5 minutes. Top the salads with the carrots and tortilla strips.

PER SERVING 514 Cal., 50% (257 Cal.) from fat; 40 g protein; 29 g fat (5.2 g sat.); 23 g carbo (3.3 g fiber); 1,739 mg sodium; 131 mg chol.

Vinaigrette

2 tbsp. lime juice

1½ tbsp. canola or vegetable oil

2 tsp. Dijon mustard

1½ tsp. honey

1 small garlic clove, minced

¼ tsp. *each* fine sea salt and pepper

Stir-Fry Sauce

½ cup teriyaki sauce

1½ tbsp. rice vinegar

1 tsp. sesame oil

1 tsp. grated fresh ginger

Salad

6 cups mixed baby greens (about 6 oz.)

2 tbsp. canola oil

1¾ lbs. boned, skinned chicken thighs, cut into ½-in. cubes

1 tbsp. finely chopped garlic (about 3 small cloves)

2 green onions, trimmed and chopped

2 medium carrots, coarsely grated

2 corn tortillas, cut in half and then into ½-in. strips

Homemade Pizza Dough

MAKES ABOUT 1³/₄ LBS. DOUGH; ENOUGH FOR TWO
12-IN. PIZZAS, EACH SERVING 2 OR 3 (OR THE DOUGH CAN
BE DIVIDED INTO 4 PIECES TO MAKE 4 INDIVIDUAL PIZZAS)
❋ 10 MINUTES, PLUS 1¹/₂ HOURS TO RISE

3¹/₃ cups (16 oz.) unbleached
all-purpose flour

¹/₄ cup whole-wheat flour

1 pkg. (2¹/₄ tsp.) fast-acting
dry yeast

1 tbsp. sugar

1 tbsp. kosher salt

2 tbsp. extra-virgin olive oil

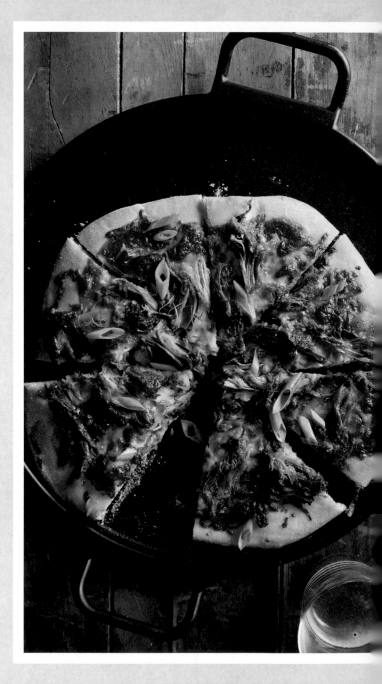

1. In a food processor, combine the flours, yeast, sugar, and
salt and pulse to blend. With the motor running, add
1 cup plus 2 tbsp. warm (110°) water and the oil quickly
in a steady stream, and pulse on and off in 2-second bursts
until the dough comes together in a rough mass. (If the
dough has not formed a ball within about 12 seconds,
remove the cover and sprinkle a tsp. or 2 of warm water
over the dough, then process again.)

2. Let the dough rest for 5 to 10 minutes, then process again
for 25 to 30 seconds more, holding the top of the food
processor with one hand. Turn the dough out onto a
lightly floured surface and form into a smooth ball. Place
the dough in a large, oiled bowl, turn over once to coat
with oil, and cover with plastic wrap. Let rise in a warm
place until doubled in bulk and very spongy, about
1¹/₂ hours (or chill overnight in a covered bowl; let come
to room temperature for 1 hour before proceeding).

3. Turn the dough out onto a lightly floured surface, punch
down, and knead into a smooth cylinder. Divide into
2 equal pieces and knead again to form 2 smooth balls,
dusting with a little flour only if the dough is sticky. Cover
with a kitchen towel and let rest for 10 minutes. Proceed
with the pizza recipe.

MAKE AHEAD: The dough may be frozen for up to 2 months,
well wrapped. Before using, allow to thaw overnight in the
refrigerator, then let stand at room temperature for 1 hour (or
thaw at room temperature for 3 hours).

PER SERVING 370 Cal., 15% (55 Cal.) from fat; 9.3 g protein; 6.7 g fat
(0.9 g sat.); 68 g carbo (3.1 g fiber); 763 mg sodium; 0 mg chol. VG

BBQ Pulled Pork Pizza

MAKES TWO 12-IN. PIZZAS; SERVES 4 TO 6 ❀ 15 MINUTES, PLUS AT LEAST 6¼ HOURS
TO SMOKE PORK AND BAKE PIZZA (PLUS TIME TO MAKE BBQ SAUCE AND DOUGH)

Sean and Chenin Carlton ran two interlinked businesses in the surf's-up, sand-swept town of Pacific City, and between the two projects, they hit all my sweet spots. Twist—still happily doing business!—is a slightly unorthodox wine bar, serving excellent wines handmade by these ex–Napa Valleyans (and also serving as the social hub for more creative locals). The Ribcage was Sean's personal dream, born after he came back from an overly long road trip to Texas profoundly and permanently changed.

Pulled Pork

1 tbsp. spice rub or chili seasoning of your choice

1 tbsp. *each* kosher salt and pepper

2½ to 3 lbs. boneless pork shoulder (Boston butt or picnic roast), some exterior fat trimmed

1½ tsp. *each* beer and apple cider vinegar

1½ tsp. Ribcage BBQ Sauce (page 179) or smoky-sweet bottled sauce

1¾ lbs. Homemade Pizza Dough or purchased pizza dough, divided into 2 balls

Olive oil

¼ cup Ribcage BBQ Sauce (page 179) or smoky-sweet bottled sauce

8 oz. low-moisture whole-milk mozzarella, grated

6 green onions, trimmed and minced

1. Prepare a smoker or a covered charcoal grill for low-heat smoking (250° to 275°). (If using a charcoal grill, follow grill instructions for low-heat smoking. Soak 2 cups wood chips in water for 30 minutes, drain, then wrap in a foil packet. When the coals are covered with ash, bank them on one side and let burn to low. Place the foil packet of wood chips directly on the coals and a small foil pan of water opposite the coals. You will need to replenish the charcoal from time to time to maintain the heat; replenish the water in the foil pan as necessary.)

2. **MAKE THE PULLED PORK:** Blend together the spice rub, salt, and pepper and rub generously all over the pork shoulder. Smoke until the pork's internal temperature reaches 200° on an instant-read thermometer, 5 to 7 hours, replenishing the wood chips as needed to maintain a low level of smoke. Let the pork cool to room temperature, then pull apart until nicely shredded. In a bowl, combine 3 tbsp. water, the beer, vinegar, and BBQ sauce, and use just enough to moisten the pulled pork until it's juicy. Let the pork stand at room temperature for at least 30 minutes and up to 1 hour.

3. Preheat oven to 425° and put a large unrimmed baking sheet (or use a rimmed sheet upside down) on an oven rack to preheat. Place a large sheet of parchment paper on a work surface and put 1 dough ball in the center. Dip your fingers in a little oil and proceed to press the dough from the center outward into a 12-in. circle of even thickness. If the dough gets springy and difficult to stretch, cover it with a kitchen towel and let it rest for a few minutes, then press on. Cover with a kitchen towel and let rise for 10 minutes.

4. Spread 2 tbsp. of the BBQ sauce evenly over the dough round, leaving a ½-in. border. Divide the mozzarella in half. Scatter one-third of the first portion over the sauce. With two forks, pull off 1 cup of the pulled pork, letting any excess liquid drain away, and spread it evenly over the cheese. Top with the remaining two-thirds portion of cheese, making sure some of the pork is uncovered. Scatter half the green onion over all.

5. Using a pizza peel or unrimmed baking sheet, slide the pizza-topped parchment onto the hot baking sheet in the oven. Cook for 15 to 20 minutes, until the edges are golden and puffed and the cheese is melted; the bottom should be fully cooked. (Prepare the second pizza while the first is cooking.) Slide the pizza onto a cutting board and cut into wedges. Bake the second pizza in the same way.

PER SERVING 942 Cal., 42% (396 Cal.) from fat; 57 g protein; 44 g fat (17 g sat.); 75 g carbo (3.8 g fiber); 1,953 mg sodium; 187 mg chol.

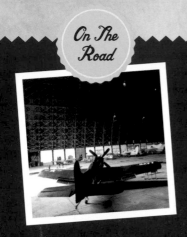

Tillamook Air Museum

NEAR TILLAMOOK

The natural world here is full of jaw-dropping sights, but make time to be totally wowed by some manmade stuff too. Inside the 7-acre hangar (the largest clear-span wooden structure in the world), feast your eyes on military and civilian aircraft, including a MiG-17 and an F-14 (sadly, sans Tom Cruise). 6030 Hangar Rd.; tillamookair.com

Roseanna's Cafe

OCEANSIDE

Get there early to ensure happiness at this no-reservations and no-online-menu funky, cute beachside space (with an awesome view!). The kitchen's ultra-fresh fish and shellfish, chowders, pastas, and fruit-forward desserts (marionberry cobbler is the go-to) are conceived of and executed with near-religious devotion. 1490 Pacific Ave. N.W.; roseannascafe.com

Smoked Baby Back Ribs

SERVES 6 TO 8 ❖ ABOUT 1 HOUR, PLUS 2 HOURS TO BAKE

At the Ribcage, Sean smoked the baby back pork ribs for 7 hours in an alderwood-fired pit smoker. This is the abbreviated, home-cooking version. There is a semi-transparent membrane on the bone side of most racks of ribs. Sean says, "Unless you remove this membrane, it is very difficult to create tender loving ribs." It's easy to pry it off yourself (see step 2 below), or you can ask your butcher to do it for you.

Ribcage BBQ Sauce

3 cups prepared tomato sauce

3/4 cup molasses

1/2 cup apple cider vinegar

1/4 cup red wine

1/4 cup balsamic vinegar

1/2 tsp. each garlic salt, onion salt, and celery salt

1/4 tsp. liquid smoke (optional)

Ribs

3 tbsp. kosher salt

1 1/2 tbsp. black pepper

2 tsp. *each* mustard powder, white pepper, and paprika

7 lbs. baby back ribs

Braising Sauce

2 tbsp. Ribcage BBQ Sauce or smoky-sweet bottled sauce

2 tbsp. apple cider vinegar

1. **MAKE THE BBQ SAUCE:** In a saucepan, combine all the ingredients and simmer until slightly thickened, stirring occasionally, about 10 minutes. Cool to room temperature, transfer to an airtight container, and chill until needed.

2. **PREPARE THE RIBS:** In a bowl, stir together the salt, black pepper, mustard powder, white pepper, and paprika. Turn a rack of ribs bone side up on a cutting board. With a knife, gently explore and pry up the membrane at the end of the first bone. Once the membrane has been separated slightly from the bone, grab the membrane with a paper towel and slowly pull it off the rack. Repeat with other racks. Turn the racks meat side up and coat the ribs with the dry rub, dividing it evenly between the racks and gently working it into the meat.

3. **GRILL THE RIBS:** *If using a charcoal grill,* prepare for indirect medium heat (325° to 350°), adding wood chunks, preferably alderwood, to the charcoal. When the coals are covered with ash, bank them on one side and set a drip pan in cleared area. Grill the ribs on the opposite side of the grill from the heat source until nicely browned, about 45 minutes. *If using a gas grill,* prepare for direct medium heat (325° to 350°), adding wood chunks to the smoker box or to a foil pan directly on the heat in a corner. Grill the ribs over direct heat for about 8 minutes on each side.

4. Meanwhile, preheat the oven to 300°.

5. **MAKE THE BRAISING SAUCE:** In a bowl, combine the ingredients for the braising sauce with 3/4 cup water.

6. Remove the ribs from the grill and wrap in heavy-duty foil. Drizzle braising sauce over each rack of ribs prior to sealing the foil, dividing the sauce between the racks, then seal up the foil and put on two rimmed baking sheets or in a roasting pan. Bake for 1 1/2 hours. Remove the ribs from the oven, open each foil package and drizzle each rack with 1/2 cup BBQ sauce. Reseal the foil packages and bake another 30 minutes, or until the meat is tender and a bone can be easily removed. Serve, passing additional BBQ sauce alongside.

MAKE AHEAD: The BBQ sauce can be kept, chilled in an airtight container, up to 2 weeks.

PER SERVING (WITHOUT ADDITIONAL BBQ SAUCE) 346 Cal., 40% (138 Cal.) from fat; 46 g protein; 15 g fat (5 g sat.); 3.4 g carbo (0.7 g fiber); 1,856 mg sodium; 116 mg chol. LC/GF

2

BLACKBIRD

Manzanita

503 Laneda Ave.
Manzanita, OR

(503) 368-7708

blackbirdmanzanita.
com

Looking like the glam vocalist in a girl band, Lee Vance wears her excitement about food on the sleeve of her chef's jacket. Cooking produce from the garden at her Italian American mom's knee was an excellent start on what became a life devoted to farm-to-table food preparation. From the Oregon Culinary Institute and cutting-edge Portland food scene, to a food truck in Oklahoma City, and back to a stand at an Oregon farmers' market, Lee has done what she does well—to growing acclaim.

At the Friday-night market in Manzanita, she would prepare dinner from the available foodstuffs; her sign proclaimed, simply, DINNER. Folks said, "Where's your restaurant?" A brief stint in the old Nehalem River Inn (just east) followed, but the feel didn't match Lee's singular style. Bravely, but with plenty of local support, she crowdfunded her own place, one that conjures her stylish quirkiness and lets her cook like no one's watching— but they are, and they like what they see and eat. If it's seasonal, local, pasture-raised, and dee-lish, Lee is a happy camper—and you will be too.

Heirloom Tomato Salad

SERVES 4 ❖ ABOUT 20 MINUTES

Lee Vance has called many towns and cities across the U.S. her home, but her heart is truly happy only in a riotous and prolific vegetable garden—all her dishes reflect her love of the earth and its bounty. Lee often adds shaved vegetables, like cucumbers, carrots, or radishes fresh from her garden, to this salad. There's no need to buy an expensive mandoline for shaving delicate shards of vegetables; a nice sharp vegetable peeler will do the trick beautifully.

1. Chill four salad plates in the refrigerator for 1 hour, or in the freezer for 5 minutes.

2. **MAKE THE VINAIGRETTE:** Whisk all the ingredients in a small bowl.

3. In a large bowl, gently toss the greens with a little vinaigrette. Mound onto the chilled plates, top with a variety of tomato slices, drizzle each salad with 1 to 2 tsp. more vinaigrette, and top with the goat cheese and, if desired, nasturtium flowers.

PER SERVING 293 Cal., 74% (217 Cal.) from fat; 8.3 g protein; 25 g fat (6.8 g sat.); 13 g carbo (4.4 g fiber); 359 mg sodium; 13 mg chol. GF/V

Champagne Vinaigrette

1½ tbsp. Champagne vinegar

½ tsp. *fleur de sel* or other medium-grain sea salt

⅓ cup best-quality extra-virgin olive oil

Freshly cracked pepper, to taste

8 oz. (about 8 cups) mixed baby greens

2 lbs. heirloom tomatoes (ideally a variety of sizes and colors), sliced

4 oz. fresh goat cheese, crumbled

Handful of nasturtium blossoms, for garnish (optional)

Roast Chicken with Bacon and Chanterelle Hash

SERVES 4 ❖ ABOUT 45 MINUTES, PLUS 24 HOURS TO AIR-DRY

Reams of recipes have been written and pondered by generations of chefs attempting to solve the age-old problem: how to achieve doneness in all parts of the chicken at the same time. Here is the answer, and you may never cook a chicken any other way. (Don't skip the air-drying process; it's part of the reason this chicken is so fantastic.) At Blackbird, Lee also serves this dish with ricotta *gnudi* (gnocchi-like dumplings), as well as a divine peach and fermented corn relish in summer. At home, you might want to serve it with corn on the cob and peach ice cream. Make the effort to secure a really wonderful pasture-raised chicken—ideally, local—for best results.

---

1 pasture-raised chicken (about 4 lbs.), quartered

1 large Yukon Gold potato (about 9 oz.), peeled and cut into 1/2-in. cubes

1 bunch rainbow Swiss chard (about 1 lb.)

5 oz. thick-sliced smoked bacon, cut crosswise into 1/4-in. strips

Fine sea salt and pepper

1 lb. fresh chanterelle or shiitake mushrooms, brushed clean and torn or cut into bite-size pieces

1 large shallot, finely chopped

6 fresh sage leaves, slivered

2 tsp. canola or vegetable oil

---

1. Rinse the chicken pieces with cold water and pat thoroughly dry. Place on a rack in the refrigerator, skin side down, and let air-dry for 24 hours.

2. In a covered steamer over simmering water, steam the potato cubes until tender but not falling apart, 10 to 11 minutes. Remove from the heat. Remove the chicken from the refrigerator and let stand at room temperature for 10 minutes, while you make the hash. Preheat the oven to 375° and place a rimmed baking sheet in the oven.

3. Remove and discard the center ribs from the chard and tear the leaves into bite-size pieces. Warm a large nonstick skillet over medium-high heat. Add the bacon and cook, stirring occasionally, until barely browned. Add the potato cubes, season with salt and pepper, and cook without moving until golden brown on the bottom, about 5 minutes. Turn with a spatula and cook without moving until golden brown on the other side, about 5 minutes more. Add the mushrooms, shallot, and sage and sauté until the mushroom liquid has evaporated, about 5 minutes more. Finally, add the chard and sauté until it has wilted, about 2 minutes more. Set the hash aside while you cook the chicken.

4. Season both sides of the chicken pieces with salt and pepper. Place a large, heavy skillet or sauté pan (ideally cast iron) over medium-high heat and let heat for 2 minutes. Add the oil and swirl to coat the pan. Sear the leg-thigh quarters, skin side down, without moving for 3 to 4 minutes, until golden. (Adjust the heat throughout the cooking time to caramelize the skin without charring.) Flip the legs briefly to the flesh side and sear for 1 minute. Turn over again and transfer to the baking sheet in the oven. Oven-roast the legs for 20 to 22 minutes while you pan-sear the breast-wing quarters for 3 minutes on the skin side, and 1 minute on the flesh side. Transfer the breast-wing pieces skin side down to the baking sheet in the oven and finish cooking for 12 to 15 minutes. The breast quarters should be 140° to 144° near the bone, and the leg quarters 158° to 162°, measured on an instant-read thermometer. Remove from the oven and let rest for 5 minutes, to gently finish the cooking. Gently rewarm the hash while the chicken is resting. Serve the chicken over the hash.

PER SERVING 831 Cal., 52% (430 Cal.) from fat; 75 g protein; 48 g fat (13 g sat.); 24 g carbo (6.8 g fiber); 1,165 mg sodium; 276 mg chol. GF

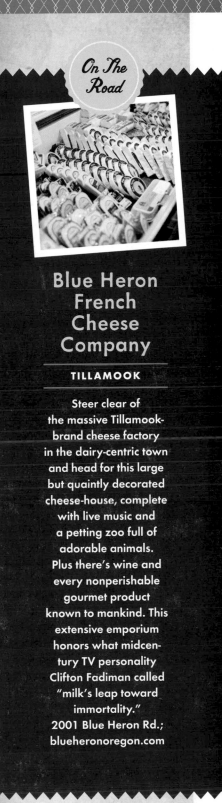

Blue Heron French Cheese Company

TILLAMOOK

Steer clear of the massive Tillamook-brand cheese factory in the dairy-centric town and head for this large but quaintly decorated cheese-house, complete with live music and a petting zoo full of adorable animals. Plus there's wine and every nonperishable gourmet product known to mankind. This extensive emporium honors what midcentury TV personality Clifton Fadiman called "milk's leap toward immortality." 2001 Blue Heron Rd.; blueheronoregon.com

Rising Star Cafe

WHEELER

A mom-'n'-pop shop for the new millennium, this cafe makes all the miles worthwhile. Ron Allen and Pepi Gabor offer big-town quality in a small, unassuming bungalow (with full bar!) in the historic town of Wheeler. While there, check out the Old Wheeler Hotel and famous sunset views. Book ahead for dinner. 92 Rorvik St.; risingstarcafe.com

Oregon Sweet Corn Bisque

SERVES 4 TO 6 ✤ ABOUT 45 MINUTES

At Blackbird, Lee Vance serves this clean and elemental soup with one of her signatures: a fermented corn relish. We've substituted an easier-to-prepare lime-juice-kissed fresh corn salsa, to add a tangy touch.

4 fresh ears corn, shucked

5½ cups whole milk

1 tsp. extra-virgin olive oil

½ medium yellow onion, finely chopped

1 small shallot, finely chopped

¼ cup dry white wine or vermouth

1 tbsp. unsalted butter

½ cup heavy cream

1½ to 2 tsp. fine sea salt, to taste

½ tsp. ground cumin

¼ tsp. red pepper flakes, plus a pinch for salsa

1 tbsp. lime juice

2 tsp. finely chopped cilantro

4 oz. fresh goat cheese, softened

1. Remove the kernels from the ears of corn with a sharp knife. Reserve ⅓ cup of corn kernels. In a large saucepan, combine the stripped corncobs and the milk and place over low heat. Partially cover and let steep for 10 to 15 minutes, while you make the soup base.

2. In a large, heavy pot, warm the oil over medium-low heat. Add the onion and shallot and cook gently, stirring occasionally and without browning, until translucent, about 5 minutes. Add the larger quantity of corn kernels and cook until tender, about 3 minutes, stirring frequently so they do not brown. Add the wine, bring to a simmer, stirring, and deglaze the pan. When the wine is almost completely evaporated, about 2 minutes, add the butter and let it melt. Stir in the cream and increase the heat to medium. Simmer until thickened, about 10 minutes; season with the salt, cumin, and ¼ tsp. red pepper flakes. Remove the corncobs from the pan of milk, and stir the milk into the corn-cream mixture. Remove from the heat and let cool for 15 minutes.

3. To make the corn salsa, combine the reserved corn kernels, the lime juice, cilantro, and a pinch of red pepper flakes in a small bowl. In a blender in two batches, purée the soup until very smooth; return to the pot. Warm gently and taste for seasoning. Ladle into bowls and garnish each with a spoonful of corn salsa and a few chunks of goat cheese.

PER SERVING 345 Cal., 58% (201 Cal.) from fat; 13 g protein; 22 g fat (13 g sat.); 26 g carbo (1.6 g fiber); 628 mg sodium; 64 mg chol. GF/V

Stop

3

CASTAWAYS RESTAURANT & TIKI BAR

Cannon Beach

316 N. Fir St.
Cannon Beach, OR

(503) 436-8777

The trim cedar-shingled building looks more like a gardening shed than the restaurant that's taken a busy vacation town by storm. How can this truly tiny hut contain a wicked-cool bar and dining room, plus a prolific kitchen? The hut started off as a stand-alone bar, brainchild of Megan Miller and her boyfriend, Josh Tuckman, who have a cocktail-centric approach to hospitality (tremendously dear to my own heart). But cocktails like food, and food crept into their bar, and Castaways is now snug in the firmament of unique, worth-a-detour dining. Megan runs the front of the house and mixes drinks like a minx, while Josh mans the stove in the tiny kitchen; his eclectic, globe-trotting cuisine is treated just as seriously as those aforementioned cocktails. Note that this place doesn't offer cookie-cutter food or ambience, like so many tourist-town eateries. The couple bill the cuisine as "Cajun & Creole," but Josh dislikes boundaries. I never feel he's veering dangerously off-track, though—his many travels and professional training are reflected throughout this diminutive structure. In truth, it's a really big place.

Mango-Strawberry Flambé with Coconut Ice Cream

SERVES 4 ❖ 10 MINUTES

It required great self-control for me to pry myself away from the bar at this teensy restaurant. The food was truly tiki-licious, and the cocktails, staff, and customers strong and smart in equal measure—no wonder it's the hottest ticket in town. If you visit—and you should—arrive early or be prepared to hang around (not the worst fate by any stretch). This is one of the most decadent desserts in this book (please use ripe strawberries, good butter, and good rum for the most ethereal result).

6 tbsp. unsalted butter

⅛ tsp. ground cinnamon

Pinch of freshly ground nutmeg

½ cup loosely packed golden brown sugar

Pinch of fine sea salt

1 small mango, peeled and sliced ¼ in. thick

8 medium-large strawberries, sliced

1½ tbsp. dark rum, such as Gosling's Black Seal

About 1 pt. coconut ice cream

1. Place a sauté pan or frying pan over medium-low heat and add the butter, cinnamon, and nutmeg. When the butter has melted and the spices are aromatic, about 2 minutes, stir in the brown sugar and salt. Stir the mixture until the sugar dissolves, 2 to 3 minutes.

2. Add the mango and strawberries to the pan and increase the heat to medium. The liquid around the edges of the pan should begin to bubble and have a caramel-like consistency.

3. Remove the pan from the heat and add the rum. Standing well away from the pan and keeping long hair out of the line of fire, light the rum with a long match. Let the rum burn off—the flame will go out in a few seconds.

4. Return the mixture to medium heat and cook for about 1 minute. Spoon the mixture over scoops of coconut ice cream. Enjoy!

PER SERVING 707 Cal., 51% (362 Cal.) from fat; 6.7 g protein; 41 g fat (26 g sat.); 78 g carbo (1.7 g fiber); 178 mg sodium; 136 mg chol. GF/LS/V

Caribbean Crab Fritters with Creole Aioli

MAKES ABOUT 20 FRITTERS; SERVES 4 TO 6 ❖ 40 MINUTES

At Castaways, Josh serves these sublime fritters with a very tiki-esque Bahamian-stew sauce, fresh mango salsa, and spicy Creole aioli. I've simplified this version to include only the aioli. Substitute blue crab if you can't find Dungeness.

Creole Aioli

- ³/₄ cup mayonnaise
- 2 tsp. lime juice
- ¹/₄ tsp. liquid smoke or smoked salt (optional)
- ³/₄ tsp. Cajun spice mix
- ³/₄ tsp. Hungarian sweet paprika
- ¹/₂ tsp. garlic powder
- ¹/₄ tsp. *each* fine sea salt and cayenne
- Tiny pinch of habanero or chipotle chile powder, or hot chili powder

Crab Fritters

- 5 oz. sourdough baguette, sliced and crusts removed
- ¹/₂ cup oyster crackers
- 1 lb. shelled cooked Dungeness crab or other fresh lump crab, pressed firmly to remove excess moisture
- ³/₄ cup finely grated Monterey jack cheese (about 2 oz.)
- 2 oz. fresh goat cheese, softened
- 1 large egg white, lightly beaten
- ¹/₂ cup finely chopped red onion
- ¹/₂ cup finely chopped red, yellow, or orange bell pepper
- 3 tbsp. mayonnaise
- ¹/₄ tsp. liquid smoke or smoked salt (optional)
- 1 tbsp. finely chopped fresh thyme or ¹/₄ tsp. dried thyme, crumbled
- 1¹/₄ tsp. garlic powder
- 1 tsp. Hungarian sweet paprika
- 1 tsp. Cajun spice mix
- ³/₄ tsp. fine sea salt
- ¹/₄ tsp. cayenne

- Canola or vegetable oil, for deep-frying
- 2 large eggs
- 1¹/₂ cups *panko* bread crumbs
- ¹/₂ tsp. ground allspice (optional)
- ¹/₄ tsp. *each* cinnamon, fine sea salt, and pepper
- 2 green onions, green parts only, thinly sliced

1. **MAKE THE AIOLI:** In a medium bowl, combine all the ingredients and whisk together until evenly blended. Transfer to a small squeeze bottle, if desired.

2. **MAKE THE FRITTERS:** Under a hot broiler or in a toaster, toast the sourdough slices until golden brown. Break into large chunks and combine in a food processor with the oyster crackers. Pulse on and off into fine crumbs. Transfer to a large bowl and add the remaining ingredients for the fritters; fold together until well blended.

3. Fill a deep-fryer or a deep, heavy pot or skillet no more than one-third full of oil and heat until it registers 375° on a deep-fry thermometer. Preheat the oven to 200°. Line a baking sheet with a double layer of paper towels and set in the oven to warm. In a large, shallow bowl, beat the eggs. In another large, shallow bowl, blend together the panko, allspice (if using), cinnamon, salt, and pepper. With clean hands, pull off pieces of fritter mixture (about 2 oz. each) and form into 2- to 2¹/₂-in. balls; the mixture will make about 20 fritters.

4. When the oil nears the desired temperature, dip the fritter balls in the beaten egg, then dredge in the panko mixture, coating all sides evenly (leave coated balls sitting in the bowl with the panko until ready to fry). Immediately and carefully add about half the fritters to the hot oil, adding in a circle around the pot. Fry for 2 to 3 minutes, nudging occasionally, until crispy and golden brown. Retrieve with a slotted spoon and transfer to the baking sheet in the oven while you fry the remaining fritters in the same way. Squeeze or drizzle aioli back and forth across the fritters (or serve alongside), scatter with green onions, and serve immediately.

MAKE AHEAD: Form the fritters up to 1 hour ahead and hold, uncovered in the refrigerator, until frying time.

PER SERVING 513 Cal., 53% (272 Cal.) from fat; 28 g protein; 30 g fat (6.5 g sat.); 34 g carbo (2 g fiber); 1,382 mg sodium; 146 mg chol.

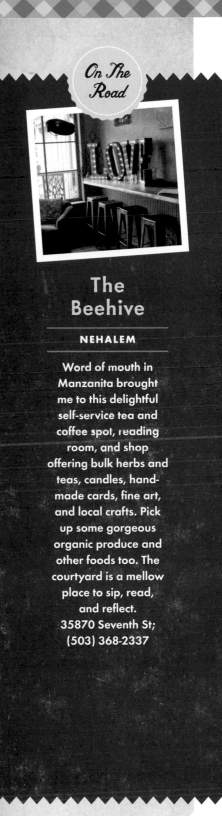

The Beehive

NEHALEM

Word of mouth in Manzanita brought me to this delightful self-service tea and coffee spot, reading room, and shop offering bulk herbs and teas, candles, handmade cards, fine art, and local crafts. Pick up some gorgeous organic produce and other foods too. The courtyard is a mellow place to sip, read, and reflect.
35870 Seventh St; (503) 368-2337

Never fried an egg roll wrapper? Your moment of outrageous crispness has arrived.

Haystack Chicken

SERVES 4 ❖ 1 HOUR

As you drive along the shore in this part of Oregon, you'll pass many tall, *Close Encounters*–like rock formations just offshore—sea stacks, which sometimes look like haystacks. There are as many Haystack Rocks as there are town names that include the word "Beach," and these tasty chicken parcels do, in a certain light, resemble the familiar formations. Megan and Josh serve their "haystacks" with mashed potatoes, sautéed vegetables, and herbed gravy. I like serving them as a light main course with mango or peach chutney, and a simple mixed green salad.

Mushrooms

2 tsp. unsalted butter

6 oz. chanterelles, shiitake, or cremini mushrooms, brushed clean, ends trimmed, and coarsely chopped

¼ tsp. fine sea salt

Pinch of pepper

Chicken

1 tbsp. extra-virgin olive oil

1 lb. boned, skinned chicken breasts, cut into eight 2-oz. pieces, avoiding pointy corners as much as possible

Fine sea salt and pepper

⅛ tsp. dried thyme

8 large egg roll wrappers (each about 6 in. square)

½ cup Caramelized Onions (page 42)

4 oz. fresh goat cheese, softened and formed into 8 small, flattened disks

Canola or vegetable oil, for frying

Your favorite purchased chutney, such as mango, for serving

1. **PREPARE THE MUSHROOMS:** In a large, heavy frying pan, warm the butter over medium-low heat. Add the mushrooms and sauté, stirring occasionally, until softened and juicy, about 4 minutes. Add the salt and pepper, and cook until the pan is almost completely dry, 2 to 3 minutes more. Transfer to a bowl and cover to keep warm.

2. **PREPARE THE CHICKEN:** In the same pan, warm the oil over medium-high heat. Season the chicken generously with salt and pepper, and sprinkle with the thyme. Add the chicken to the pan and cook, turning over occasionally, until firm and just barely cooked through at the center, about 10 minutes. Transfer the chicken to a plate and let cool for 5 minutes.

3. **ASSEMBLE THE "HAYSTACKS":** Place the egg roll wrappers on a dry surface, on a diagonal. Trim any pointy ends from the chicken breasts, to create a more oval shape. Set a piece of chicken in the middle of each egg roll wrapper and top with about 1 tbsp. of caramelized onions in an even layer. Top the onions with a thin layer of sautéed mushrooms, about 1 tbsp. (do not overload, or it will be difficult to seal the packet). Top the mushrooms with a disk of goat cheese. Wet all the edges of the wrappers with cold water, using a pastry brush or fingertips. Seal the "haystacks" by folding the bottom point up to the center. Then fold the side flaps to the center, overlapping, and finish by folding down the top flap. Repeat to seal the remaining packets.

4. Preheat the oven to 200°. In a large, deep-sided frying pan, heat 1 in. of oil to 350° on a deep-fry thermometer. Place 4 of the packets into the oil, seam side down. Fry for 1½ to 2 minutes, until golden and crispy. Turn over and cook the other side until golden brown, 1½ to 2 minutes more. With tongs, stand each packet on its sides for a few seconds, to ensure that the sides are crispy too. Transfer to a paper towel–lined baking sheet and set in the oven to keep warm while you fry the remaining packages in the same way. Serve 2 haystacks per person with a dollop of chutney alongside.

PER SERVING (WITHOUT CHUTNEY) 447 Cal., 43% (190 Cal.) from fat; 34 g protein; 22 g fat (7.5 g sat.); 30 g carbo (2.9 g fiber); 723 mg sodium; 87 mg chol. LC

ASTORIA COFFEEHOUSE & BISTRO

Astoria

243 11th St.
Astoria, OR

(503) 325-1787

astoriacoffeehouse.com

Jim Defeo and his partner of 25 years, Anthony Danton, moved to Astoria to "retire" in 2006. "Portland was getting too big and gentrified," Jim says. "Astoria had an out-of-time vibe, like a forgotten island full of friendly people and great architecture." A restaurateur in Portland and Seattle ("I was into vegan and organic then—not so much now"), Jim initially intended simply to convert a garage into an espresso bar. That happened. Panini and breakfast followed—Jim cooked and Anthony baked—then beer and wine, and suddenly live music. The locals were starving for a community gathering place with good food, alcohol, and coffee. "I never wanted to do a typical restaurant, but we realized we had something," Jim says. The interior evolved somewhat organically into a space combining garage aesthetics with those of a granny's parlor. As the enterprise grew, talented and fish-loving chef Sean Whittaker came aboard to take the food to another level. The empire has expanded across the street, with an art gallery and a quirky import shop called Cargo. Retirement, apparently, has been postponed.

Monte Cristo Breakfast Sandwiches

SERVES 4 HUNGRY PEOPLE ❖ ABOUT 25 MINUTES

This decadent sandwich is a hybrid of French toast and the venerable Monte Cristo. Both are great dishes in their own right, but Sean Whittaker's take gives wild and crazy new meaning to the concept of breakfast.

1. **MAKE THE FRENCH TOAST:** In a large baking dish, place the bread slices in a single layer. In a large glass measuring pitcher, thoroughly whisk together the eggs, cream, spices, orange zest, and vanilla. Pour evenly over the bread and let stand for 1 minute; turn the bread over. Cover the dish with plastic wrap and let stand for 20 minutes, turning several times during the soaking time.

2. Place a large nonstick frying pan over medium heat and melt 1 tbsp. of the butter. Add the soaked bread (as many slices as fit in the pan without overlapping). Cook, turning once halfway through, until golden brown, about 6 minutes. Transfer to a baking sheet and repeat with the remaining slices, adding the remaining butter and adjusting the heat as necessary to toast the bread. Wipe out the pan with a paper towel.

3. **ASSEMBLE THE SANDWICHES:** Place 4 slices of French toast on a work surface and layer with the filling in this order, dividing evenly: cheese, turkey, ham, and bacon. Spread the other 4 slices on one side with mayo, then place, mayo side down, over the filling.

4. Lightly oil the frying pan or a griddle and place over medium-low heat. "Grill" the sandwiches for 4 to 5 minutes, then carefully turn over and cook 4 to 5 minutes more, until golden brown and beginning to crisp on both sides and the cheese is melting at the edges. Remove from the heat, slice each sandwich in half, and dust the tops with powdered sugar. If you like, serve with the lingonberry preserves on the side, for dipping.

PER SERVING (WITHOUT PRESERVES) 1,488 Cal., 48% (713 Cal.) from fat; 72 g protein; 80 g fat (35 g sat.); 120 g carbo (4.8 g fiber); 3,006 mg sodium; 543 mg chol.

French Toast

8 slices sourdough bread (about 5 in. wide and ½ in. thick)

6 large eggs

1 cup heavy cream

¼ tsp. *each* ground cardamom and cinnamon

1 tsp. finely grated orange zest

½ tsp. vanilla extract

2 tbsp. unsalted butter

8 oz. thinly sliced Swiss cheese

8 oz. thinly sliced smoked turkey breast

6 oz. thinly sliced smoked ham

6 oz. peppered bacon slices, cooked until crisp

4 tbsp. mayonnaise

Canola or vegetable oil, for "grilling"

Powdered sugar, for dusting

Swedish lingonberry preserves (optional), for serving

Astoria

Many East or West Coast urbanites have relocated to this tiny metropolis—named after John Jacob Astor—at the mouth of the Columbia River. Indie bookstores jostle with smoked-fish emporiums and funky coffeehouses, and finite geographical boundaries mean no future sprawl; everyone seems open-minded, smart, and healthy, and the 1920s architecture is a joy. travelastoria.com

Astoria Surf Melt

SERVES 4 ✤ ABOUT 1 HOUR

As in many small cities and towns in the Northwest, coffee is king in Astoria. With the plethora of caffeine outlets, it takes something special to stand out from the rest, and this buzzing spot excels not just with food, but with decor and ambience as well. I am always on the lookout for new and inventive ways to convey melted cheese to my mouth, and if said comestible can be combined with shellfish, I'm in heaven. Choose one or all of the following cheeses (or another cheese of your choice): Swiss, gruyère, cheddar, jack, or muenster. Serve your melt with a side of coleslaw and potato chips for the welcome crunch factor, if desired.

Sandwiches

Four 5-in. lengths French baguette

1/2 lb. cooked Oregon pink shrimp or bay shrimp, cut into bite-size pieces if large

2 tbsp. each finely diced yellow and red bell peppers

4 green onions, finely chopped

1/2 cup very finely chopped celery

1 1/4 tsp. Old Bay Seasoning, plus more to taste

3 tbsp. lemon juice

Mornay Sauce

1 1/2 tbsp. butter

2 1/2 tbsp. all-purpose flour

1 cup whole milk, warmed

1/4 tsp. fine sea salt

Ground black or white pepper, to taste

1/2 cup grated cheese (see note above)

2 oz. (1/2 cup) coarsely grated parmesan cheese

Lemon wedges, for serving

1. **START THE SANDWICHES:** Preheat the oven to 400° and line a baking sheet with foil. Cut each length of baguette in half lengthwise. Using a fork, hollow out all the baguette halves, keeping the shells intact and reserving the crumbs for another use. Toast the baguette shells on the prepared baking sheet in the oven until lightly browned and crisp, 4 to 6 minutes. Set aside until needed. Turn the oven to broil. In a large bowl, combine the shrimp, bell peppers, green onions, celery, Old Bay, and lemon juice; taste for seasoning.

2. **MAKE THE MORNAY SAUCE:** In a heavy saucepan, melt the butter over medium heat. Using a whisk, blend in the flour to make a paste. Stir constantly until the paste has bubbled for 2 minutes; do not brown (reduce to medium-low heat if it boils too vigorously). Remove from the heat. When the paste stops bubbling, pour in all the milk and whisk vigorously until blended, with no lumps. Return to the heat and bring to a simmer. Simmer gently until thickened, 2 to 3 minutes, stirring occasionally, then remove from the heat and whisk in the salt and pepper. Let stand for 2 to 3 minutes, then whisk in the cheese.

3. **ASSEMBLE THE SANDWICHES:** Fold the Mornay sauce into the shrimp mixture until blended. Mound the mixture in the hollowed bread, and scatter with parmesan. Place on the baking sheet and toast 6 in. from the broiler until the tops are golden brown in several spots and the filling is warmed through, about 5 minutes. Let stand 5 minutes before serving. Serve with lemon wedges.

PER SANDWICH 428 Cal., 31% (134 Cal.) from fat; 31 g protein; 15 g fat (8.5 g sat.); 42 g carbo (2.2 g fiber); 1,230 mg sodium; 149 mg chol. LC

Smoked Salmon "Hash"

SERVES 4 ❖ 1¼ HOURS

Astoria's position at the mouth of the Columbia River means smoked fish is big business. Styles abound; you can taste a variety in the area's smokehouses, with many of the preparations based on old family recipes. Stock up on vacuum-packed portions to take or send home. (Try Josephson's Smokehouse, right on the river and only a few blocks from Astoria Coffeehouse, for fish with a view.) Each and every breakfast in the coffeehouse is served with the potatoes that are the basis of this smoky, satisfying dish.

Coffeehouse Potatoes

2 lbs. small red potatoes (each about the size of a golf ball), cut into quarters

1½ tbsp. plus 2 tsp. extra-virgin olive oil

½ tsp. *each* paprika and granulated garlic

¾ tsp. fine sea salt, plus more to taste

½ tsp. pepper, plus more to taste

½ cup diced white or yellow onion (about ¼ of a large onion)

1 red, yellow, or green bell pepper, stemmed, seeded, and cut into ½-in. chunks (or use a combination)

12 oz. hot smoked salmon (sometimes called kippered), in chunks

Hollandaise Sauce

Finely grated zest of 1 lemon

¼ cup lemon juice

2 large egg yolks

14 tbsp. (7 oz.) unsalted butter, cut into small chunks, and softened

¼ tsp. fine sea salt

Tiny pinch of cayenne

1 tsp. white vinegar or cider vinegar

8 large eggs

1. **MAKE THE POTATOES:** Preheat the oven to 350°. Put the potatoes in a large metal roasting pan and drizzle with 1½ tbsp. oil. Season with the paprika, garlic, salt, and pepper and toss to mix; spread into an even layer. Drizzle ¾ cup water around the edges, and wrap the pan securely with foil, crimping the edges. Bake until the potatoes are tender, 45 to 50 minutes. Remove the foil and bake for 5 to 10 minutes more, to evaporate the remaining water.

2. **MAKE THE HOLLANDAISE SAUCE:** In a nonreactive double boiler over barely simmering water, combine the lemon zest, juice, and egg yolks. Whisk gently for 1 to 2 minutes, until the mixture has just barely begun to thicken to a thin, yogurtlike consistency. Whisk in a piece of butter, and continue whisking in the butter a piece at a time, whisking all the time and allowing 1 piece to be absorbed before adding the next. Do not let the mixture get so hot that it boils. (If it does get too hot, remove the bowl from the heat for a minute or 2 while still whisking.) Whisk in the salt and cayenne, cover, and set aside at the back of the stove, off the heat, until serving, up to 15 minutes. Stir the sauce before serving.

3. In a large, heavy frying pan, warm the remaining 2 tsp. oil over medium-high heat. Sauté the onion and bell pepper until tender and slightly golden, 2 to 3 minutes. Fold in the potatoes and cook for 2 to 3 minutes, pressing down on the mixture gently to help the browning process. Fold in the salmon and cook for 1 to 2 minutes more to warm through without drying out the salmon. Taste for seasoning and adjust with salt and pepper.

4. Meanwhile, in a wide saucepan with a tight-fitting lid, bring 3 in. of water to a very gentle simmer and add the vinegar. Crack 4 eggs, 1 at a time, just above the surface of the water. Cover the pan and cook for 3 minutes, or until the whites are just set. With a slotted spoon, remove the eggs from the poaching water, resting the spoon on a folded paper towel for a moment to drain excess water. Repeat with the remaining eggs.

5. To serve, divide the hash among 4 individual plates. Top each portion with 2 poached eggs, then spoon some of the hollandaise sauce over the top.

PER SERVING 915 Cal., 62% (568 Cal.) from fat; 36 g protein; 64 g fat (31 g sat.); 51 g carbo (5.4 g fiber); 1,380 mg sodium; 653 mg chol.

Frite & Scoop

ASTORIA

Seattle refugees Kevin and Lisa settled on Astoria's glittering Riverwalk with the intention of making the best possible ice cream with the most impeccable ingredients available. Every. Single. Day. Say "Hello!" to Salted Caramel and Peanut Butter Cookie, and then "Why Not?" to Kindergarten Pop and Hokey Pokey. (Check Facebook for today's flavors.) Craving equal time for salty snacks, Lisa recently added authentic Belgian frites to the menu. 175 14th St.; (503) 468-0416; friteandscoop.com

ington

Route 10

CROSSING INTO WASHINGTON, there's an immediate sense that something is different. Although the entire Pacific Coast is and will always be popular with vacationers and retirees, it's less populated up here.

Long Beach Peninsula is an improbable 28 miles of lovely beaches strung together by a charm bracelet of small towns—Oysterville is the oldest, *Long Beach* the biggest—featuring attractions like the World's Largest Frying Pan, peep shows, and penny arcades.

Farther north, approaching South Bend ("Oyster Capital of the World"), you drive along a huge protected body of water: Willapa Bay, which separates Long Beach Peninsula from the mainland. Here, salt marshes and cattle ranches are punctuated with vast swaths of clear-cut timber. All along this route you'll see enormous piles of stripped trees on their way to somewhere else. If you're in a hurry, stick with 101 as it cuts inland; or hug the coast on 105 toward Westport, onetime "Salmon Capital of the World." (Beginning to sense a theme?)

After the twin—and diametrically opposite—towns of Hoquiam (historic, quaint) and Aberdeen (heavily industrialized), you are officially on the Olympic Peninsula—OP to the locals. Sleepy but fast-developing *Pacific Beach* boasts one of the biggest beaches I've ever seen. Dogs frolic, kites fly, and driftwood fires burn; you can drive right onto the beach, should the need arise. In nearby *Moclips*, tree-clad bluffs tower over the beach, requiring intrepid beachgoers to either hike down to the landscape or perch up top and just drink it in. Ideally, with an excellent glass of Washington wine.

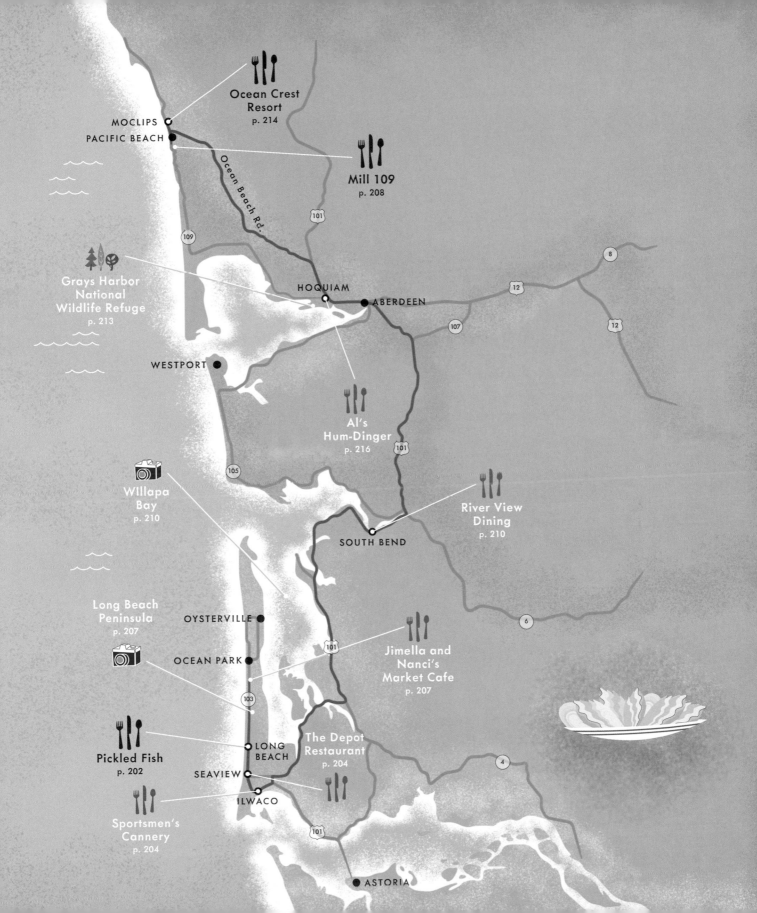

Ocean Crest
Resort
p. 214

MOCLIPS

PACIFIC BEACH

Ocean Beach Rd.

Mill 109
p. 208

101

109

8

Grays Harbor
National
Wildlife Refuge
p. 213

HOQUIAM

12

ABERDEEN

107

12

WESTPORT

Al's
Hum-Dinger
p. 216

101

105

River View
Dining
p. 210

WIllapa
Bay
p. 210

SOUTH BEND

Long Beach
Peninsula
p. 207

OYSTERVILLE

6

OCEAN PARK

101

Jimella and
Nanci's
Market Cafe
p. 207

103

Pickled Fish
p. 202

LONG
BEACH

The Depot
Restaurant
p. 204

SEAVIEW

4

Sportsmen's
Cannery
p. 204

ILWACO

101

ASTORIA

Stop 1

PICKLED FISH

Long Beach

409 Sid Snyder Dr.
Long Beach, WA

(360) 642-2344

adrifthotel.com

Charlie Zorich stuffed his first mushroom at 10. "My grandmother was a cateress," he says. He was also lucky enough to grow up right here on the Long Beach Peninsula, frequently eating at legendary restaurant The Ark, helmed by Jimella Lucas. (James Beard was a big fan, and Lucas is credited with putting the area on the culinary map in the 1980s.) Charlie never had any doubts about his career and started culinary school right out of high school. Stints in various restaurants followed (including an apprenticeship with Jimella Lucas herself, who passed away in 2013). After running his own place for four years (Epicure, in Portland), Charlie let the accessibility of fresh and foraged produce on this peninsula lure him back home to a stunning space set dune-side atop the green-and-modern Adrift Hotel, with natural wood, towering windows, and forever-views. "I get wild berries, fiddlehead ferns, nettles ... I know everyone who delivers my seafood," he says. Visitors from Portland and Seattle are thrilled to discover this bastion of carefully curated and lovingly prepared food offered by Charlie and baking and pastry partner Matt Richardson.

Winter Kale Salad with Roasted Squash and Cranberries

SERVES 4 ✦ ABOUT 30 MINUTES

Pickled Fish hadn't been open long when I stumbled onto Long Beach Peninsula. The narrow, eight-town-long strip has been a beach destination for denizens of the Northwest for generations (as evidenced by the rows of neatly kept Victorian beach cottages lining the sidewalk-free streets, each one ending in a dune). "Where can I have a glass of wine within view of the ocean?"—my usual opening gambit—was rewarded with this unexpected bonanza: impeccable beach and sunset views, great wines and beers by the glass, and a passionate chef not long out of the culinary mecca of Portland. Doing great things with the abundant local produce, I might add.

1. **COOK THE SQUASH AND TOAST THE PEPITAS:** Preheat the oven to 350°. In a small roasting pan, toss the squash with the oil and season with salt and pepper. Roast for 20 to 25 minutes, until golden and fork-tender; toss once or twice during cooking time to color evenly. In a small, dry nonstick skillet over medium heat, toast the pepitas until aromatic, 2 to 3 minutes, jiggling the pan so they don't scorch.

2. **MEANWHILE, MAKE THE DRESSING:** In a small bowl, whisk together all the ingredients until smooth and creamy.

3. Remove and discard the center ribs from the kale. Slice the kale leaves into 1/4-in. ribbons; you should have about 5 cups. In a large bowl, toss together the kale, squash, and cranberries. Add just enough of the dressing to coat the ingredients lightly. Divide salad among four plates, top with the toasted pepitas, and serve.

PER SERVING 345 Cal., 56% (192 Cal.) from fat; 3.2 g protein; 22 g fat (2.7 g sat.); 35 g carbo (0.4 g fiber); 283 mg sodium; 0 mg chol. LC/LS/VG

Squash and Pepitas

8 to 9 oz. butternut squash, peeled and cut into 3/4-in. pieces

1 tbsp. extra-virgin olive oil

1/4 cup *pepitas* (pumpkin seeds)

Apple Cider Dressing

1 small garlic clove, minced

1/4 cup apple juice

1/2 tsp. fine sea salt

1/4 tsp. pepper

2 tbsp. apple cider vinegar

1 green onion, trimmed and minced

2 tsp. stone-ground Dijon mustard

2 tbsp. canola oil

2 tbsp. extra-virgin olive oil

1 bunch (8 oz.) Lacinato (also called Tuscan) kale

3/4 cup dried cranberries

Sportsmen's Cannery

ILWACO

It's possible that someday this insider's gem will have a website, but for now you must go in person (or call) to buy the legendary canned garlic tuna, as well as smoked sturgeon, smoked salmon, and oysters. Think canned fish is meh? Not here. They will also clean and package your hand-dug razor clams. 211 S.E. Howerton Way; (360) 642-3340

The Depot Restaurant

SEAVIEW

Tucked away on a side street in a 125-year-old red wooden train station, this is another gem in the peninsula's sparkling crown. Chef-owner Michael Lalewicz has a deft hand with game and seafood, plus a sense of humor (Oysters 'Scargot, anyone?). The wide-ranging, reasonable wine list had me at the half-bottle of Dry Creek Fumé Blanc. 1208 38th Place; depotrestaurantdining.com

My discovery of the sublime eatery Pickled Fish was true serendipity— the kind all roadfoodies strive and drive for.

Wild Cod Poppers with Rémoulade

MAKES 12 POPPERS; SERVES 4 AS AN APPETIZER ❖ ABOUT 25 MINUTES

Sometimes I think I may have eaten enough fried seafood to last a lifetime. And then I come across something like this. Golden brown, shatter-crisp nuggets of cod cooked to perfection in nice hot oil, served with the tastiest rémoulade sauce this cook/roadfoodie has ever encountered. (Rémoulade is to tartar sauce what aioli is to mayo.) You'll be (re)hooked for life. This recipe makes more rémoulade than necessary, but you'll find plenty of uses for the leftovers.

Rémoulade Sauce

1 cup mayonnaise

2 tsp. Dijon mustard

1 tbsp. finely chopped yellow onion

1 small garlic clove, minced

1/8 tsp. granulated garlic

2 tbsp. capers, roughly chopped

1 1/2 tsp. caper juice

2 tsp. lemon juice, plus more to taste

3/4 tsp. red wine vinegar

1/4 tsp. Worcestershire sauce

1 1/2 tsp. *each* finely chopped fresh dill and finely chopped fresh flat-leaf Italian parsley

Fine sea salt and pepper

Poppers

Canola or rice bran oil, for deep-frying

3/4 cup all-purpose flour

1/4 tsp. fine sea salt, plus more for sprinkling

1/2 tsp. *each* pepper, granulated garlic, and sweet paprika

1 cup buttermilk

1 cup *panko* bread crumbs

12 oz. Pacific cod, cut into 12 equal pieces

1. **MAKE THE RÉMOULADE:** In a bowl, whisk together all the ingredients except the salt and pepper. Taste for seasoning and adjust with salt, pepper, and/or lemon juice as desired.

2. **MAKE THE POPPERS:** Prepare a deep-fryer or deep, heavy pot no more than one-third full of oil for deep-frying. Heat the oil to 350° on a deep-fry thermometer. Place a baking sheet lined with a double layer of paper towels in a low (200°) oven.

3. In a medium-size shallow bowl or baking dish, blend the flour, salt, pepper, granulated garlic, and paprika. Put the buttermilk in a similar bowl, and the panko in a third. When the oil reaches 350°, dust 6 pieces of cod in the seasoned flour, then dredge in the buttermilk, letting the excess drain away. Finally, toss in the panko to coat evenly.

4. Add the cod gently to the hot oil, working in a clockwise circle. Fry for 2 to 3 minutes, until deep golden brown. Retrieve with a slotted spoon and transfer to the oven while you fry the remaining pieces of cod in the same way. Sprinkle with sea salt and serve immediately, with the rémoulade sauce on the side.

PER 3-POPPER SERVING WITH RÉMOULADE 457 Cal., 53% (251 Cal.) from fat; 19 g protein; 28 g fat (3.8 g sat.); 34 g carbo (0.8 g fiber); 912 mg sodium; 45 mg chol.

Dungeness Crab Mac 'n' Cheese

SERVES 4 TO 6 ❖ ABOUT 30 MINUTES

Is this my number one favorite dish in this book? I'm hereby taking the Fifth! But I will say that I prefer it served in individual gratin dishes to ensure democratic distribution of the crispy-cheesy bread crumbs. (You'll need four shallow dishes of about 1½-cup capacity.) Or just smooth the creamy, crabby mixture into a wide baking dish and try to distribute the goodness equitably. Imagine my glee when presented with this amazing dish, against the background of setting sun on Pacific Ocean, all reflected through a prism of Mount Baker Oyster Blanc in a pristine glass.

Kosher salt, for the pasta

Softened butter or oil, for the baking dish(es)

Seasoned Bread Crumbs

1 cup fresh bread crumbs

¼ tsp. *each* fine sea salt and paprika

¼ tsp. ground white or black pepper

1 tbsp. finely chopped fresh flat-leaf Italian parsley

¼ cup (2 oz.) unsalted butter, melted

1 lb. ditalini or miniature penne pasta

3 cups heavy cream

½ cup grated sharp white cheddar

¼ cup grated parmigiano-reggiano cheese

1 tsp. hot sauce, such as Tabasco

¼ tsp. fine sea salt

¼ tsp. ground white or black pepper

½ tsp. dry mustard

12 oz. shelled cooked Dungeness crab, flaked

1. Preheat the oven to 400°. Bring a large pot of lightly salted water to a boil. Butter four individual porcelain or ceramic gratin dishes, or one 9- by 13-in. baking dish.

2. **MAKE THE SEASONED BREAD CRUMBS:** Place the fresh bread crumbs on a rimmed baking sheet and toast until golden, stirring occasionally, 10 to 12 minutes. Transfer to a bowl and toss with the salt, paprika, pepper, parsley, and melted butter.

3. Add the pasta to the boiling water and cook according to package instructions; drain well in a colander. Rinse with cold water to prevent sticking.

4. Place a large saucepan over medium-high heat and add the cream. As soon as the cream comes to a fast boil, quickly stir in the cheeses, hot sauce, salt, pepper, and mustard. Continue stirring until the mixture thickens, about 2 minutes. Add the pasta and toss to coat evenly. Scoop the mixture into the prepared baking dish(es), smooth flat, and nestle the crab evenly on top of the pasta, pressing it in slightly. Scatter with seasoned bread crumbs. Transfer to the oven and cook until the crab is warmed and the bread crumbs are browned, 10 to 12 minutes.

PER SERVING 900 Cal., 60% (537 Cal.) from fat; 29 g protein; 60 g fat (37 g sat.); 64 g carbo (2.7 g fiber); 711 mg sodium; 243 mg chol.

Long Beach Peninsula

This is beach life at its unspoiled, nostalgic best (in California, these 28 miles would be lined with McMansions): drive-on, dog-friendly beaches; Victorian beach cottages; Marsh's Free Museum and the World Kite Museum; plus the meandering, Hamptons-like bike and hike Discovery Trail and Boardwalk. My fave spot: the historic Shelburne Inn (with a pub!). funbeach.com

Jimella and Nanci's Market Cafe

OCEAN PARK

Nanci Main and Jimella Lucas pioneered clean, local, fresh, and seasonal cuisine on this peninsula long before such became standard fare, attracting the attention of James Beard when they helmed the Shelburne Inn, and later at the revered Ark Restaurant. Jimella's now gone to the great kitchen in Heaven, but the fine flavors remain here, and are worth the wait. 21742 Pacific Way; jimellaandnancis.com

Stop 2

5 W. Myrtle Lane
Pacific Beach, WA

(360) 276-4884

mill109.com

MILL 109

Pacific Beach

At 15, Rob Paylor had a French teacher who railroaded him into a temporary dish-washing job at an Aberdeen Swiss-Italian restaurant, Parma. That was the day his life changed. Owner/chef/patriarch Pierre Gabelli became a lifetime mentor to Rob, and the Gabelli clan became his second family, helping support him through culinary school and beyond. Rob then bounced around the local culinary world, spending 10 years as the chef-manager of an Irish pub in Ocean Shores. "I tried to buy the pub, but that deal fell through." The developers of nearby Seabrook offered him the chef's position at the main (then, the only) restaurant in the beachy, dog-friendly community about a mile south of Pacific Beach. A year and a half after taking over, Rob bought the restaurant and established his kingdom in the kitchen of this friendly, rustic-industrial space, with huge windows looking out toward one of the biggest beaches I've ever seen. Here, activities long banned farther south (beach driving, dog-running, drift-wood fires) are still A-OK. Stunning sunsets draw in visitors and homeowners for Rob's excellent Tuaca-liqueur-laced margarita, the seafood is only hours old, and there's a daily mac and cheese that's beloved by kids (and me).

Spiced Berry Pancakes

MAKES ABOUT 24 (4-IN.) PANCAKES; SERVES 6 ❖ 25 MINUTES

The entire Northwest is a virtual cornucopia of berries. At Mill 109, the chef uses marionberries for this bright Northwest-centric breakfast; choose from what's available in your area. The drained-off juice from the berries makes an excellent base for a berry mimosa: Just add 1 tsp. of the juice to a Champagne flute and top with chilled Washington sparkling wine.

1. **PREPARE THE BERRIES:** In a medium bowl, using a potato masher or fork, lightly break up the berries. Stir in the brown sugar, cinnamon, allspice, nutmeg, ginger, and vanilla. Drain in a sieve to remove any excess juice, reserving it for another use (see note above).

2. **MAKE THE PANCAKES:** In a large bowl, combine the flour, sugar, baking powder, and salt. In another bowl, whisk together the milk and eggs, then stir into the dry ingredients. Whisk in the melted butter. Very gently fold in the berry mixture.

3. Preheat the oven to the lowest heat and put in a platter and four plates. Preheat a nonstick or well-seasoned cast-iron griddle to medium-high heat, until a drop of water flicked onto the surface dances and evaporates instantly. Brush the griddle with melted butter. Use a 2-oz. ladle or $1/4$ cup dry measure to scoop up some batter and pour it onto the griddle. Continue ladling to make as many pancakes as you can without letting them touch. When the pancakes have begun to bubble in the center (the undersides will be golden), use a spatula to flip them to the other side. Cook for 1 minute more, then transfer to the platter in the oven while you cook the remaining pancakes, adding more butter and adjusting the heat as necessary throughout the cooking time. Serve on warmed plates, with whipped butter and warm syrup, if desired.

PER 4-PANCAKE SERVING 332 Cal., 33% (109 Cal.) from fat; 9.1 g protein; 12 g fat (6.7 g sat.); 47 g carbo (3.7 g fiber); 553 mg sodium; 98 mg chol. LC/V

Spiced Berries

8 oz. (about $1^{1}/2$ cups) fresh or thawed frozen seasonal berries, such as raspberries, blackberries, and blueberries

$1^{1}/2$ tbsp. brown sugar

$1/8$ tsp. ground cinnamon

Pinch *each* of ground allspice, ground nutmeg, and ground ginger

$1/2$ tsp. best-quality vanilla extract

Pancakes

2 cups all-purpose flour

$1^{1}/2$ tbsp. sugar

1 tbsp. baking powder

1 tsp. fine sea salt

$1^{2}/3$ cups whole milk

2 large eggs, lightly beaten

$1/4$ cup unsalted butter, melted, plus additional melted butter for brushing the griddle

Whipped butter and boysenberry or maple syrup, for serving (optional)

River View Dining

SOUTH BEND

The only thing that is not gritty here are the excellent oysters, lovingly harvested nearby and then coddled to smoky goodness on a rusty grill—or served gloriously raw. The somewhat cranky chef occasionally rants, and the dining room is a little (okay, a lot) low on charm, but the proof is on the (paper) plate. 618 Robert Bush Dr. W.; (360) 875-6155

Willapa Bay

The Long Beach Peninsula separates this massive but shallow estuary from the Pacific, and much of the bay is protected as a wildlife refuge. The many oysters (Kumamoto, Pacific, and Olympia) filter the water, helping the bay to keep its designation as "cleanest in the USA." Über-tasty Dungeness crab thrive here too. fws.gov/refuge/willapa

I'm a butter lover from waaay back, so a good hollandaise is like having money in the bank: You just ain't gonna fail with this one.

Seabrook Benedict

SERVES 2 AS A SUBSTANTIAL BREAKFAST, OR 4 AS PART OF A LARGER BREAKFAST SPREAD ❖ 15 MINUTES

Arguably, the best part of any road trip is breakfast, and I encountered many great ones on my drive. Since riffs on the Benedict theme abound, many morning meals involved hollandaise (my own favorite food group). For those who have a hollandaise phobia, making it in the blender is an easy and foolproof route. However, the sauce must either be made at the last moment (due to all the moving parts, a fiddly proposition with any Benedict-style breakfast) or warmed in a double boiler, to ensure warm sauce (warm sauce being, of course, crucial)*.

½ lb. shelled cooked Dungeness crab, picked over for shell fragments

Dijon Hollandaise Sauce

½ cup (4 oz.) best-quality unsalted butter

2 large egg yolks

1 tbsp. lemon juice

2 tsp. Dijon mustard

½ tsp. fine sea salt, or to taste

Dash of hot sauce, plus more to taste

1 tsp. distilled white vinegar or cider vinegar

4 large eggs, preferably from pasture-raised hens

2 English muffins, homemade (page 59) or purchased, split and toasted

1. Preheat the oven to the lowest setting and put in plates to warm. Remove the crab from the refrigerator to take the chill off.

2. **MAKE THE HOLLANDAISE:** In a small saucepan, melt the butter over medium-low heat. Remove from the heat and let cool for 2 minutes. Meanwhile, put the remaining sauce ingredients and 1 tbsp. water in a blender. Turn on the blender and slowly pour the warm butter over the yolk mixture; it will thicken immediately. If serving right away, leave in the blender pitcher*. Taste for seasoning and adjust with salt and hot sauce if desired.

3. **POACH THE EGGS:** In a large saucepan with a tight-fitting lid, bring 3 in. of water to a very gentle simmer and add the vinegar. Crack the eggs, 1 at a time, just above the surface of the water. Cover the pan and cook for 3 minutes.

4. Place the toasted muffin halves on the plates. Top each muffin with an even layer of crab. With a slotted spoon, remove the eggs from the poaching water, resting the spoon on a paper towel for a moment to drain excess water. Transfer the eggs to the waiting crab-topped muffins. Immediately nap the eggs generously with a blanket of warm hollandaise sauce.

*If you plan to make the hollandaise ahead of time, place a double boiler insert or metal bowl over, but not touching, a pot of gently simmering water; remove the pot from the heat and cover to keep warm. Transfer the sauce from the blender to the double boiler as soon as it's nicely thickened. It may then be held in the double boiler over the hot—but not simmering—water for up to 30 minutes.

PER SERVING 507 Cal., 59% (300 Cal.) from fat; 25 g protein; 34 g fat (19 g sat.); 26 g carbo (1 g fiber); 601 mg sodium; 436 mg chol.

Roosevelt Beach Razor Clams

SERVES 4 AS AN APPETIZER ❖ 45 MINUTES, PLUS 2 HOURS TO STAND

Roosevelt Beach, 5 miles south of Pacific Beach, is a prime place for clamming. To protect the valuable resource, there is a limit to how many razor clams one person can dig in a day—currently 15 (each digger must keep the first 15 he or she digs; you're not allowed to throw them back and look for bigger/better clams). Rob Paylor's family has lived in the area for a long time, and at Mill 109 his recipe for breaded fresh clams is just slightly modified from the one his family has always followed. Here, the clams are served very simply with a wedge of lemon as an appetizer. You could also pair them with a starch and vegetables, to make a main course for two.

1/3 cup kosher salt

1/4 cup coarse cornmeal

15 freshly dug live Pacific razor clams (the daily limit) or Atlantic jackknife clams*

1 1/2 cups all-purpose flour

3 large eggs

Juice of 1 lemon

1 1/2 cups *panko* bread crumbs

1 1/2 cups finely grated parmesan cheese

Canola or vegetable oil, for frying

Extra-virgin olive oil, for frying

2 tsp. fine sea salt

1 1/2 tsp. pepper

Lemon wedges, for serving

1. **TO PURGE AND CLEAN THE RAZOR CLAMS:** Mix the kosher salt with 1 gal. cold water until the salt dissolves; add the cornmeal. Add the clams and let stand for 2 hours. Bring a pot of water to boiling, and fill a large bowl with very cold water. Put your clams in a large colander in the sink. Slowly pour boiling water over the clams, long enough for the shells to pop open, 5 to 10 seconds. Do not soak in the boiling water, or the meat will become tough. Immediately transfer the clams to the bowl of cold water, and remove the meat from the shells. With small scissors, snip and trim away the dark parts of the clams: the tip of the siphon, then, after cutting the clam lengthwise, the gills and the digestive tract.

2. Put the flour in a wide, shallow bowl. In a second bowl, whisk the eggs with the lemon juice. In a mini food processor, combine the panko and parmesan and pulse to a fine texture. Transfer to a third bowl.

3. Preheat the oven to its lowest setting and put a paper towel–lined baking sheet inside to warm. In a large nonstick sauté pan or large deep skillet (such as well-seasoned cast iron), bring 2 in. of combined canola and olive oil to 360°, measured on a deep-fry thermometer. Working with half of the clams, season them with half the salt and pepper. Dredge each clam in flour, then the egg mixture, then coat with the panko mixture, pressing crumbs into clams; gently shake off the extra, and transfer the breaded clams to a baking sheet. (The breading will be quite thick.) Repeat to season and bread the other half of the clams.

4. Slide several of the clams gently into the hot oil, working around the pan in a clockwise direction. When the bottom of the first piece is deep golden brown, gently turn over with a metal spatula in order to catch any crust that might try to stick. Repeat with the other pieces and cook until the other side is also deep golden brown, 1 to 2 minutes total. When done, transfer to the baking sheet, reheat the oil to 360°, then fry the remaining clams. Serve immediately, with wedges of lemon.

*Atlantic jackknife clams are also known as Atlantic razor clams or bamboo clams. Pacific and Atlantic razor clams are very different from hard-shell clams such as littlenecks; don't sub in hard-shell clams for this recipe. Razor clams can be very sandy, so be sure to purge and clean them.

PER SERVING 584 Cal., 55% (324 Cal.) from fat; 32 g protein; 37 g fat (9.3 g sat.); 32 g carbo (1.3 g fiber); 1,632 mg sodium; 154 mg chol.

Grays Harbor National Wildlife Refuge

HOQUIAM

This quiet and beautiful haven is a superb spot for bird-watching any time, but especially during the spring migration of shorebirds. The Sandpiper Trail, a wooden boardwalk that's 2 miles round-trip, leads out to the estuary, mudflats, and salt marshes through a forest full of willow, alder, cottonwood— and songbirds. Precious habitats, preserved. Paulson Rd., south of State 109; fws.gov/ refuge/grays_harbor

Stop 3

OCEAN CREST RESORT

Moclips

4659 State 109
Moclips, WA

(360) 276-4465

oceancrestresort.com

The calamitous June 2011 electrical fire that destroyed the restaurant at this cedar-sided, dog-friendly beachside resort took more than just a structure. "The original restaurant grew up from Grandma's one-bedroom home, where she raised her four children," says Jess Owen, grandson of the resort's founder, Barbara Curtright. "There was a lot of history there." (He had started working in the kitchen at age 11.) Jess, with his extended family, including his wife, Sara, and mother (another Barbara), worked tirelessly to rebuild the restaurant on the same footprint (with the same incredible views), to make it a shiny, well-equipped reality (with a much larger kitchen). Back in 1953, Grandma Barbara and her first husband bought what were then called the Ocean Crest Cottages. In 1963, when Barbara's second husband (the first Jess) convinced her to open a restaurant in their house, guests ordered dinner upon reserving a room. Now the extensive wine list wins awards and the food is perhaps the best you'll encounter in this corner of Washington. At sunset, relax in the beautiful new dining room and watch the silhouetted shadows of dogs and their humans frolicking on the huge beach at the foot of the tree-edged bluffs.

Peppered Wild Salmon
with Balsamic Strawberries

SERVES 4 ❖ 15 MINUTES

Sometimes, restaurant dishes don't translate to the home cook in user-friendly fashion, but this is one of those glorious examples that illustrate the precise opposite: a sublimely simple and delicious dish that requires no fancy equipment or hard-to-find ingredients. Indeed, there are so few parts here, it's of utmost importance that every item is of top quality and seasonality.

2 tbsp. best-quality maple syrup

2 tbsp. best-quality balsamic vinegar

4 ripe, in-season strawberries (about 4 oz.), thinly sliced, vertically

Four 7- to 8-oz. fillets wild salmon (about 1 in. thick at the widest point), skin removed, very cold

Extra-virgin olive-oil cooking spray

1¼ tsp. fine sea salt

1 tsp. pepper, or more to taste

2 tsp. slivered fresh basil

1. Prepare a charcoal or gas grill for medium-high heat (about 450°). In a small grill-proof saucepan, combine the maple syrup and balsamic vinegar; add the strawberries and swirl to coat. Brush the grill grates clean.

2. Coat both sides of each salmon fillet with oil spray, and season evenly with salt and pepper. Place the fillets on the grill with the flesh side (the prettier side) down. Grill for 3 minutes without moving or shifting, then turn with a metal spatula and grill until firm to the touch and opaque at the center, 3 to 5 minutes more (cooking times will depend on the thickness of the fillets, temperature of the grill, and desired doneness). Transfer to plates and immediately place the pan of maple-balsamic strawberries on the hottest part of the grill; swirl for a minute or 2, until the liquid is steaming. Spoon some strawberries and plenty of juices over each salmon fillet, and scatter with a little basil.

PER SERVING 365 Cal., 36% (130 Cal.) from fat; 45 g protein; 14 g fat (2.2 g sat.); 10 g carbo (0.7 g fiber); 557 mg sodium; 125 mg chol. GF/LC

Al's Hum-Dinger

HOQUIAM

The teensy clapboard building (no indoor seating) looks like it would fly away in a high wind, and the staff is low on people skills, but the shakes are made with real ice cream, the fries are fresh (don't forget the "fry sauce"), and the burgers will take you back to the '60s. 104 Lincoln St.; (360) 533-2754

Lots of lodgings claim a "family-style" welcome; OCR just kinda naturally feels like home—only nicer.

Grandma's Famous Clam Chowder

SERVES 6 TO 8 ❋ 2 HOURS, 20 MINUTES

Early on, the Ocean Crest Cottages did a brisk business only on Saturday nights. To encourage visitors to come out earlier, Barbara served her version of clam chowder, gratis, to Friday night guests—and it worked! Her clam chowder has never been off the menu since. She still runs and provisions the resort gift shop, bringing along the sharp eye for decor she developed as owner of a gift shop in the Sea-Tac area after WWII.

3 slices thick-cut smoked bacon, cut into ¼-in. dice

3 fresh flat-leaf parsley sprigs

2 fresh thyme sprigs

2 bay leaves

2 pts. shelled fresh clams, chopped, with all their liquor; or 2 pts. best-quality clam strips, chopped; or 2 (6.5-oz.) cans best-quality chopped clams

12 oz. Yukon Gold potatoes (about 4 small), peeled and cut into ½-in. dice

1 small white or yellow onion, cut into ½-in. dice

1 stalk celery, cut into ¼-in. dice

1 tsp. fine sea salt, or your favorite seasoning salt, plus more to taste

¼ tsp. pepper, plus more to taste

2 cups heavy cream

2 tbsp. finely snipped chives

1. In a dutch oven set over medium heat, fry the bacon until crisp. Using a slotted spoon, transfer to a doubled layer of paper towels.

2. Make a bouquet garni using a small piece of kitchen string: Tie the parsley sprigs, thyme sprigs, and bay leaves together. Put in the dutch oven and add 3 cups cold water, the clams, potatoes, onion, celery, salt, and pepper. Set over medium heat, add the cooked bacon, and bring to a simmer. Reduce the heat to its lowest setting and keep the soup at a bare simmer (use a heat diffuser if necessary to keep the soup just below an active simmer). Cook, partially covered, for 2 hours, stirring occasionally.

3. Keep the heat at the lowest possible setting, discard the bouquet garni, and stir in the cream. Allow the chowder to heat through, stirring, for 2 to 3 minutes. Remove from the heat; taste for seasoning and adjust with salt and pepper if necessary. Ladle the chowder into warm bowls and scatter with chives.

PER SERVING 284 Cal., 76% (217 Cal.) from fat; 7.2 g protein; 24 g fat (14 g sat.); 11 g carbo (0.9 g fiber); 618 mg sodium; 94 mg chol. GF

Route 11

WINDING UP THE eastern edge of the huge Olympic Peninsula (OP), the Hood Canal's protected waters and currents create an ideal environment for oysters. Tiny towns cater to tourists who come for views, oysters, and water sports. At Brinnon, the road begins angling up into a mountainous interior and toward the tiny town of *Quilcene*. Here, oyster hatcheries have replaced the old timber industry, which left its massive relics behind.

Port Townsend was once envisioned as the largest harbor on the West Coast—city fathers imagined an elegant "City of Dreams." Imposing brick and stone Victorian buildings were begun, then when things went bust because the railroad stopped short of town, owners pulled down the upper stories (thus, many of them look oddly short for their scale). The historic downtown abounds with bookstores, yoga and massage centers, coffeehouses, galleries, and an impressive choice of eateries. It's now a City of Dreams for refugees from Seattle, who cherish the stunning architecture yet enjoy the small-city feel.

Heading west along the top of the OP, the Olympic range towers on the left; on the right, the terrain slopes gently down to the sea, leaving plenty of room for arable land. The charming little town of *Sequim* ("Lavender Capital of the World") boasts a mild climate—nourishing to animals as well as produce. There's a strong presence of Native American tribal art, language, and culture, plus roadside stands selling elk and buffalo jerky. Now busy with tourists rather than lumberjacks, the still rather industrial city of *Port Angeles* is a jumping-off point for ferries to Vancouver Island, B.C., and the perfect base for exploring Olympic National Park.

Dungeness Spit
p. 235

Olympic National
Park Visitor Center
p. 241

Sweet Laurette
Café & Bistro
p. 226

Owl Sprit
Cafe
p. 228

PORT ANGELES

SEQUIM

PORT TOWNSEND

101

20

19

Michael's
Seafood &
Steakhouse
p. 238

Alder
Wood
Bistro
p. 232

Blondie's
Plate
p. 235

104

101
Brewery
p. 222

Hurricane
Ridge
p. 242

Timberhouse
p. 220

101

QUILCENE

Mt. Walker
Viewpoint
p. 225

BRINNON

Hama Hama
Oyster
Company
p. 222

101

LILLIWAUP

TIMBERHOUSE

Quilcene

295534 U.S. 101
Quilcene, WA

(360) 765-0129

olympictimberhouse.
com

Virtually every surface in this massive rustic lodge is wood, and most of it came from Quilcene. Refurbished farm tools and locally hunted animal heads adorn the cedar-paneled walls, while huge Doug fir beams hold up the soaring roof. Table-tops are 4-inch-thick, live-edge old-growth fir and maple. In 1977, timber crew boss Wally Pederson wanted a place for his men to eat, so he brought his sawmill, cut and milled the trees, and built this imposing yet warmly welcoming eatery.

Paul Schmidt bought the place in 2000, thinking he might live in it, but "the locals didn't take too well to that idea." So Paul spent a year polishing up the incredible smorgasbord of wood and adding a new kitchen and hardwood floors. It's definitely a destination restaurant (the population of Quilcene is 591), and repeat customers always want "their" server and "their" table, often for anniversaries and birth-days. The wait staff are of the long-term variety (20 to 30 years!), and there's an inviting family feeling in this elegant space, where the quality of food and chilled adult beverages is paramount.

Quilcene Blackberry Cobbler

SERVES 8 TO 10 ❖ **ABOUT 40 MINUTES**

Washington is berry country, but—though it pains me to admit it—this dark and richly fruity, crunchy-sweet dessert also works very well with frozen blackberries. In the restaurant, the cobbler is served in individual baking dishes—which I just love because you don't have to fight over who got more topping. To serve it this way at home, divide the filling among eight individual baking dishes, spooning 1 cup of filling into each, then divide the topping among the dishes and bake for about 20 minutes.

1. Preheat the oven to 375°. Butter a 9- by 13-in. baking dish.

2. **MAKE THE FILLING:** In a large mixing bowl, gently stir together the blackberries, sugar, flour, and lemon zest until thoroughly combined. Smooth the blackberry mixture into the prepared baking dish.

3. **MAKE THE TOPPING:** In a bowl, combine the dry ingredients and blend together well. Whisk the egg and cream in a small glass measuring pitcher. Scatter the butter over the dry ingredients and cut in with two knives or a pastry cutter. When the mixture resembles coarse meal, add the egg mixture and blend with a fork, just until it comes together. (It will be the consistency of thick drop batter.)

4. Drop the topping by the spoonful evenly over the filling. Bake until the topping is golden and cooked through, about 25 to 35 minutes. Serve hot, topped with ice cream.

PER SERVING (WITHOUT ICE CREAM) 270 Cal., 34% (92 Cal.) from fat; 4.3 g protein; 10 g fat (5.9 g sat.); 43 g carbo (7.2 g fiber); 177 mg sodium; 50 mg chol. LC/LS/V

Filling

3 lbs. fresh or thawed frozen blackberries

3/4 cup sugar

3 tbsp. all-purpose flour

Zest of 1/2 lemon

Topping

1 cup all-purpose flour

3/4 tsp. kosher salt

2 tbsp. sugar

1 tsp. baking powder

1 large egg

1/2 cup heavy cream

1/4 cup very cold unsalted butter, cut into small pieces

Vanilla-bean ice cream, for serving

Hama Hama Oyster Company

LILLIWAUP

After you tire of saying "Lilliwaup" over and over, stop for cold beer and perfect oysters right beside the Hood Canal (outdoors only; indoors is just a tiny shop). Expertly grilled, they're topped with garlic-herb or garlic-chipotle butter, and these may have been the best of the drive. With shucked-just-for-you-raw, stick to lemon and Tabasco. 35846 U.S. 101; hamahamaoysters.com

101 Brewery at Twana Roadhouse

QUILCENE

It seems fair to say most people who stop to eat in the tiny town of Quilcene are on their way to somewhere else. Happily, this unpretentious little family-run brewery is tailor-made for feeding and watering hungry travelers. Housemade microbrews go down nicely with the fried oysters and handmade burgers. 294793 U.S. 101; 101brewery.com

Pan-Fried Oysters

SERVES 2 TO 4 AS AN APPETIZER ❖ ABOUT 10 MINUTES (IF OYSTERS HAVE BEEN SHUCKED)

I'm hard-pressed to remember anything more idyllic from my Big Drive than sitting at the woodsy bar at the Timberhouse, sipping a glass of dry Washington Sauvignon Blanc, and sinking my teeth into crispy Hama Hama oysters from just down Route 101. If you can secure wonderful tiny Pacific oysters, and fry them in very clean, very hot oil, you can easily reproduce this at home, even if your house doesn't boast a soaring cedar-paneled bar. But don't forget the Washington wine. Turn these into a main course with coleslaw and French fries.

Canola or vegetable oil, for frying

1 cup club soda, plus more as needed

¾ cup rice flour

¾ tsp. fine sea salt

¼ tsp. pepper

⅛ tsp. cayenne

12 extra-small Pacific oysters, preferably Hama Hama, shucked

Lemon wedges and cocktail sauce, for serving

1. Preheat the oven to 200°. Line a baking sheet with a double layer of paper towels and set in oven to warm. In a small saucepan or small deep frying pan over medium-high heat, warm 2 in. of oil until it registers 380° on a deep-fry thermometer. Ideally, have on hand a splatter screen.

2. In a shallow bowl, gently mix the club soda into the rice flour. Add more soda if needed to make the batter the consistency of heavy cream. Season with salt, pepper, and cayenne. When the oil is hot, quickly dredge an oyster in the seasoned rice flour mix and shake off the excess. Very gently slide the oyster into the hot oil and proceed to dredge and fry the remaining oysters, 1 at a time. Be sure not to crowd the pan, and don't let the oil cool down too much.

3. Do not turn the oysters over; as soon as the bottom side is crisp and slightly golden, 45 to 60 seconds, transfer each oyster cooked side up to the baking sheet and keep warm while you fry the remaining oysters. Serve the oysters with lemon wedges and cocktail sauce.

PER 3-OYSTER SERVING 275 Cal., 44% (121 Cal.) from fat; 13 g protein; 14 g fat (1.5 g sat.); 24 g carbo (0.6 g fiber); 355 mg sodium; 63 mg chol. GF/LC

Cedar-Planked Wild Salmon with Beurre Blanc

SERVES 4 ❖ 15 MINUTES, PLUS 1 HOUR TO SOAK

At the Timberhouse, this dish is served with seasonal veggies and herb-roasted potatoes. You will need four small food-safe cedar planks, or one large plank that will fit in your oven. If the plank has a rough and a smooth side, cook the salmon on the smoother side. Have all the beurre blanc ingredients ready and make it while the salmon is in the oven, as it does not hold well.

Salmon

1 large or 4 small smooth cedar planks

4 (8-oz.) wild salmon fillets, about 1 in. thick

Extra-virgin olive oil

2 tsp. seafood rub

Beurre Blanc

1/2 cup medium-dry white wine, such as Chardonnay or Viognier

1 shallot, thinly sliced

1/3 cup heavy cream

10 tbsp. very cold unsalted butter, cut into 10 pieces

Pinch *each* of ground white pepper and sugar

1/4 tsp. fine sea salt

1 lemon wedge

1 tbsp. snipped chives

1. Soak a 1/2-in.-thick cedar plank in warm water for 1 hour. Preheat the oven to 450°. Warm the dinner plates briefly in the oven.

2. COOK THE SALMON: Rub the salmon with some oil and the seafood rub, then set on the plank skin side down. Put the plank directly on the oven rack and roast for 8 to 12 minutes, or until salmon is almost opaque. Transfer to warm plates.

3. WHILE THE SALMON IS ROASTING, MAKE THE BEURRE BLANC: In a small saucepan, combine the wine and shallot. Over medium heat, bring to a simmer and cook until almost all the wine has evaporated, 4 to 5 minutes; retrieve the shallot with a slotted spoon and discard. Add the cream and reduce over medium heat until thickened, 2 to 3 minutes. Reduce the heat to medium-low and stir in the butter, 2 pieces at a time, stirring constantly, until all the butter has been absorbed. Season with the pepper, sugar, salt, and a squeeze of lemon.

4. Spoon some of the beurre blanc over the salmon. Scatter with the chives and serve, passing any additional sauce alongside.

PER SERVING 776 Cal., 71% (553 Cal.) from fat; 50 g protein; 62 g fat (29 g sat.); 2.4 g carbo (0 g fiber); 299 mg sodium; 267 mg chol. GF/LS

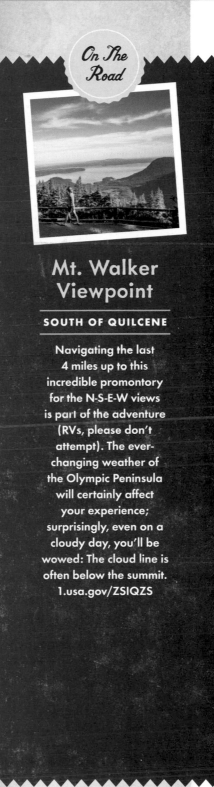

Mt. Walker Viewpoint

SOUTH OF QUILCENE

Navigating the last 4 miles up to this incredible promontory for the N-S-E-W views is part of the adventure (RVs, please don't attempt). The ever-changing weather of the Olympic Peninsula will certainly affect your experience; surprisingly, even on a cloudy day, you'll be wowed: The cloud line is often below the summit. 1.usa.gov/ZSIQZS

SWEET LAURETTE CAFÉ & BISTRO

Port Townsend

1029 Lawrence St.
Port Townsend, WA

(360) 385-4886

sweetlaurette.com

Laurette Feit's slice of homestyle goodness, on an eclectic/charming shopping street in uptown Port Townsend, is slightly schizo, but that only makes me love it more. The Carhartt's Breakfast Special offers a $1 discount to anyone who comes in wearing those quintessential overalls. And yet (in a sign of immense class, IMHO), the tea comes in a Real Porcelain Pot. Laurette started out across the street in a tiny storefront, where she made cakes and pastries from scratch and fulfilled all viable requests at the two minuscule tables. Nothing's changed now that she's upgraded to the current shabby-chic space with mix-and-match tablecloths, high ceilings with windows to match, and dark wainscoting above a scuffed wood floor. But it's not just breakfast anymore. "We outgrew the new space the day we opened in 2002," she says. Adding a bistro next door allowed for dinner service and a small bar, and this ex–organic farmer and refugee from Chicago still cooks almost everything herself.

Farmers' Market Scramble

SERVES 4 ❖ 15 MINUTES

The mix of vegetables in this recipe is firmly dictated by the seasonal farmers' market bounty. Some of Laurette's favorites include broccolini, kale, purple cabbage, thinly sliced delicata squash, cherry tomatoes, green beans, and sugar snap peas. Laurette says, "Cooking the eggs separately ensures a beautiful scramble, with fluffy, fully cooked eggs. I think when the eggs are cooked with the veggies, you lose the definition of the dish and the individual identity of the very colorful produce. If the eggs are scrambled right onto the veggies, it's a bit more work to fully cook them, and you risk overcooking everything."

1. **MAKE THE BASIL PESTO:** Layer the ingredients in a food processor in the order listed. Pulse until smooth and creamy. Use immediately, or transfer to a glass or ceramic container, cover with plastic wrap actually touching the surface of the pesto, and chill. The pesto may discolor slightly.

2. In a large nonstick frying pan, warm half of the oil over medium heat. Sauté the vegetables until almost completely cooked through but still with a little bite and bright color, 3 to 5 minutes depending on the variety and size of the vegetables chosen. Remove from the heat and stir in the feta and 1/2 cup basil pesto; season very lightly with salt (the feta is salty) and pepper. Cover the pan.

3. Place a medium nonstick frying pan over medium-high heat and add the remaining oil. Whisk the eggs with 1/4 cup water. When the pan is nice and hot, pour in the eggs and use a heatproof rubber spatula to stir constantly until the eggs are fluffy and set to your liking. Pour the cooked eggs into the vegetables and stir gently to blend; do not overmix. Serve at once.

PER SERVING 661 Cal., 83% (549 Cal.) from fat; 21 g protein; 63 g fat (13 g sat.); 9 g carbo (2.9 g fiber); 585 mg sodium; 445 mg chol. GF/V

Basil Pesto

1/2 cup extra-virgin olive oil

2 garlic cloves

1 1/2 cups (about 1 1/2 oz.) fresh basil leaves, stems removed

1 cup (about 1 oz.) fresh spinach leaves, stems removed

1/4 cup grated parmesan cheese

1/4 cup walnuts, coarsely chopped

1/4 tsp. *each* kosher or fine sea salt and pepper

1/4 cup extra-virgin olive oil or unsalted butter

4 cups mixed vegetables (see note), cut into bite-size pieces

1/2 cup feta cheese, crumbled

Fine sea salt and pepper

8 large eggs, preferably organic and free-range

On The Road

Owl Sprit Cafe

PORT TOWNSEND

Fine-dining spots have an edge on local sourcing because they can pass on the cost to patrons. But the casual Owl Sprit Cafe local-sources ingredients because it's important; even the beef for burgers comes from 10 miles away. PT peeps know the cafe's exceptional soups, salads, and sandwiches are top-notch, the prices are fair, and the welcome is warm. 218 Polk St.; owlsprit.com

Blueberry Dutch Baby with Lemon Curd

SERVES 3 TO 4 ❖ 45 MINUTES, PLUS 1 HOUR TO REST

Laurette Feit has tapped into the artistic heart of historic, picturesque Port Townsend with her neighborhoody, homey spot. This showstopping breakfast "pancake" will amply reward the intrepid traveler who seeks out her very personal restaurant, on a block filled with similarly unique shops and services. Or make it at home! You'll be amazed at the puff of this tasty treat.

Lemon Curd

Zest of 2 lemons

1/2 cup lemon juice

3/4 cup sugar

2 large eggs

1/2 cup unsalted butter, cut into 4 pieces

Batter

3/4 cup all-purpose flour

1 tbsp. sugar

1/4 tsp. fine sea salt

3 large eggs

3/4 cup whole milk

1 tsp. vanilla extract

2 tbsp. melted unsalted butter or vegetable oil

1 cup fresh or frozen blueberries

Powdered sugar, for serving

1. **MAKE THE LEMON CURD:** In the top of a double boiler or in a heatproof bowl, whisk together the lemon zest, juice, sugar, and eggs. Add the butter and set the bowl over a saucepan of simmering water. Cook the mixture, whisking constantly, until thickened, about 20 minutes. Strain through a fine-mesh sieve into a bowl. Put into an airtight container and chill until ready to use.

2. **MAKE THE BATTER:** In a large bowl, combine flour, sugar, and salt. In a large glass measuring pitcher, whisk together the eggs, milk, and vanilla. Gently whisk the wet ingredients into the dry ingredients until everything is thoroughly blended. Cover and let stand at room temperature for 1 hour or, preferably, transfer to the refrigerator and let rest for 2 to 3 hours.

3. About 20 minutes before the end of the resting time, preheat the oven to 450°. When the oven is very hot, put in a 10-in. cast-iron skillet for 10 minutes, to thoroughly preheat. Working quickly, with all ingredients at hand, pull the skillet out of the oven with oven mitts and set on the stovetop or a heatproof trivet. Pour in the melted butter and swirl the pan (use caution; it will spatter). Whisk the batter to smooth out. Pour in the batter, scatter the blueberries over the top, and return the pan to the oven.

4. Bake until the Dutch baby is puffed up and golden brown around the edges and set in the center, about 15 minutes. Sift with powdered sugar. Divide among plates and top with lemon curd. Yum!

MAKE AHEAD: The batter can be kept, covered and chilled, up to 3 hours. The lemon curd can be kept, covered and chilled, up to 2 weeks.

PER SERVING 648 Cal., 50% (327 Cal.) from fat; 12 g protein; 37 g fat (21 g sat.); 70 g carbo (1.9 g fiber); 208 mg sodium; 345 mg chol. LS/V

Eggs Rosa

SERVES 4 ❖ ABOUT 20 MINUTES, PLUS 35 MINUTES TO COOK AND 2 HOURS TO COOL POLENTA (OPTIONAL)

Laurette makes her own polenta for this filling, colorful dish, and you may want to try it yourself if you have time to prepare it the night before, so it will set up nice and firm. Supermarkets now sell tubes of firm polenta, which can easily be sliced into nice thick disks and substituted, if you are in a pinch.

Polenta (see note)

1½ tbsp. unsalted butter

1 tsp. fine sea salt

¼ tsp. white or black pepper

1 cup polenta

2 tbsp. extra-virgin olive oil

6 tbsp. coarsely grated parmesan cheese, plus extra for garnish

4 sweet or hot Italian chicken sausages, fully cooked, halved lengthwise

2 tsp. white vinegar

8 large eggs

Pepper

1 cup pico de gallo

2 tbsp. slivered fresh basil

1. **IF YOU ARE MAKING THE POLENTA:** In a large saucepan, combine 4 cups water, the butter, salt, and pepper; bring to a boil. Reduce the heat so the water is just simmering. Whisking all the time, pour the polenta into the water in a thin stream. When all the polenta has been incorporated and the mixture is smooth, 3 to 5 minutes, switch to a wooden spoon.

2. Reduce the heat to very, very low and stir frequently for about 30 minutes, until the polenta is so thick that the spoon will stand upright for a second or 2. Remove from the heat and scoop the hot polenta into a 7- by 10-in. roasting pan or baking dish, smoothing to a 1-in. thickness. Cool for about 2 hours at room temperature, or overnight in the refrigerator.

3. Preheat the oven to 200°. Cut 4 slices of polenta, each about 3½ by 5 in. and 1 in. thick. Put a large, heavy frying pan over medium-high heat and add 1 tbsp. oil. Add the polenta slices and cook until crisp and golden brown on both sides, about 6 minutes, turning over once. Scatter the top of each piece with 1½ tbsp. parmesan. Cover the pan with a lid and remove from the heat. Let stand for 1 to 2 minutes, until the cheese melts. Transfer the polenta slices to a large platter and keep warm in the oven; warm four plates too.

4. Wipe out the pan with a paper towel and add the remaining tbsp. oil. Over medium heat, cook the sausage halves until browned on both sides and warmed through, 4 to 5 minutes. Transfer to the platter with the polenta slices, and keep warm.

5. In a wide saucepan with a tight-fitting lid, bring 3 in. of water to a very gentle simmer and add the vinegar. Crack the eggs 1 at a time just above the surface of the water. Cover the pan and cook for 3 minutes, or until the whites are just set.

6. **WHILE THE EGGS ARE POACHING, ASSEMBLE THE PLATES:** Place a slice of polenta on each of the warm plates, season with pepper, and top with 2 sausage halves. With a slotted spoon, remove the eggs from the poaching water; rest the spoon on a folded paper towel for a moment to drain excess water, before placing 2 eggs atop the sausages on each plate. Top with pico de gallo. Scatter with fresh basil and additional parmesan.

PER SERVING (INCLUDING POLENTA) 595 Cal., 50% (299 Cal.) from fat; 36 g protein; 34 g fat (11 g sat.); 39 g carbo (2.7 g fiber); 1,792 mg sodium; 513 mg chol.

ALDER WOOD BISTRO

Sequim

139 W. Alder St.
Sequim, WA

(360) 683-4321

alderwoodbistro.com

For years, residents of Sequim (say *skwim*) believed their peaceful little community of 6,600 people wasn't big—or touristy—enough to support a fine eatery staunchly committed to using the amazing culinary bounty of the OP. Then Gabriel and Jessica Schuenemann landed here from the San Francisco Bay Area by way of Spain, Italy, France, Turkey, Indonesia, and Switzerland—and that concept died; Alder Wood is consistently packed with locals. It's a light and airy dining room in what first appears to be a private home; walk inside and the wood-burning oven immediately clues you in: This is not *garagiste* cuisine. The wood oven is featured but not overused on the menu, and Nash Huber—a prominent local farmer—might be sitting at the table next to yours as you blissfully devour his superlative beets, broccoli, and greens. Gabriel takes a hand in every aspect of his restaurant, carefully sourcing Tamworth hogs and blending beer with a local brewery, while Jessica helms the front of house. "It takes a community to nourish a restaurant the way we choose to do it," she says. "Our people come in the back door and the front door too."

Pickled Beet Salad with Pumpkin Seeds and Goat Cheese

SERVES 4 ❖ 20 MINUTES,
PLUS AT LEAST 45 MINUTES TO ROAST AND 2 DAYS TO MARINATE

Perhaps my newfound love affair is only with golden beets (my lips are sealed). If you choose to use both red and golden beets for this salad, as at Alder Wood Bistro, they must be roasted and pickled separately, to avoid bleeding the color from the red onto the golden beets. (Unsurprisingly, I prefer using all golden beets.)

1. **PREPARE THE BEETS:** Preheat the oven to 350°. Trim off the beet greens and reserve for another use. Scrub the beets and place them in a small roasting pan. Add 1/2 cup water and cover with foil. Roast for 45 to 60 minutes, until fork-tender. Uncover and let cool slightly. When the beets are cool enough to handle, peel and cut into bite-size pieces. Transfer to a nonreactive container and add the onion.

2. In a nonreactive saucepan, combine 3/4 cup water, the vinegar, sugar, salt, and ginger. Place over low heat and stir until the sugar and salt have dissolved. Remove from the heat and let stand for 10 minutes; stir in the ice. Pour over the beets and onion, cover the container, and chill for 2 days, so the flavor can develop.

3. **MAKE THE VINAIGRETTE:** In a small bowl, whisk together the vinegar, shallot, mustard, honey, salt, and pepper until smooth. Drizzle in the oils, whisking until creamy; stir in the parsley.

4. In a large bowl, toss the salad greens with enough vinaigrette to coat them lightly. Fold in the beets (reserve the pickled onions for garnish). Divide the salad among four plates and top each portion with pumpkin seeds and goat cheese. Top with pickled onion rings, and pass the remaining vinaigrette at the table.

PER SERVING 327 Cal., 71% (232 Cal.) from fat; 7.7 g protein; 26 g fat (6.4 g sat.); 17 g carbo (3.5 g fiber); 409 mg sodium; 11 mg chol. V

Pickled Beets

4 medium or
6 small organic
red or golden beets

1/2 small red onion, thinly sliced and separated into rings

1 cup apple cider vinegar or rice vinegar

1/4 cup sugar

1 1/2 tsp. kosher salt

Walnut-size piece of fresh ginger, peeled and cut into 4 pieces

1 cup ice

Vinaigrette

2 tbsp. sherry vinegar

1 small shallot, finely chopped

3/4 tsp. Dijon mustard

1 1/2 tsp. honey

1/8 tsp. *each* fine sea salt and pepper

1/4 cup extra-virgin olive oil

1 1/2 tbsp. canola or vegetable oil

1 1/2 tsp. finely chopped fresh flat-leaf parsley

4 cups (about 4 oz.) loosely packed mixed organic salad greens, ideally local

2 tbsp. pumpkin seeds

3 to 4 oz. soft fresh goat cheese, crumbled

Marinated Roasted Veggie Pizza

MAKES 2 LARGE PIZZAS; SERVES 4 TO 6 ❧ 1 HOUR, PLUS 2 HOURS TO LET DOUGH RISE AND TO ROAST VEGETABLES

I'm not even going to ask how Jessica and Gabriel got a permit to put a wood-burning oven on a residential street in *Skwim*, but the rabid devotion of their repeat clientele shows it was worth whatever magic was involved. (Crammed with people at 6 p.m. on a Tuesday in October? Um ... these are locals.) If you've never made pizza at home, try the tips and tricks detailed here, and you'll be a convert.

Marinated Roasted Vegetables

2 small organic garlic cloves, peeled

1/2 tsp. lemon zest

2 tbsp. firmly packed mixed fresh herbs (choose from dill, oregano, parsley, tarragon, thyme)

1/4 tsp. fine sea salt

1/2 tsp. pepper

1/4 cup *each* organic extra-virgin olive oil and organic safflower oil

1 1/4 to 1 1/2 lbs. assorted seasonal organic vegetables (such as broccoli, brussels sprouts, carrots, cauliflower, fennel, red onion, rutabaga, summer squash, turnips)

1/2 cup ricotta cheese

1 tsp. white or black truffle oil or truffle salt, plus more to taste

1 3/4 lbs. Homemade Pizza Dough (page 176) or purchased pizza dough, divided into 2 balls

Extra-virgin olive oil

1/2 cup your favorite tomato sauce

8 oz. low-moisture whole-milk mozzarella, shredded

4 tsp. roughly chopped fresh oregano leaves

1. **MAKE THE MARINATED ROASTED VEGETABLES:** Preheat the oven to 500°. In a small food processor, combine the garlic, lemon zest, herbs, salt, pepper, and the oils. Pulse until the garlic is slightly chunky. (Or chop the garlic and herbs by hand and combine with the remaining ingredients.)

2. Trim the ends of the vegetables and cut them into bite-size pieces, keeping each vegetable separate from the rest; halve the brussels sprouts and slice the onions about 1/3 in. thick. Toss the longest-cooking vegetables (root vegetables such as carrots, rutabaga, and turnips) with just enough of the marinade to lightly coat all sides. Spread in an even layer on a rimmed baking sheet and roast until al dente, a total of about 10 minutes, tossing occasionally to promote even cooking. Toss the quicker-cooking vegetables (broccoli, brussels sprouts, cauliflower, fennel, onion rings) in the marinade; spread on a second rimmed baking sheet and roast for about 8 minutes. About halfway through the roasting time, toss the quickest-cooking vegetables (rapini, summer squash) in the marinade and add to the second baking sheet; roast for the final few minutes of cooking time. Cool completely, then combine in a large bowl.

3. In a small bowl, whisk the ricotta with 1 tsp. truffle oil. Taste, then add additional oil if needed (truffle oil varies in intensity; it's easier to add more than take it away).

4. Put a large unrimmed baking sheet (or use a rimmed sheet upside down) on an oven rack to preheat (it should still be at 500°; if you made the veggies ahead, preheat the oven first). Place a large sheet of parchment paper on a work surface and put 1 dough ball in the center. Dip your fingers in a little oil and proceed to press the dough from the center outward into a 15- by 10-in. oval of even thickness. If the dough gets springy and difficult to stretch, just cover with a kitchen towel and let it rest a few minutes, then press on. If you like a thick-crust pizza, allow it to rise for 10 minutes before topping.

5. Spread 1/4 cup tomato sauce evenly over the top of the pizza, leaving a 1/2-in. border. Divide the mozzarella in half. Using two-thirds of 1 portion of the mozzarella, scatter over the sauce. Arrange half of the roasted vegetables evenly over the pizza, then dollop with half of the truffled ricotta here and there. Finish with the remaining mozzarella from the first portion.

6. Using a pizza peel or unrimmed baking sheet, slide the sheet of pizza-topped parchment onto the hot baking sheet in the oven. Cook until the edges are golden and puffed and the cheese has melted; the bottom should be fully cooked. This will take between 10 and 15 minutes, depending on your oven. (Prepare the second pizza while the first is cooking.) Slide the parchment paper holding the cooked pizza onto a cooling rack so the bottom won't get soggy. After 2 to 3 minutes, slide onto a cutting board. Scatter with half the oregano and drizzle with a little olive oil; cut into wedges for serving. Bake and finish the second pizza in the same way.

PER SERVING 771 Cal., 47% (360 Cal.) from fat; 23 g protein; 41 g fat (11 g sat.); 79 g carbo (6.6 g fiber); 1,119 mg sodium; 44 mg chol. V

On The Road

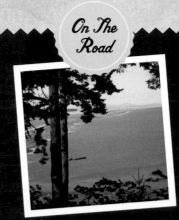

Dungeness Spit

NEAR SEQUIM

This, the longest natural sandspit in the U.S. and part of the Dungeness National Wildlife Refuge, heads 5.5 miles straight out into the Strait of Juan de Fuca. Precious habitat for salmon and seabirds and home to outrageous driftwood shapes, it's one of the most stunning hikes this occasional trekker has ever experienced (low tide only, please). Voice of America Rd. W.; fws. gov/washingtonmaritime/dungeness

Blondie's Plate

SEQUIM

A midcentury-modern eatery in a sensitively remodeled old clapboard church, Blondie's has a sophisticated menu mixing game, fish, salad, and an awesome mac 'n' cheese with more eclectic fare like pork belly and poutine. Order a Moscow Mule from the full bar, and it comes in an iced copper mug, just as it should. 134 S. Second Ave.; (360) 683-2233

Smoked Salmon Pasta "Carbonara"

SERVES 4 ❖ 1 HOUR, 20 MINUTES

Sequim hardly seems the sort of community where you'd find an oasis of creative, local-sustainable cuisine, but do go out of your way to discover this very civilized spot. Although most cookbook authors will deny this in public, we all have a short list of favorite dishes in each book. (No one wants the other recipes to feel unloved, but this is unavoidable and very personal.) This dish is at the tippy-top of "my eyes only" fave list. Make it your own.

Fried Bread Crumbs

1 tbsp. extra-virgin olive oil

1 large or 2 small garlic cloves, minced

3 oz. country-style white bread (about two 3- by 5-in. slices), crusts removed, chopped in a mini food processor

1/4 tsp. fine sea salt

Pinch of pepper

Custard

1 1/2 cups organic heavy cream

4 large whole eggs

2 large egg yolks

1 1/2 cups finely grated grana padano (about 2 oz.)

Zest of 1 lemon

1 tsp. fine sea salt

1 1/2 tsp. pepper

Carbonara

1/2 cup Caramelized Onions (page 42)

3/4 to 1 cup Marinated Roasted Vegetables (optional; page 234)

2 oz. thinly sliced prosciutto, slivered

3 garlic cloves, minced

3 tbsp. chopped mixed herbs (chives, oregano, parsley)

Pinch of red chile flakes

2 tbsp. vegetable stock or water

8 oz. dried penne pasta

8 oz. cold smoked wild salmon, slivered

Fine sea salt to taste

1/2 tsp. pepper, or to taste

1/4 cup shaved grana padano

1. **MAKE THE FRIED BREAD CRUMBS:** In a small frying pan, warm the oil over medium-low heat. Add the garlic, bread crumbs, salt, and pepper, and stir frequently until golden brown, 2 to 3 minutes; do not allow the garlic to burn. Measure out 1/2 cup bread crumbs and set aside. Cool the remaining bread crumbs, place in an airtight container, and freeze (almost indefinitely) for another use.

2. **MAKE THE CUSTARD:** In a medium saucepan, warm the cream over medium heat until it is just beginning to simmer (do not allow it to boil); remove from the heat. In a mixing bowl, whisk together the eggs and egg yolks. Whisking all the time, drizzle in about one-quarter of the warm cream mixture. Now return the egg-cream mixture to the saucepan with the remaining cream. Place over medium-low heat and whisk until the mixture thickens just enough to coat the back of a spoon (about 170° on an instant-read thermometer), about 3 minutes. Remove from the heat and let stand for 5 minutes. Strain through a fine-mesh sieve into a bowl; stir in the cheese, lemon zest, salt, and pepper.

3. Bring a large pot of lightly salted water to a boil for the pasta. In a large frying pan or sauté pan, combine the caramelized onions, roasted vegetables if using, prosciutto, garlic, herbs, and chile flakes. Place over medium heat and warm through for 2 minutes, until fragrant. Stir in the stock and remove from the heat.

4. Cook the pasta until al dente, according to the package instructions. Drain well, and add to the pan with the caramelized onions; place the pan over medium-low heat. With a rubber spatula, fold in the custard and salmon; warm through for 1 to 2 minutes, but do not allow to boil or the custard will separate. Taste for seasoning and adjust with salt and pepper if necessary (the salmon is salty). Divide among warm plates and top with the reserved 1/2 cup fried bread crumbs and the shaved cheese.

PER SERVING (NOT INCLUDING ROASTED VEGETABLES) 1,109 Cal., 55% (609 Cal.) from fat; 66 g protein; 68 g fat (31 g sat.); 62 g carbo (4 g fiber); 1,311 mg sodium; 551 mg chol.

Stop 4

MICHAEL'S SEAFOOD & STEAKHOUSE

Port Angeles

117B E. First St.
Port Angeles, WA

(360) 417-6929

michaelsdining.com

I'm thinking "speakeasy" as I finally locate the door of Michael's in the historic downtown of this ex–timber-hub city. Descending narrow stairs, the intrepid traveler to this far-northwestern spit of the continental USA is rewarded with a clubby, rich interior festooned with old album covers, vintage bar games, and Euro-bistro posters. Happily, the bar is small and cozy, the house wine ("Cuvée de Michael's") is estimable, and I get to chew the fat (figuratively) with Michael Lynch himself. Owner-proprietor since 2001, he tends bar, mans the phone, and often cooks too. The bar menu runs the gamut from duck confit to Philly cheesesteak flatbread; annual events include Michaelmas in September. It's clear this is a restaurant festively wrapped in the personality of its owner—plus his 85-year-old dad, who's a frequent fixture. Michael had no formal training except at the school of hard knocks, and the imaginative, well-executed menu has evolved from his hands-on collaboration with "three or four" chefs. Most customers are in PA for the ferry to Victoria, B.C., or access to the national park, but this spot is fast approaching the title of Destination.

Crab, Artichoke, and Spinach Dip

SERVES 6 TO 8 ❖ 20 MINUTES, PLUS 25 MINUTES TO BAKE

Sweet, tender Dungeness crab has been pricey in recent years—but of course we all believe in our Pacific Coast fisheries and want to support them so our grandchildren will still be able to taste the unique flavor of the revered Dungeness. The crustacean is superior, at least from *this* West Coaster's point of view, to the more economical Atlantic blue crab, which may be substituted in a pinch. At Michael's, this addictive dip is served in individual shallow gratin dishes, but here we make the dip in a large gratin one.

1 tsp. extra-virgin olive oil

4 oz. (about 4 cups, loosely packed) baby spinach leaves

4 oz. thawed frozen or canned artichoke hearts (about 6 small whole hearts, or half a 14-oz. can), finely chopped

2 tbsp. finely chopped jarred roasted red bell pepper

2 garlic cloves, minced

1 cup mayonnaise

2/3 cup (1 oz.) plus 2 cups (3 oz.) finely grated parmesan cheese

2/3 cup (2 oz.) coarsely shredded low-moisture mozzarella cheese

1 tsp. lemon zest

1 1/2 tsp. lemon juice

1/4 tsp. Old Bay Seasoning

1/2 tsp. fine sea salt

1/4 tsp. pepper

1 lb. fresh shelled cooked Dungeness crab, firmly squeezed to remove any excess water

Chopped fresh flat-leaf parsley leaves, for garnish

Lemon wedges, for serving

12 slices ciabatta bread (1/4 in. thick), lightly toasted

1. Warm the oil in a large nonstick pan over low heat. Add the spinach and sauté, stirring occasionally, until wilted but still bright green, 2 to 3 minutes. Remove from the heat and transfer to a fine sieve. Press down firmly with a wooden spoon to extract as much water as possible. Finely chop the spinach. Place the artichoke hearts and bell pepper in the sieve and press down firmly to remove as much water as possible. In a large bowl, mix together the spinach mixture, garlic, mayonnaise, 2/3 cup parmesan, the mozzarella, lemon zest and juice, Old Bay, salt, and pepper.

2. Preheat the oven to 375° and butter an 11- or 12-in. oval gratin or baking dish. Spread the crab in an even layer in the dish. Top with an even layer of the dip, dropping the dip in spoonfuls evenly over the crab, to avoid overblending the two mixtures when spreading. Smooth the top. Bake for 20 minutes, then scatter the remaining 2 cups parmesan evenly over the top and bake until golden brown in places and bubbling, about 5 minutes longer (or turn on the broiler and broil the top for 3 to 5 minutes until golden brown). Garnish with parsley and place lemon wedges around the edge. Serve warm with the toasted ciabatta.

PER SERVING (INCLUDING CIABATTA) 445 Cal., 46% (205 Cal.) from fat; 32 g protein; 23 g fat (7.5 g sat.); 30 g carbo (2.3 g fiber); 1,361 mg sodium; 78 mg chol.

Michael's Caesar

This recipe falls into the category of Gilding the Lily, but I have no problem with that. If we are going to town, let's go all the way. Caesar has been my go-to dinner for ages, but it hadn't ever occurred to me that blue cheese, bacon, and even steak could be right at home on a (big) plate with the Most Popular Salad of All Time. (First invented down in Tijuana—as legend has it— only a few miles south of this book's southernmost outpost, Vamos a Texcoco, page 14, i.e., firmly and gloriously on the West Coast.)

Dressing

½ cup extra-virgin olive oil

¼ cup lemon juice

3 tbsp. mayonnaise

2 tbsp. Dijon mustard

8 anchovy filets

6 garlic cloves, minced

2 tsp. red wine vinegar

2 tsp. Worcestershire sauce

½ tsp. pepper

½ cup finely grated parmesan cheese

1 (1¾-lb.) beef sirloin, or 4 individual sirloin steaks, about 7 oz. each

Extra-virgin olive oil, for brushing

Fine sea salt and pepper

4 hearts of romaine lettuce, very cold

6 oz. parmesan, shaved with a vegetable peeler

1 cup garlic croutons

4 oz. blue cheese, crumbled (optional)

8 strips thick-sliced bacon, cooked and crumbled

1 lemon, cut into wedges

1. **MAKE THE DRESSING:** In a mini food processor, combine all the ingredients for the dressing except the parmesan. Pulse to blend thoroughly. Transfer to a very large mixing bowl; fold in the parmesan.

2. Brush the steak with oil, and season all over with salt and pepper. Let stand at room temperature for 30 minutes. Prepare a charcoal or gas grill for medium-high heat (about 450°). Assemble the remaining ingredients, a steak-carving knife, and plates (but leave the romaine hearts in the refrigerator).

3. Grill the steak on each of all 4 sides, turning occasionally, until the center reaches 120° for rare or 135° for medium-rare on an instant-read thermometer. Depending on the thickness of the steak and the heat of your grill, this could take between 8 and 15 minutes total; use your thermometer to ensure success. Transfer to a cutting board and tent loosely with foil; let stand for 5 to 6 minutes while you assemble the salads.

4. Trim the root end of the romaine hearts and slice in half lengthwise. Perch one half atop the other, on a diagonal, on each of four plates (if serving more than four, slice romaine more thinly to divide evenly among plates). Drizzle the lettuce generously with the dressing. Sprinkle with parmesan, croutons, blue cheese (if using), and bacon, dividing evenly. Slice the steak about ¼ in. thick on the diagonal and overlap on top of the salad. Garnish each salad with a wedge of lemon and pass additional dressing at the table.

PER SERVING 731 Cal., 58% (427 Cal.) from fat; 59 g protein; 49 g fat (14 g sat.); 17 g carbo (4.3 g fiber); 1,292 mg sodium; 125 mg chol.

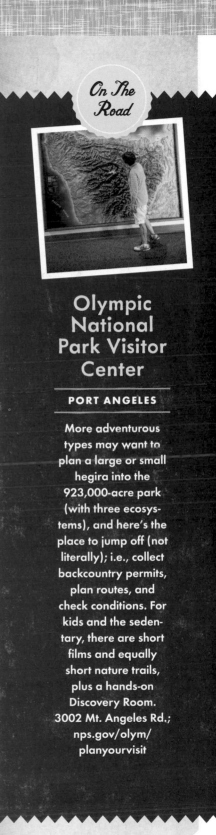

Olympic National Park Visitor Center

PORT ANGELES

More adventurous types may want to plan a large or small hegira into the 923,000-acre park (with three ecosystems), and here's the place to jump off (not literally); i.e., collect backcountry permits, plan routes, and check conditions. For kids and the sedentary, there are short films and equally short nature trails, plus a hands-on Discovery Room. 3002 Mt. Angeles Rd.; nps.gov/olym/planyourvisit

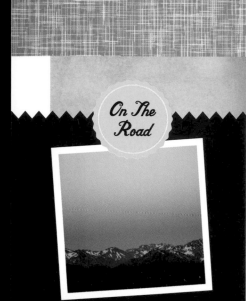

Hurricane Ridge

NEAR PORT ANGELES

At only 17 miles south of Port Angeles, this is one of the easiest ways to experience the majestic mountains of the Olympic Peninsula. Picnic areas make the viewpoint the perfect spot to take it all in, without putting on skis or boots. At 5,242 feet, the ridge is subject to dramatic weather variations. nps.gov/olym (search "Hurricane Ridge")

Bacon-Wrapped Pork Tenderloin with Worcestershire Butter

SERVES 4 ❖ 20 MINUTES, PLUS AT LEAST 30 MINUTES TO CHILL

Here is one of those restaurant dishes old-fashioned chefs used to call *à la minute* (meaning prepared to order), and it translates particularly well to the home kitchen, with spectacular results. The slow oven-finish to the pork medallions yields tender, juicy meat. And the sauce really showcases the complexity of Worcestershire—perhaps finally explaining why the method for making Worcestershire (say *whatsthisheresauce*) has been such an intensely guarded secret for multiple generations: Who would part with a recipe this great? And who knew that adding cold butter tames this punchy liquid just enough to yield a highly sophisticated sauce? Keeper! Remember to hold the butter in the refrigerator until just before serving time.

Quick Pickled Onions

½ cup *each* red wine vinegar and apple cider vinegar

1 tbsp. brown sugar

½ tsp. red chile flakes

½ tsp. kosher salt

1 small red onion, cut into rings just less than ¼ in. thick

1 (1¼-lb.) pork tenderloin

4 strips smoked bacon, halved crosswise

¼ tsp. *each* fine sea salt and pepper

½ cup Worcestershire sauce

¼ cup very cold unsalted butter, cut into 4 pieces

2 tsp. canola or vegetable oil

1. **MAKE THE PICKLED ONIONS:** In a small saucepan, combine the vinegars, brown sugar, chile flakes, and salt. Over medium-low heat, stir just until the sugar dissolves. Remove from the heat and cool to room temperature. Bring 2½ cups of water to a boil in a saucepan. Place the onions in a sieve, and slowly pour boiling water over the top, to blanch them. Put the onions in a clean pint-size glass jar and pour the vinegar mixture over the top. Chill for at least 30 minutes before using, or ideally, 2 hours.

2. Cut the pork crosswise into 8 equal medallions, each about 1½ in. thick. Wrap each medallion with a strip of bacon and secure it with a toothpick, to hold the bacon in place (don't worry if it doesn't go all the way around). Season the cut sides with a little salt and pepper. Pour the Worcestershire into a small, heavy saucepan and set aside on the stove. Put the pieces of butter on a small plate, and keep refrigerated.

3. Preheat the oven to 325°. Place a large ovenproof cast-iron skillet or heavy frying pan over medium-high heat and let it get very hot, about 2 minutes. Add the oil to the pan, and swirl. Add the medallions to the pan and sear for 1½ to 2 minutes per side, turning them in the order added to the pan. With tongs, turn each medallion on its edge for about 30 seconds, rotating to sear the edges in 2 to 3 places. Transfer the skillet to the oven to finish cooking, until the pork is almost firm to the touch and reaches 145° in the center on an instant-read thermometer, about 8 minutes. Remove from the oven and let rest for 5 minutes; remove toothpicks. (While meat is resting, warm four plates in the oven.)

4. While the medallions finish cooking in the oven, warm the Worcestershire over medium-high heat, until steaming; remove from the heat and add the pieces of butter all at once, swirling the pan constantly until the mixture is smooth and glossy; do not return to the heat or the sauce will separate. Serve 2 medallions on each warm plate. Spoon some of the sauce over the top and scatter with pickled onion rings.

PER SERVING 357 Cal., 50% (178 Cal.) from fat; 30 g protein; 20 g fat (9.6 g sat.); 12 g carbo (0.4 g fiber); 659 mg sodium; 115 mg chol. GF/LC

Route 12

VICTORIA

ON THE CAR FERRY FROM Port Townsend to Whidbey Island, sparkling sun-on-water lures me to the prow with a few other newbies; the regulars stay indoors. Once on the island, before I reach the town of *Langley*, I stop at the (proclaimed-by-me) Driftwood Capital of the World, on the spit that separates Admiralty Inlet from Crockett Lake. This veritable carpet of driftwood is 2 feet deep and stretches for miles.

Langley is only an hour from Seattle, and that is evident in the shop and restaurant offerings on the main street, as well as with the presence of the exclusive Inn at Langley, and the generally well-kept look to the residential streets.

At the north end of Whidbey, at Deception Pass, a bridge conveys me to Fidalgo Island (too bad; I could get used to ferries), and the road affords stunning views of inlets and bays. After the mountains, *Anacortes* at first appears oddly flat, but the vibe is decidedly cutting edge in this "Brooklyn West," where live music flows freely along with community theater, coffee, tequila, and Anacortes Brewery's finest nectar. (Ignore the *Blade Runner*–esque skyline to your east; it's a massive refinery. Or try to see it as a hip sculpture-cum–light show.)

Again there's no need for a ferry, as I make my way back to the mainland. I adore the radical-rural town of Edison, where tattoos abound and young bikers (the kind with motors) and farmers tend to be one and the same. I head up to *Chuckanut Drive*—often called "Washington's Big Sur"—and it lives up to its glowing press; sea sparkles between the trees, and every deep curve conceals a pocket beach.

(Postscript: The Canadian border is only 35 miles away, so I think I'll drift to a stop, slurp oysters pulled from the tidal flats, and sip a glass of icy Chablis at one of the "Best Places to Kiss.")

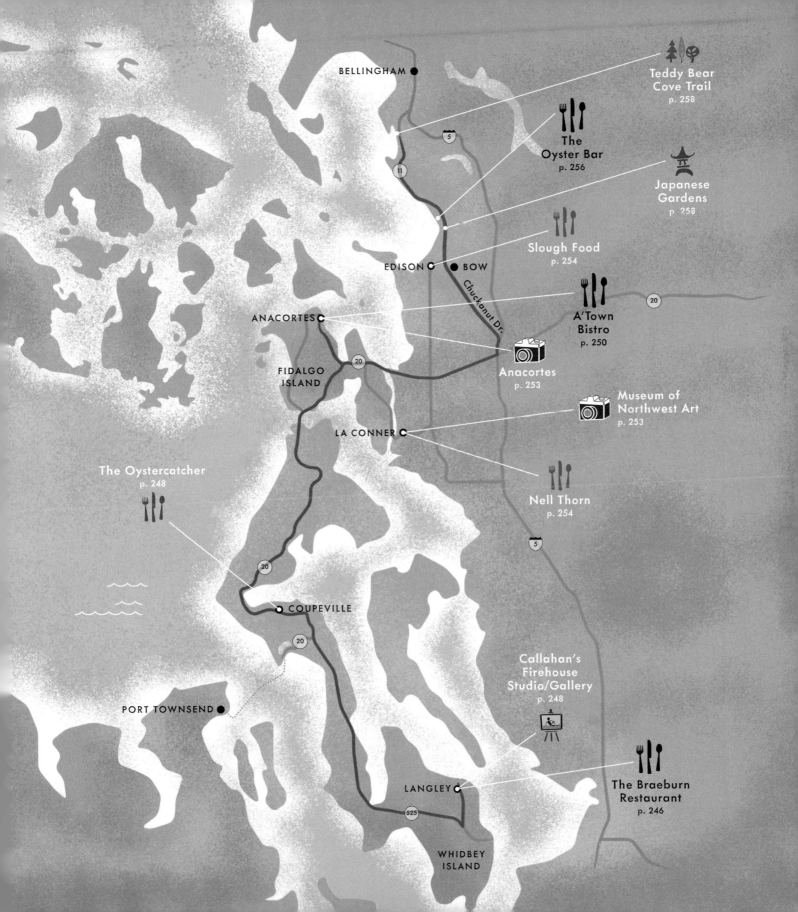

BELLINGHAM

Teddy Bear
Cove Trail
p. 258

The Oyster Bar
p. 256

Japanese
Gardens
p. 258

Slough Food
p. 254

EDISON   BOW

Chuckanut Dr.

A'Town
Bistro
p. 250

ANACORTES

FIDALGO
ISLAND

Anacortes
p. 253

Museum of
Northwest Art
p. 253

LA CONNER

The Oystercatcher
p. 248

Nell Thorn
p. 254

COUPEVILLE

Callahan's
Firehouse
Studio/Gallery
p. 248

PORT TOWNSEND

The Braeburn
Restaurant
p. 246

LANGLEY

WHIDBEY
ISLAND

THE BRAEBURN RESTAURANT

Langley, Whidbey Island

197D Second St.
Langley, WA

(360) 221-3211

braeburnlangley.com

The decor is blond wood ladder-back chairs, melamine tables, and colorful '70s-era cute, but the open kitchen reveals tattooed and do-rag–wearing chefs discussing the provenance of their produce, and the menu confirms a rapt attention to local bounty, plus a sense of humor (the Three-Digit Grilled Cheese Sandwich: three slices of raisin bread layered with crisp bacon and extra-sharp cheddar). In good weather, there's a dog-friendly patio in back, plus seating in front on busy-adorable Second Street. When it's chilly, belly up to the potbellied stove in the art-filled front room. Owner Lisa Carvey once waited tables here, so she has an insider's intuition for what works, and mason-jar mimosas definitely do. "I followed a boy here from Vermont," she says, "and fell in love instantly." My visit to The Braeburn happened on an autumnal midweek morning, when the sleepy charm of Langley town was at its best; I fell for the Cowboy Burrito. Via the Mukilteo ferry, Langley is only "an hour from Seattle"; on weekends, be warned. The corned-beef mash (on mashed potatoes) has made headlines, and even if you have to wait, can be yours just for the asking.

Cowboy Burritos

SERVES 4 ❖ 20 MINUTES

Whether you are driving the coast in search of adventure or enjoying a quiet weekend at home, these ultra-plump burritos will set you up for a day of bike riding, hang gliding, surfing, or just shopping. (Langley is a shopper's paradise—if, that is, you eschew chain stores and prefer the personal and passionate.)

1. Place the tortillas on a work surface and distribute the cheese over each, leaving a 1/4-in. border.

2. In a large cast-iron skillet or nonstick frying pan, warm the oil over medium heat. Add the bacon, jalapeño, and black beans, and sauté until the chiles are tender, about 4 minutes. Scrape into a heatproof bowl, cover with foil, and keep warm until needed. Wipe the skillet clean, return it to the heat, and add the butter. As soon as the butter melts, add the eggs and scramble until they are done to your liking.

3. Divide the scrambled eggs among the cheese-topped tortillas and sprinkle with cilantro. Top each tortilla with one-quarter of the warm bean mixture. Roll up burrito-style, tucking in the ends snugly. Wipe the skillet with a paper towel and return it to medium heat. Place the burritos seam side down in the skillet and toast until light golden brown on all sides, 1 to 2 minutes per side, using tongs to turn them (this will melt the cheese). Cut each burrito in half crosswise and serve with pico de gallo and sour cream.

4 large flour tortillas (about 12 in.)

8 oz. pepper jack cheese, shredded (2 cups)

2 tsp. canola or vegetable oil

10 to 12 slices bacon, cooked, drained on paper towels, and crumbled

1 to 3 jalapeño or other green chiles, stemmed, seeded, and finely chopped

1 (14-oz.) can black beans, well rinsed and drained

1 tbsp. butter

12 large eggs, preferably pasture-raised, lightly beaten

1/4 cup finely chopped cilantro

Pico de gallo and sour cream, for serving

PER BURRITO 995 Cal., 46% (460 Cal.) from fat; 51 g protein; 51 g fat (20 g sat.); 76 g carbo (6.6 g fiber); 1,642 mg sodium; 713 mg chol.

Callahan's Firehouse Studio/Gallery

LANGLEY, WHIDBEY ISLAND

I defy any human being to walk into this cavernous ex-firehouse turned working glass-blowing studio and not want to buy a recently cooled-off work of art. Or three. Light, color, and smoothly evocative curves combine in a kaleidoscope that captures the eye, heart, and soul. Also gives all-age glass-blowing classes. 179 Second St.; callahansfirehouse.com

The Oystercatcher

COUPEVILLE, WHIDBEY ISLAND

This sophisticated spot walks the fresh-local-seasonal walk with a barely perceptible edginess. Lamb sweetbreads jostle with albacore Niçoise (when in season) and the area's game competes for attention with exquisite seafood. Seattle-adjacency means top-notch atmosphere and service in the simple clapboard house close to the harbor. 901 Grace St.; oystercatcherwhidbey.com

Veggie Hash

This popular dish varies daily, depending on what's fresh and local. When I visited, the current hash featured farm-fresh winter veggies from Willowood Farm and Deep Harvest Farm, both nearby on Whidbey Island. This rustic hash is perfect with sprouted-wheat toast and your favorite style of eggs.

Roasted Vegetables

4 oz. brussels sprouts, trimmed and halved

1 small bunch golden beets (about 6 oz.), trimmed, peeled, and roughly chopped

1 medium carrot, cut into 1-in. chunks

1 medium parsnip, cut into 1-in. chunks

3½ tbsp. extra-virgin olive oil

Fine sea salt and pepper

1 large garlic clove, minced

½ large delicata squash (about 12 oz.), sliced ¾-in. thick and slices halved crosswise, or ½ butternut squash, peeled, seeded, and cubed

1 small leek, white and light green parts only, trimmed and roughly chopped

1 small bunch (about 5 oz.) Lacinato (also called Tuscan) kale, washed and roughly chopped (including ribs)

1 small bunch (about 5 oz.) rainbow Swiss chard, washed and roughly chopped (including ribs)

1½ tsp. fine sea salt

¼ tsp. pepper

1¼ tsp. best-quality curry powder or curry paste

2 tsp. medium-dry or sweet sherry

Toasted bread of your choice and 2 eggs per person, cooked any style, for serving

1. **MAKE THE ROASTED VEGETABLES:** Preheat oven to 350°. In a large metal roasting pan, combine the brussels sprouts, beets, carrot, and parsnip. Toss with 2 tbsp. oil, then season with salt and pepper to taste. Add a pinch of the garlic and roast, tossing occasionally, until caramelized and fork-tender, 45 to 50 minutes.

2. In a large frying pan, heat 1½ tbsp. oil over medium-high heat. Add the squash and leek and sauté until golden brown and tender, tossing occasionally. Add the kale, chard, salt, pepper, and the remaining garlic; toss until the greens begin to break down, 2 to 3 minutes.

3. Add the roasted vegetables, curry powder, and sherry to the frying pan. Cook for 3 to 5 minutes more, until caramelized and slightly crisp but still colorful. Serve with toast and eggs.

PER SERVING (WITHOUT TOAST AND EGGS) 177 Cal., 42% (75 Cal.) from fat; 3.0 g protein; 8.8 g fat (1.3 g sat.); 25 g carbo (5.6 g fiber); 546 mg sodium; 0 mg chol. LC/GF/VG

Stop 2

A'TOWN BISTRO

Anacortes, Fidalgo Island

418 Commercial Ave.
Anacortes, WA

(360) 899-4001

atownbistro.com

I was a goner the moment I spotted the waist-high, double-sided fireplace inside the front door of this high-ceilinged locavore haven. The decor is polished industrial barn-chic, with old tools, raw blond wood, and rustic-eclectic artwork. The burlwood bar offers a highly curated selection of spirits, seemingly every beer within a day's drive (Lost Coast Alleycat Amber is one of them), and wines from all over. Owner L. M. Libby—known as "Libby"—grew up in Maine and taught fish cooking techniques in Alaska, so seafood has been her life.

Driven from the East Coast by encroaching urbanization, she happened upon this island and knew immediately it was the place to raise her two daughters. Intending to semiretire from culinary consulting, instead she gave in to the locals, and created a restaurant. "I slept on the floor for two nights, studying the fireplace issue." An ex-president of the Anacortes Farmers Market, Libby's local/sustainable street cred is 24 karat, and the menu changes weekly, although the regulars would riot without the clam chowder or Irish pâté.

Braised Lamb Shanks with Red Wine Gravy

SERVES 4 ❖ ABOUT 30 MINUTES, PLUS 2 HOURS TO BRAISE

A few doors down from A'Town, there's a dark and mysterious tequila bar lurking invitingly behind a Mexican restaurant, like a speakeasy in Capone's Chicago. I invite you to seek it out prior to bellying up to the fantastic bar at A'Town for some warming, meaty sustenance. At the restaurant, Libby serves the lamb shanks over cheesy polenta and roasted root vegetables, but you can also serve them atop egg noodles or mashed potatoes.

4 lamb shanks
(1 lb. each)

Fine sea salt and pepper

1 tbsp. extra-virgin olive oil

1 yellow onion, coarsely chopped

1 medium parsnip, peeled and cut into 1-in. lengths

2 medium carrots, peeled and cut into 1-in. lengths

3 stalks celery, thickly sliced

5 garlic cloves, peeled

3 cups dry red wine

1 tsp. red wine vinegar, plus more to taste

12 black peppercorns

3 bay leaves

3 sprigs fresh thyme, plus chopped leaves for garnish

1. Preheat the oven to 325°. Season the lamb shanks with salt and pepper. In a large dutch oven or braising pan, warm the oil over medium-high heat. Sear the lamb on all sides until golden, about 4 minutes total. Add the onion, parsnip, carrots, celery, garlic, red wine, 1 cup water, vinegar, peppercorns, bay leaves, and thyme sprigs. Bring to a simmer.

2. Cover the pan and transfer to the oven; cook for 1½ to 2 hours, until the lamb is very tender. Remove the pan from the oven and remove the shanks from the pan. Strain the pan juices into a large heatproof pitcher; discard the thyme and bay leaves and reserve the vegetables. Spoon off the fat from the braising juices.

3. In a blender, combine 2 cups of the braising juices with the vegetables and blend thoroughly, until completely smooth. Add any additional juices if desired, to make a smooth gravy. Return to a clean saucepan and taste for seasoning; adjust to taste with salt, pepper, and a drop or 2 of vinegar. Serve the shanks in warm bowls with the gravy, garnished with a sprinkle of thyme leaves.

PER SERVING 946 Cal., 47% (445 Cal.) from fat; 99 g protein; 50 g fat (20 g sat.); 21 g carbo (4.4 g fiber); 446 mg sodium; 361 mg chol. GF/LS

Blue Cheese Polenta Fries
with Curry Ketchup and Garlic Aioli

SERVES 4 ❖ 1 HOUR, PLUS 45 MINUTES TO ROAST AND OVERNIGHT TO CHILL

Polenta is good luck for me—my very first cookbook was all about polenta—so when I saw this dish on the menu at A'Town Bistro in funky-licious Anacortes, I was immediately sold. Sure, you have to make the polenta ahead of time, but that just means less prep time on the night you'll be serving. And don't try to serve more than four people, or everyone will wish they had more. This is insanely good!

Curry Ketchup

2 tbsp. best-quality curry powder or yellow curry paste, plus more to taste

2 tsp. lime juice, plus more to taste

1½ cups ketchup

Roasted Garlic Aioli

15 garlic cloves, unpeeled

2 tbsp. extra-virgin olive oil

½ tsp. *each* fine sea salt and pepper

1⅓ cups mayonnaise

2 tsp. finely snipped chives

Polenta Fries

2 tsp. fine sea salt

½ tsp. pepper

3 tbsp. unsalted butter

2 cups polenta

¾ cup (about 4 oz.) crumbled dry gorgonzola, or other dry blue cheese

½ cup cilantro leaves, finely chopped

Canola or vegetable oil, for deep-frying

About 1 cup corn flour

1. **MAKE THE CURRY KETCHUP:** In a bowl, whisk the curry and lime juice into a paste. Add the ketchup and blend thoroughly. Taste for flavor and adjust with curry powder and/or lime juice.

2. **MAKE THE GARLIC AIOLI:** Preheat the oven to 350°. Make a doubled layer of foil into a 6- by 6-in. square. Put the garlic in the center and bring up the sides to form a cup; place on a small rimmed baking sheet. Drizzle the cloves with the oil and sprinkle with the salt and pepper. Bring the sides all the way up and twist together to make a firm seal. Place the baking sheet in the oven and roast the garlic for 35 minutes. It should be tender and golden but not dark brown. Remove from the oven and open the top to stop the cooking. When cool enough to handle, squeeze the garlic cloves from their skins. Purée the garlic in a small food processor until smooth. Set aside 1 tbsp. garlic purée for the polenta. In a bowl, whisk the remaining puréed garlic with the mayonnaise until evenly blended. Fold in the chives.

3. **MAKE THE POLENTA FRIES:** In a large saucepan, combine 8 cups water with the reserved garlic purée, salt, pepper, and butter, and bring to a boil. Reduce the heat so the water is just simmering. Whisking all the time, pour the polenta into the water in a thin stream. When all the polenta has been incorporated and the mixture is smooth, 3 to 5 minutes, switch to a wooden spoon. Reduce the heat to very, very low and stir frequently for about 30 minutes, until the polenta is so thick that the spoon will stand upright. Remove from the heat and stir in half the blue cheese and the cilantro. Scoop the hot polenta into a 10- by 14-in. rimmed baking sheet, and smooth to a 1-in. thickness. Chill overnight in the refrigerator. Keep chilled until just before cutting and frying.

4. Prepare a deep-fryer or deep, heavy pot one-third full of oil for deep-frying. Heat the oil to 350° on a deep-fry thermometer. Cut the polenta into 3- by ½-in. sticks and arrange on a parchment paper–lined baking sheet. Dredge in corn flour to coat well. Shake off the excess and set on a clean dry baking sheet until ready to fry. In batches to avoid crowding the pan, fry the polenta sticks until golden brown, about 4 minutes per batch. Retrieve from the oil with a flat skimmer, and drain briefly on paper towels. Crisscross on plates or a platter and scatter with the remaining blue cheese. Serve with the ketchup and aioli.

PER SERVING (WITHOUT CURRY KETCHUP OR AIOLI) 753 Cal., 46% (343 Cal.) from fat; 20 g protein; 38 g fat (15 g sat.); 84 g carbo (9.2 g fiber); 1,881 mg sodium; 55 mg chol. V

Museum of Northwest Art

LA CONNER

Located in a historic waterfront town, this small museum focuses on contemporary art—mostly mid-20th century—from the entire region, ranging from found-object installations to art glass. Classes (such as foundations of feltmaking, or whimsical animals crafted in mixed media) serve the community and travelers. The shop offers nice non-cookie-cutter jewelry and crafts. 121 S. First St.; monamuseum.org

Anacortes

FIDALGO ISLAND

The vibe is shockingly hip for a town of just 15,928, perhaps because it's the jumping-off point for ferries to the San Juan Islands. Mild weather (it's in the rain shadow of Olympic Mountains) means a thriving indoor-outdoor ocean-centric lifestyle. My fave: speakeasy-esque Frida's, with a huge selection of tequilas and a historic bar. anacortes.org

On The Road

Slough Food

EDISON

In perhaps one of the smallest foodie towns in history, this spot is more wine/gourmet shop than restaurant, and the tiny menu is filled with carefully sourced and crafted salumi, cheeses, soups, and salads. In fine weather, snack on the bench out back, overlooking the soft-flowing eponymous slough. The beer and wine are mighty fine too. 5766 Cains Court; sloughfood.com

Nell Thorn

LA CONNER

Outdoor seating and a full bar complement this woodsy, locals-love-it, upscale yet casual eatery with a shady, dog-friendly deck right on the waterfront (happy hour here is a true delight). The menu is creative and meat-and-seafood-forward with some nice twists. Try the lovingly crafted seafood pastas. Whenever possible, ingredients are organic and sourced locally. 116 S. First St.; nellthorn.com

Pan-Seared Halibut with Beurre Blanc and Sweet Potato Mash

SERVES 4 ❖ 30 MINUTES

My favorite part about dining at the bar in this rustic-elegant eatery is the see-through fireplace that's the first thing you encounter upon entering—it presages all the warm and comforting things to come. Once ensconced at the bar, you can enjoy the reverse side, and glimpse incoming patrons around the edges of the live flames. At A'Town, this halibut dish is served with slices of roasted delicata squash and either sweet potato mash or diced roasted sweet potatoes—and sometimes, if you are lucky, candied hazelnuts. Feel free to garnish with lightly dressed micro greens to really take it over the top.

Sweet Potato Mash

1 large sweet potato (about 12 oz.), peeled and cut into 1-in. chunks

3 tbsp. unsalted butter

2 tbsp. heavy cream

1/2 tsp. fine sea salt

1/4 tsp. white pepper

Fish and Sauce

2 medium shallots, minced

1 cup dry white wine

1 tsp. lemon juice

4 (1 1/2- to 2-in.) halibut steaks (6 to 7 oz. each)

Fine sea salt and black pepper

3 tbsp. extra-virgin olive oil

4 oz. unsalted butter, cut into 8 pieces and softened

2 tbsp. heavy cream

1. **MAKE THE SWEET POTATO MASH:** Place a steamer basket over a pot of simmering water. Steam the sweet potato until tender, 8 to 10 minutes. Transfer to a bowl and add the butter, cream, salt, and pepper. Mash with a fork until almost smooth. Cover and keep warm.

2. **BEGIN THE BEURRE BLANC:** Preheat the oven to 400°. Place a small saucepan over medium heat and add the shallots, wine, and lemon juice. Bring to a simmer and reduce slightly. Remove from the heat.

3. **PREPARE THE FISH:** Season the fillets very lightly with salt and pepper. Place a large, oven-safe skillet or sauté pan (cast iron works best) over high heat and add the oil. When it is very hot, sear the halibut fillets on one side only, about 4 minutes. With a metal spatula, carefully turn over the halibut, making sure to keep the fillets intact. Transfer to the oven to finish cooking for 2 to 4 minutes, until opaque through to the center. Be careful not to overcook.

4. **FINISH THE BEURRE BLANC:** While the fish is in the oven, warm the shallot-wine mixture until just steaming, then whisk in the butter until creamy. Remove from the heat and whisk the cream into the beurre blanc. Serve the fillets atop a mound of the sweet potato mash, with the beurre blanc spooned around the edges. Drizzle any pan juices over the fish.

PER SERVING 662 Cal., 69% (458 Cal.) from fat; 40 g protein; 52 g fat (26 g sat.); 9.5 g carbo (1 g fiber); 320 mg sodium; 163 mg chol. GF/LS

Stop 3

2578 Chuckanut Dr.
Bow, WA

(360) 766-6185

theoysterbar.net

THE OYSTER BAR

Chuckanut Drive, near Bow

Widely touted as the most romantic
restaurant in Washington, the elegant
Oyster Bar has a distinct *Swiss Family
Robinson* feel; you'll imagine you've found
your Friday when the winding road brings
you to this stunning glass box suspended
on a forested slope above the ocean. From
your impeccably laid table, sparkling
seawater is visible between the trees—and
virtually no amenity is missing. Pinch
yourself: Owners Guy and Linda Colbert
have nearly a century of combined restaurant experience between them; they know
how to make a place really special. While
at college in San Diego, both worked their
way up from the menial to the managerial,
and then they owned a 22-seat eatery in
Balboa Island. In 1987, the desire to raise
their kids in a less populated spot brought
them to Bow, and a serendipitously for-sale
restaurant they'd loved one night 10 years
prior. Now empty-nesters, the two credit
their gifted chef, Justin Gordon—who
plays with the region's flawless seafood
with talented glee—for their ability to
travel in the winter with no worries.

The Oyster Bar Crab & Cheddar Melt

SERVES 4 ❖ 10 MINUTES

At The Oyster Bar, this simple but sublime seafood sandwich is served with sweet potato fries and a little pot of aioli. If you don't have a nonstick skillet (or a nonstick griddle) large enough to fit four slices of bread in an even layer, cook the sandwiches in two batches, brushing with additional oil-butter mixture as necessary.

1. In a large bowl, combine the green onions, bell pepper, mustard, mayonnaise, lemon juice, salt, and pepper. Blend together, then gently fold in the crab.

2. Put a large nonstick skillet or griddle over medium-low heat. Combine the oil and butter and brush the cooking surface with the mixture. Spread the crab mixture in an even layer over 4 of the bread slices and immediately place, filling side up, in the skillet. Distribute the cheese slices and then the avocado slices evenly over the crab mixture. Place the remaining slices of bread on top of each sandwich, press down firmly, and brush the top with a little more oil-butter mixture. When the bottom is golden brown, about 2½ minutes, carefully flip each sandwich and cook the other side until browned and the cheese is oozing slightly from the sides, about 2 minutes more. Transfer to plates and cut in half on the diagonal.

2 green onions, trimmed and finely chopped

2 tbsp. finely diced red bell pepper

1 tbsp. Dijon mustard

½ cup mayonnaise

1 tbsp. lemon juice

¼ tsp. *each* fine sea salt and pepper

12 oz. shelled cooked Dungeness crab

1½ tbsp. canola or vegetable oil

1½ tbsp. melted butter

8 (½-in.-thick) slices large sourdough bread (4- by 6-in. slices), crusts removed

5 to 6 oz. medium-sharp cheddar cheese, sliced ¼ in. thick

1 ripe avocado, pitted, peeled, and sliced

PER SANDWICH 1,068 Cal., 37% (396 Cal.) from fat; 50 g protein; 44 g fat (15 g sat.); 121 g carbo (7.9 g fiber); 2,242 mg sodium; 122 mg chol.

Japanese Gardens

CHUCKANUT DRIVE

This large but jewel-like garden may be
the finest spot for Zen contemplation
in the Western Hemisphere. The grounds
are often deserted, but you can browse in
the library or find a kimono in the gift
shop. For a quarter, you can buy some fish
food and make new piscine friends.
3533 Chuckanut Dr.; (360) 399-1646

Teddy Bear Cove Trail

CHUCKANUT DRIVE

Follow the switchbacks on a 1.3-mile
(one way) trail through a forest of madrona
and Garry oaks to the shore, with great
views of Chuckanut Bay and Clark's Point.
Clamshells crushed by centuries of Native
Americans and the tides resulted in a stunning
white sand beach. Commune with majestic
herons and marine life in the crystal-clear
tidepools. Trailhead parking: Chuckanut Dr.
near California St., S. Bellingham;
co.whatcom.wa.us/parks/teddy-bear

Baked Oysters

12 OYSTERS; SERVES 4 AS AN APPETIZER

15 MINUTES (IF THE OYSTERS HAVE BEEN SHUCKED), PLUS 15 MINUTES TO BAKE

This simple dish perfectly expresses the goodness of the Northwest. It depends on great oysters and those dependable standbys in the deliciousness department: bacon and cream. Yet each oyster is crisp, briny, and rich—a mother lode of flavor. Note that you will need about 3 pounds of rock salt as a base for the oysters. The rock salt may be reused.

2 slices best-quality bacon

2 tbsp. finely chopped shallot (1 medium)

1 tbsp. Pernod or sherry

1/2 cup heavy cream

1 cup baby spinach leaves, roughly chopped

Dash of hot sauce, such as Tabasco

1/4 tsp. fine sea salt

1/4 tsp. ground white or black pepper

About 3 lbs. rock salt

1 dozen fresh oysters, shucked and on the half-shell

2 tbsp. finely diced tomato

6 tbsp. dried bread crumbs, such as *panko*

Snipped chives and lemon wedges, for serving

1. Preheat the oven to 400°. In a medium frying pan over medium-low heat, cook the bacon until crispy and golden brown. Transfer to a paper towel–lined plate, and pour off all but about 1 tbsp. of bacon fat from the pan. Add the shallot and sauté over medium heat, stirring, until golden brown.

2. Add the Pernod to the skillet and deglaze, stirring around the edges and base of the pan. Simmer for 1 minute, to burn off the alcohol. Stir in the cream and simmer gently until slightly reduced, with thick bubbles, 2 to 3 minutes. Remove from the heat and add the chopped spinach; stir constantly until the spinach wilts, 1 to 2 minutes. Season with the hot sauce, salt, and pepper.

3. Make a thin layer of rock salt on a large rimmed baking sheet (this helps keep the oysters upright while baking). Place the oysters-in-their-shells on the rock salt and top each with 1 tbsp. of the creamed spinach mixture, covering the oyster completely. Top each oyster with 1/2 tsp. tomato, crumble bacon onto each oyster, and finish with a generous sprinkle of bread crumbs. Bake for 15 to 20 minutes, until golden on top and bubbly around the edges. Transfer to plates and top with chives; serve with a lemon wedge on the side.

PER 3-OYSTER SERVING 196 Cal., 77% (150 Cal.) from fat; 5.3 g protein; 17 g fat (9 g sat.); 6.7 g carbo (0.5 g fiber); 320 mg sodium; 63 mg chol.

Cascadia Mushroom Tartlets

SERVES 4 ❖ 40 MINUTES, PLUS 1¼ HOURS TO ROAST AND BAKE

In fall, winter, and spring, The Oyster Bar takes advantage of the rich treasure of wild fungus in the Northwest, such as lion's mane, oyster mushrooms, and cinnamon caps. Choose from the wild mushrooms available in your area, or use portobello, cremini, and/or shiitake. You'll need four 5-in. tartlet pans.

Savory Tart Dough

1¾ cups all-purpose flour

½ tsp. fine sea salt

½ cup unsalted butter, cut into ½-in. chunks and frozen for 10 minutes

1 large egg, lightly beaten

2 tsp. lemon juice

3 tbsp. ice water, plus 1 to 3 additional tbsp. as needed

Roasted Garlic

15 garlic cloves, unpeeled

2 tbsp. extra-virgin olive oil

½ tsp. dried oregano, crumbled

½ tsp. *each* fine sea salt and pepper

Whipped Goat Cheese

4 oz. fresh goat cheese, softened

⅓ cup heavy cream

½ tsp. lemon juice

Fine sea salt and pepper

Basil Oil

½ cup (packed) fresh basil leaves, roughly chopped

½ cup extra-virgin olive oil

1 small garlic clove, roughly chopped

¼ tsp. lemon juice

¼ tsp. fine sea salt

Mushrooms

¼ cup unsalted butter

1 medium leek, white and tender green parts only, rinsed and thinly sliced

1½ lbs. assorted seasonal mushrooms, brushed clean, stem ends trimmed, and quartered if large

½ tbsp. fresh thyme leaves

½ cup dry sherry

½ tsp. fine sea salt

Pepper, to taste

1. **MAKE THE TART DOUGH:** In a food processor, combine the flour and salt. Pulse to blend evenly. Add the butter and pulse on and off 10 to 15 times, until the larger pieces of butter are broken down and the mixture resembles coarse cornmeal. In a measuring cup, briefly whisk together the egg, lemon juice, and 2 tbsp. ice water. With the motor running, drizzle in the egg mixture quickly, and process for a few seconds more. Remove the cover and sprinkle 1 tbsp. water evenly over the mixture. Pulse 5 or 6 times; the dough will be crumbly, but should begin to hold together when a small amount is picked up and pressed together. Sprinkle on more water, 2 tsp. at a time, with 2 to 3 quick pulses after each addition, adding just enough water for the dough to hold together easily when pressed into a ball. (Add the liquid sparingly so that the dough doesn't get sticky. Be careful not to overprocess, or the pastry will be tough.) Transfer the crumbly mass to a lightly floured work surface and shape into a smooth cylinder. Cut into 4 portions and shape into 4 disks. If using the dough right away, wrap securely in plastic wrap and chill for 1 hour before rolling out.

2. **MAKE THE ROASTED GARLIC:** Preheat the oven to 350°. Make a doubled layer of foil into a 12- by 12-in. square. Put the garlic in the center and bring up the sides to form a cup; place on a small rimmed baking sheet. Drizzle the oil over the cloves and add the oregano, salt, and pepper. Bring the sides all the way up and twist together to make a firm seal. Place the baking sheet in the oven and roast the garlic for 35 minutes. It should be tender and golden but not dark brown. Remove from the oven and open the top so the garlic will stop cooking. Keep the oven on. When ready to use, squeeze the cloves from the skins.

3. **MEANWHILE, MAKE THE WHIPPED GOAT CHEESE:** In a bowl with a mixer on high speed, whip the goat cheese, cream, and lemon juice until light and fluffy. Season with salt and pepper. Set aside.

4. **MAKE THE BASIL OIL:** In a blender or small food processor, combine the basil, oil, garlic, lemon juice, and salt. Pulse until blended. Set aside.

5. On a lightly floured work surface, roll out each disk of dough into a 1/4-in.-thick round. Fit each round into a 5-in. tartlet pan, pressing into the corners and up the sides. Roll the rolling pin over the tops of the pans to cut away excess dough. Fit a piece of foil into each tartlet, overhanging on all sides, and fill with pie weights or dried beans. Transfer to a large baking sheet and bake 10 minutes. Remove the foil and weights and return to oven. Bake 20 to 30 minutes more, until golden and cooked through.

6. **WHILE THE TART SHELLS ARE BAKING, COOK THE MUSHROOMS:** Place a large frying pan over the lowest possible heat and add the butter. When it has melted, add the leek, cover the pan, and cook gently, stirring occasionally, until tender and slightly golden, about 4 minutes. Add the mushrooms, turn heat to high, and cook, stirring occasionally, until tender, about 8 minutes. Add the thyme, sherry, salt, and pepper and cook for 2 minutes. Remove from the heat and fold in the roasted garlic.

7. Fill the warm tart shells with the warm mushroom mixture. Place a dollop of whipped goat cheese on each and drizzle with basil oil. Serve immediately, passing additional goat cheese and basil oil alongside.

MAKE AHEAD: The tart dough disks can be kept, frozen, wrapped in plastic wrap and put in a resealable plastic bag, for up to 3 months. Thaw at room temperature for 2 1/2 hours before using, until workable but still slightly chilled.

PER TARTLET 1,074 Cal., 69% (745 Cal.) from fat; 19 g protein; 85 g fat (36 g sat.); 63 g carbo (3.5 g fiber); 1,177 mg sodium; 185 mg chol. V

A Guide to
Our Nutrition Footnotes

Every *Sunset* recipe comes with an analysis of its main energy-yielding components, based on USDA guidelines: fat, protein, and carbohydrates, plus a tally of its sodium, saturated fat, and cholesterol content. And when appropriate, each recipe also has abbreviations indicating whether it meets criteria for special diets. Generally, the analysis is for a single serving; if a range is given, the analysis is for the larger number of servings. Also, if an ingredient is listed with a substitution, only the ingredient listed first is analyzed. Optional ingredients, and those for which no stated amount is given, aren't included in the calculations.

Here's how to decode our nutritional footnotes:

CAL. (CALORIES). How many you need to maintain your current weight depends on your height, on how active you are, and on how your body burns energy. As a benchmark for the calories an average person requires per day, the USDA suggests 2,000.

CAL. FROM FAT. The current advice from the USDA's Dietary Guidelines for Americans (health.gov/dietary guidelines) is that 20 to 35 percent of your total daily calories come from fat. However, numbers can be misleading: Take, for instance, a green salad tossed with vinaigrette. Because the main ingredients are so low-calorie, most of the calories come from the vinaigrette, and the percentage of fat can make the salad seem like a high-fat food.

PROTEIN. The USDA recommendation is for 46 grams per day for adult women and 56 grams per day for adult men, based on a 2,000-calorie diet.

FAT. While fat can and should be part of a healthful diet, the type of fat makes a difference. Monounsaturated and poly-unsaturated—which come primarily from fish, nuts, seeds, and vegetable oils—promote heart health. Saturated fats, which come mainly from animal sources, and especially trans fats, mostly coming from the hydrogenation of oils, are linked to heart disease. For now, the official recommendation is that no more than one-third of total calories should come from fat (less than 10 percent of calories should come from saturated fats, with trans fats as low as possible).

CARBO (CARBOHYDRATES). These provide the main energy source for our bodies and are the only source of fiber, which helps digestion and protects against heart disease, obesity, and diabetes. Whole-grain sources of carbohydrates have much higher levels of fiber and nutrients than refined sources. The USDA suggests that carbs should make up 45 to 65 percent of total daily calories, with 25 grams of fiber in a 2,000-calorie diet.

SODIUM. A major mineral, it is essential to nerve and muscle function. Salt is the main form of sodium in our diets, and too much of it can contribute to high blood pressure. The recommended daily maximum for sodium is 2,300 mg (about 1 teaspoon of table salt), but for adults over 51, all African Americans, and anyone with diabetes, hypertension, or chronic kidney disease, the recommendation is 1,500 mg.

CHOL. Cholesterol is a fatty substance found in all animal products. The relationship between dietary cholesterol (from the foods we eat) and cholesterol made by our bodies is influenced by our genes and not totally understood. The current guideline is to consume no more than 300 mg a day.

GF (GLUTEN-FREE). No wheat, rye, barley, or oats. Check any processed food ingredients you use to verify they're gluten-free.

LC (LOW-CALORIE). Less than 500 calories for a main dish, 250 for a side dish, 150 for an appetizer, and 350 for dessert.

LS (LOW-SODIUM). Less than 500 mg for a main dish, and 350 for a side dish, appetizer, or dessert.

V (VEGETARIAN). Contains no meat or fish products.

VG (VEGAN). Contains no animal products (including eggs and dairy).

Measurement Equivalents

REFER TO THE FOLLOWING CHARTS FOR METRIC CONVERSIONS AS WELL AS COMMON COOKING EQUIVALENTS. ALL EQUIVALENTS ARE APPROXIMATE.

Cooking/Oven Temperatures

	Fahrenheit	Celsius	Gas Mark
Freeze Water	32°F	0°C	
Room Temp.	68°F	20°C	
Boil Water	212°F	100°C	
Bake	325°F	160°C	3
	350°F	180°C	4
	375°F	190°C	5
	400°F	200°C	6
	425°F	220°C	7
	450°F	230°C	8
Broil			Grill

Liquid Ingredients by Volume

¼ tsp.	=					1 ml.	
½ tsp.	=					2 ml.	
1 tsp.	=					5 ml.	
3 tsp.	=	1 tbsp.	=	½ fl. oz.	=	15 ml.	
2 tbsp.	=	⅛ cup	=	1 fl. oz.	=	30 ml.	
4 tbsp.	=	¼ cup	=	2 fl. oz.	=	60 ml.	
5⅓ tbsp.	=	⅓ cup	=	3 fl. oz.	=	80 ml.	
8 tbsp.	=	½ cup	=	4 fl. oz.	=	120 ml.	
10⅔ tbsp.	=	⅔ cup	=	5 fl. oz.	=	160 ml.	
12 tbsp.	=	¾ cup	=	6 fl. oz.	=	180 ml.	
16 tbsp.	=	1 cup	=	8 fl. oz	=	240 ml.	
1 pt.	=	2 cups	=	16 fl. oz.	=	480 ml.	
1 qt.	=	4 cups	=	32 fl. oz.	=	960 ml.	
				33 fl. oz.	=	1,000 ml.	= 1 l.

Dry Ingredients by Weight

1 oz.	=	1/16 lb.	=	30 g.
4 oz.	=	¼ lb.	=	120 g.
8 oz.	=	½ lb.	=	240 g.
12 oz.	=	¾ lb.	=	360 g.
16 oz.	=	1 lb.	=	480 g.

(To convert ounces to grams, multiply the number of ounces by 30.)

Length

1 in.	=					2.5 cm.	
6 in.	=	½ ft.	=		=	15 cm.	
12 in.	=	1 ft.	=		=	30 cm.	
36 in.	=	3 ft.	=	1 yd.	=	90 cm.	
40 in.	=					100 cm.	= 1 m.

Equivalents for Different Types of Ingredients

Standard Cup	Fine Powder (e.g., flour)	Grain (e.g., rice)	Granular (e.g., sugar)	Liquid Solids (e.g., butter)	Liquid (e.g., milk)
1	140 g.	150 g.	190 g.	200 g.	240 ml.
¾	105 g.	113 g.	143 g.	150 g.	180 ml.
⅔	93 g.	100 g.	125 g.	133 g.	160 ml.
½	70 g.	75 g.	95 g.	100 g.	120 ml.
⅓	47 g.	50 g.	63 g.	67 g.	80 ml.
¼	35 g.	38 g.	48 g.	50 g.	60 ml.
⅛	18 g.	19 g.	24 g.	25 g.	30 ml.

Recipe Index

Location Index

Acknowledgments

It takes a pretty big village to make a book like this A. Informative, B. Beautiful, C. Fun, D. Timely, and E. Correct. Thanks to:

AT OXMOOR HOUSE: Leah McLaughlin, the woman with the vision; Hélène Dujardin for her excellent food photography, plus Susan Hettleman and Courtney Greenhalgh.

AT TIME INC: Erica Sanders-Foege, a true joy to noodle with.

AT SUNSET: Peggy Northrop, whose enquiring mind always wants to know—more; Margo True, for her encyclopedic, hungry-girl knowledge about the nooks and crannies of the West Coast—many entries leapt straight from her mind to my itinerary; Linda Bouchard, for cheerful and *huge* attention to detail; Maili Holiman, for her artist's eye; Peter Fish and Bruce Anderson for great tips; and Carol Shih.

Carole Bidnick, My Person (and agent), for tireless belief in me even when my own wanes. As always, you made it real.

Kim Laidlaw, a true and longtime collaborator, I was so lucky to have this angel perched on my shoulder, for every mile and every meal.

Alanna Kinne and Leslie Porcelli for help with nitty-gritty and perfectionist recipe testing locally, and to the legendary Grace Parisi for overseeing testing at Oxmoor House.

The best traveling companions any roadfoodie could ever desire: Stella and, occasionally, Casey Biggs.

All the chefs, restaurateurs, bartenders, and helpful folks who patiently attended to my endless queries, in order from South to North, as the crow flies—ish: Roberto Cuin; Debbie Gaudette; Jennifer and Jonathan Arbel; Katie McBride; David Skaggs; Andria Jacobs, Brianna Cromer and Michael Cherney; Jamie Gluck and John Wentworth, Clark Staub; Dana Ashlock, Sandy and Mike Knotts; Liz Lynch and Tim Begovich; Dr. Tedone (in memoriam); Mark Tognazzini; Eric Gonzales, Tony DeGarimore, and Antonio Landin; Ali Rush Carscaden; Jeff and Lindsay Jackson and family; Chris and Shandi Kobayashi; Neil Collins and Jackie Meisinger; Jacob Lovejoy, Ted and Lisa Plemons, and Steve and Alice Cass; Kevin and Genoa Riley, and Ken Fuller; Jim Clarke and Steve Kniffen; Ian McPhee and Jim Saunders; Torrey Waag, Linda Jones, and Domingo Santamaria; Christian Caiazzo; Shannon Gregory; Evelyn Casini, Gwenyth Prosser, and Mark Malicki; Barbara Burkey and Franny Burkey; Kevin and Sandy VanderBes; Nick Petti and Jaimi Parsons; Doug Bryan and Laurel Radloff; Chris Smith, Bill Chino, and Lauren Vucci; Vernon and Charlene Rollins; Devon and Michelle Morgante; Chris Hawthorne and family; Brian and Lia Menten; Laura Anderson and Charlie Branford; Jeff and Lynne England, and Linda Owings; Chenin and Sean Carlton; Lee Vance; Megan Miller and Josh Tuckman (plus hugely informative "bar-fly" Jim Litherland); Jim Defeo, Anthony Danton, and Sean Whittaker; Charlie Zorich and Eileah Wright; Rob Paylor; Jess Owen and Sara Owen, and Barbara Matson; Paul Schmidt, Steven Serbousek, and Tammy; Bill Dewey from Taylor Seafood; Laurette Feit; Gabriel and Jessica Schuenemann; Michael Lynch; Lisa Carvey and Patrick Boin; L. M. Libby and Tim Moffitt; Guy and Linda Colbert, and Justin Gordon.

Special shout-outs to Eric Gonzales at Pier 46 in Templeton for all the export info on West Coast seafood; to Celia Sack and Paula Harris, Shannon Hughes, and Vivien Straus for insider insights to the Mendocino coast, plus comfy beds, great pizza, and doggie kisses; to Drew Ross for tips along the Lost Coast; and to Melinda Handy and my niece Melissa Davison for superb Oregonian and Washingtonian finds.

The tasters during research and recipe test-tasting (very difficult job!): Robert Lombardi, Michael and Andrea DeWit, Mary Lou and John Splittorf, and Casey Biggs.

LOCATION PHOTOGRAPHERS: Lisa Corson, Thomas J. Story, Justin Bailie, Michael Hanson.